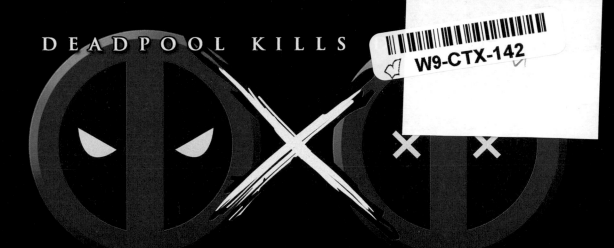

DEADPOOL KILLS

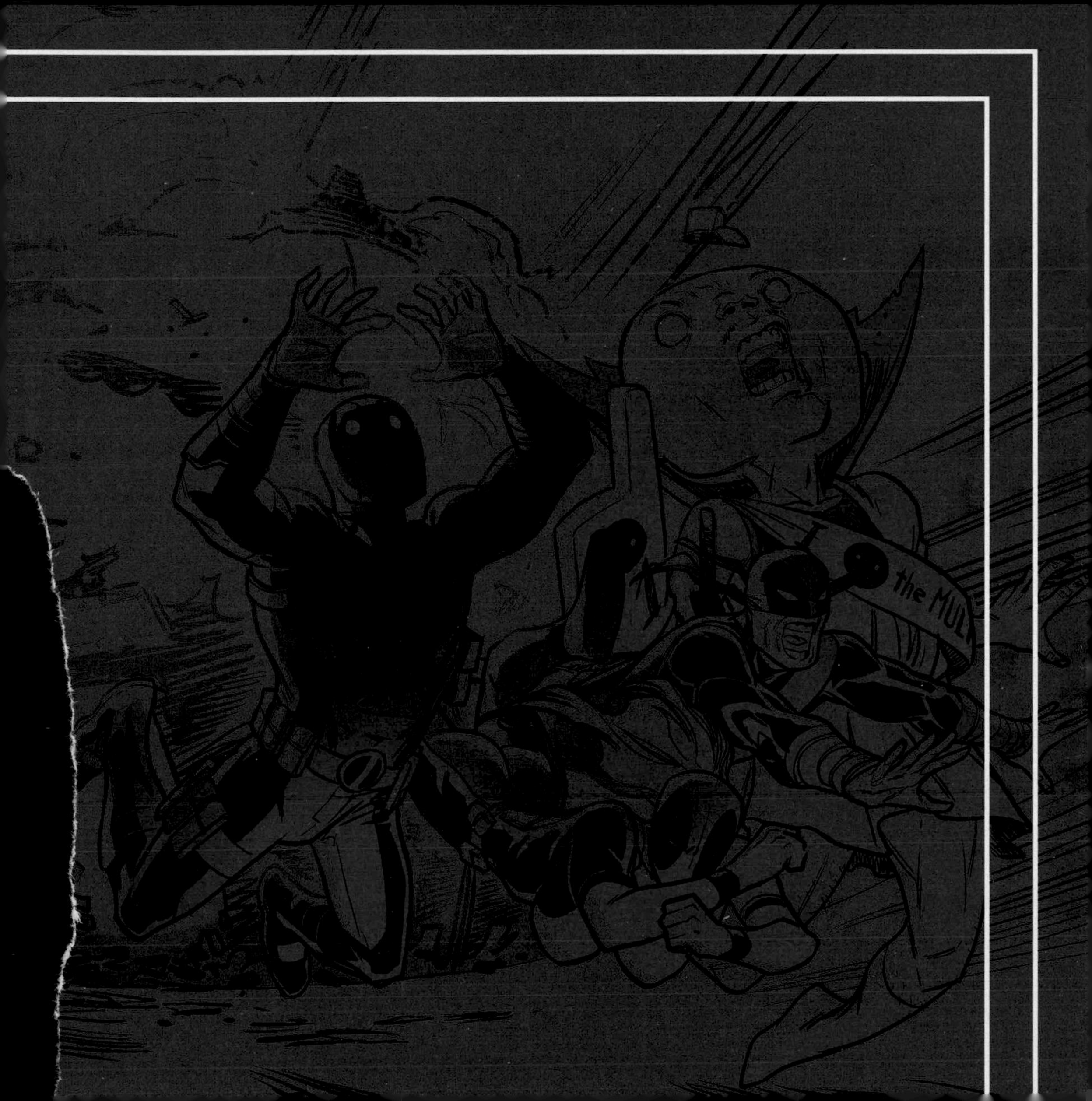

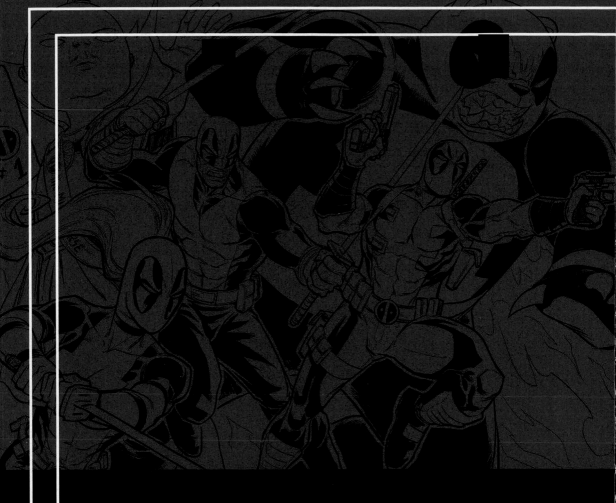

WRITER
CULLEN BUNN

ARTIST
SALVA ESPIN

COLOR ARTIST
VERONICA GANDINI

LETTERER
VC'S JOE SABINO

COVER ART
MIKE DEL MUNDO

EDITOR
JORDAN D. WHITE

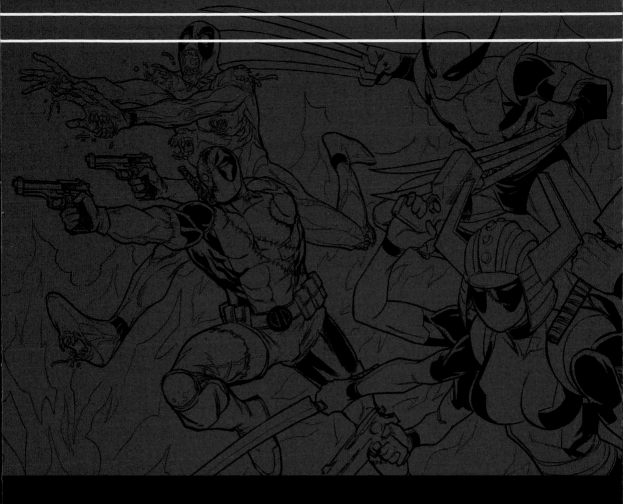

COLLECTION EDITOR & DESIGN
CORY LEVINE
ASSISTANT EDITOR
SARAH BRUNSTAD
ASSOCAIATE MANAGING EDITOR
ALEX STARBUCK
EDITORS, SPECIAL PROJECTS
JENNIFER GRÜNWALD & MARK D. BEAZLEY
SENIOR EDITOR, SPECIAL PROJECTS
JEFF YOUNGQUIST
SVP PRINT, SALES & MARKETING
DAVID GABRIEL

EDITOR IN CHIEF
AXEL ALONSO
PUBLISHER
DAN BUCKLEY
CHIEF CREATIVE OFFICER
JOE QUESADA
EXECUTIVE PRODUCER
ALAN FINE

DEADPOOL KILLS DEADPOOL. Contains material originally published in magazine form as DEADPOOL KILLS DEADPOOL #1-4. Second printing 2015. ISBN# 978-0-7851-8493-5. Published by MARVEL WORLDWIDE, INC., a subsidiary of MARVEL ENTERTAINMENT, LLC. OFFICE OF PUBLICATION: 135 West 50th Street, New York, NY 10020. Copyright © 2013 Marvel Characters, Inc. All rights reserved. All characters featured in this issue and the distinctive names and likenesses thereof, and all related indicia are trademarks of Marvel Characters, Inc. No similarity between any of the names, characters, persons, and/or institutions in this magazine with those of any living or dead person or institution is intended, and any such similarity which may exist is purely coincidental. **Printed in Canada.** ALAN FINE, EVP - Office of the President, Marvel Worldwide, Inc. and EVP & CMO Marvel Characters B.V.; DAN BUCKLEY, Publisher & President - Print, Animation & Digital Divisions; JOE QUESADA, Chief Creative Officer; TOM BREVOORT, SVP of Publishing; DAVID BOGART, SVP of Operations & Procurement, Publishing; C.B. CEBULSKI, SVP of Creator & Content Development; DAVID GABRIEL, SVP Print, Sales & Marketing; JIM O'KEEFE, VP of Operations & Logistics; DAN CARR, Executive Director of Publishing Technology; SUSAN CRESPI, Editorial Operations Manager; ALEX MORALES, Publishing Operations Manager; STAN LEE, Chairman Emeritus. For information regarding advertising in Marvel Comics or on Marvel.com, please contact Niza Disla, Director of Marvel Partnerships, at ndisla@marvel.com. For Marvel subscription inquiries, please call 800-217-9158. **Manufactured between 12/10/2014 and 1/12/15 by SOLISCO PRINTERS, SCOTT, QC, CANADA.**

1 0 9 8 7 6 5 4 3 2

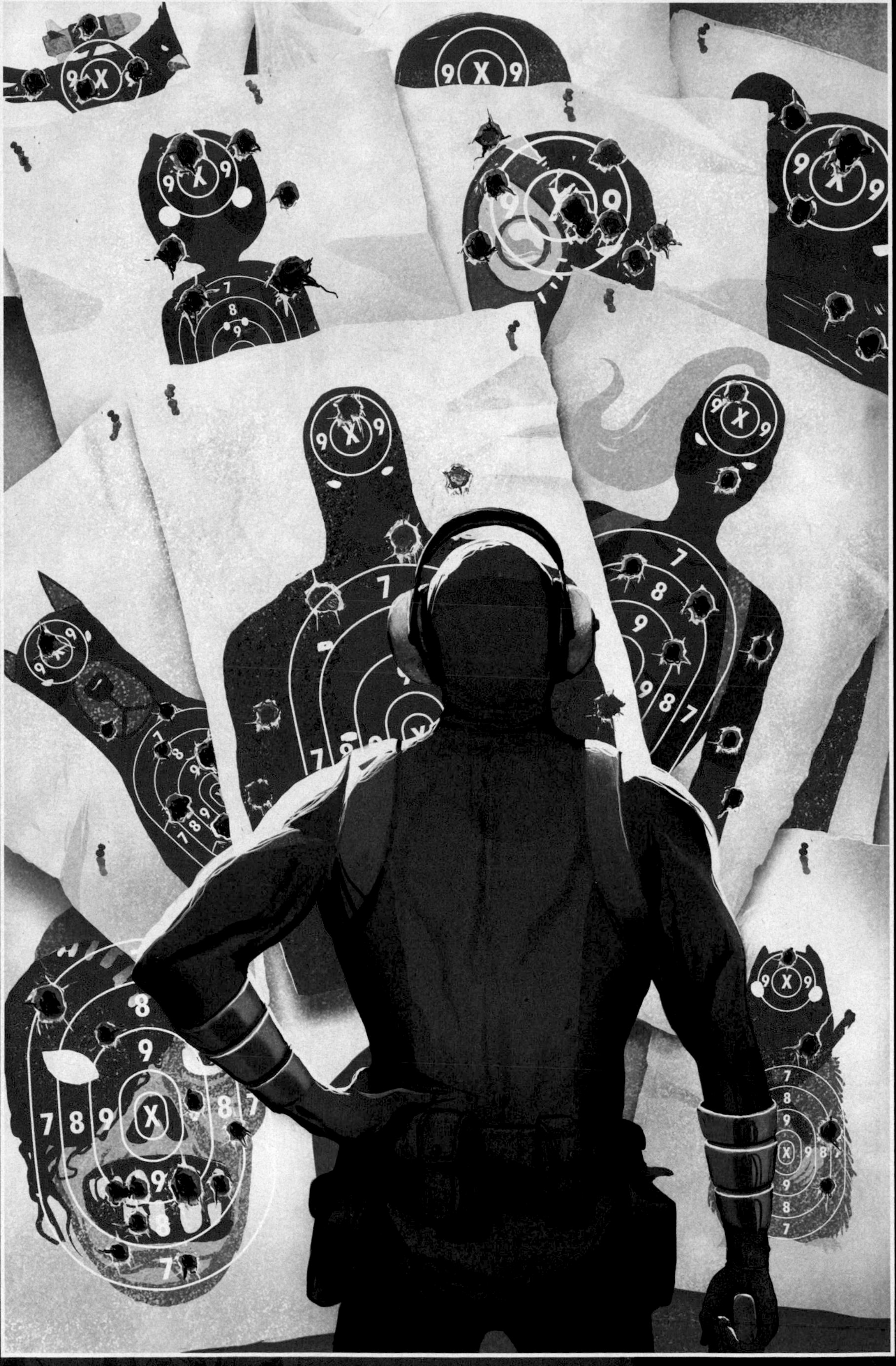

9 X 9
7 8 9 X 9 8 7

ONE

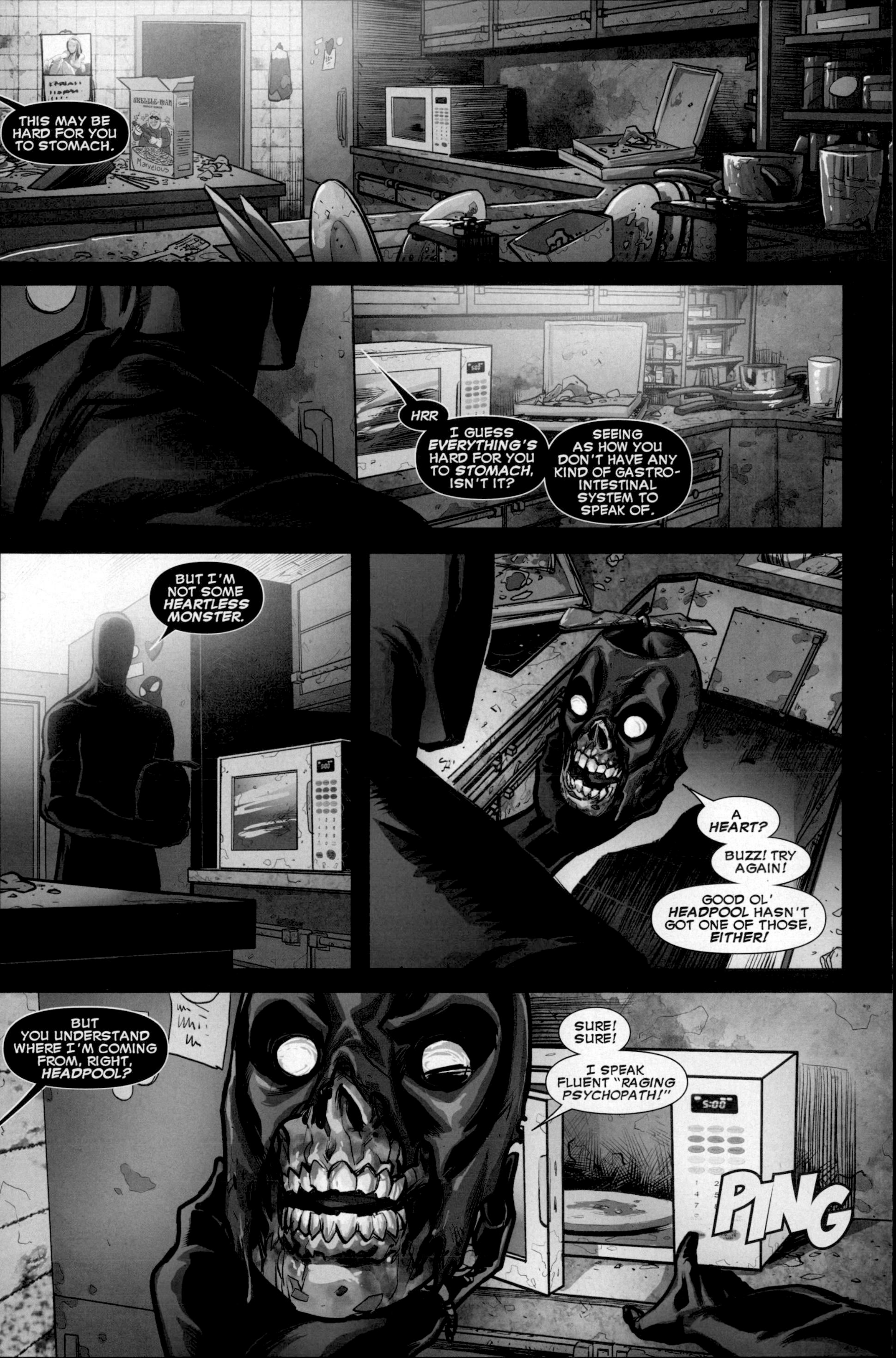
THIS MAY BE HARD FOR YOU TO STOMACH.
HRR
I GUESS EVERYTHING'S HARD FOR YOU TO STOMACH, ISN'T IT?
SEEING AS HOW YOU DON'T HAVE ANY KIND OF GASTRO-INTESTINAL SYSTEM TO SPEAK OF.
BUT I'M NOT SOME HEARTLESS MONSTER.
A HEART?
BUZZ! TRY AGAIN!
GOOD OL' HEADPOOL HASN'T GOT ONE OF THOSE, EITHER!
BUT YOU UNDERSTAND WHERE I'M COMING FROM, RIGHT, HEADPOOL?
SURE! SURE!
I SPEAK FLUENT "RAGING PSYCHOPATH!"
PING

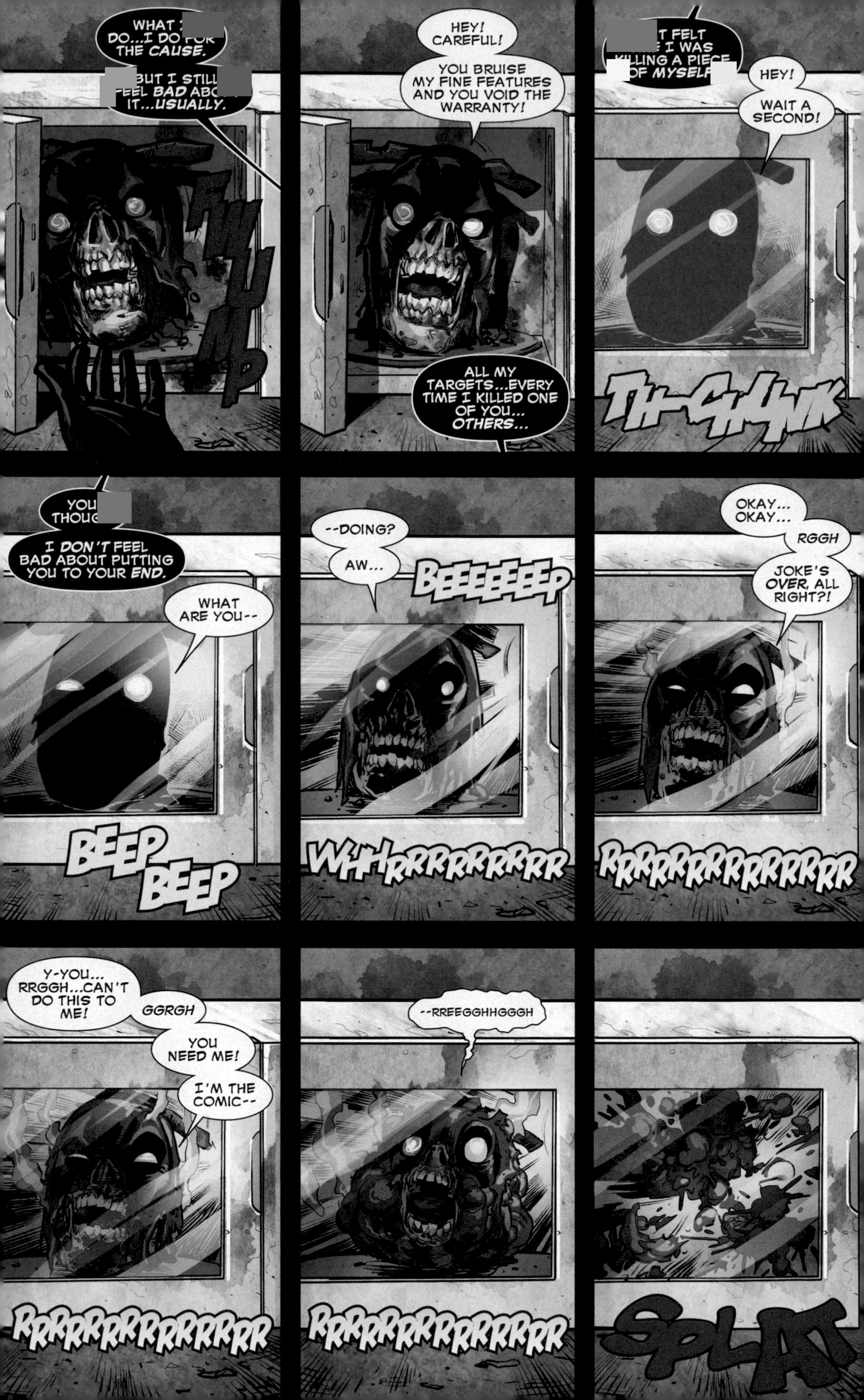

WHAT [redacted] DO...I DO FOR THE CAUSE.
[redacted]BUT I STILL [redacted]EEL BAD ABO[redacted] IT...USUALLY.
FWUMP
HEY! CAREFUL!
YOU BRUISE MY FINE FEATURES AND YOU VOID THE WARRANTY!
ALL MY TARGETS...EVERY TIME I KILLED ONE OF YOU... OTHERS...
[redacted]T FELT [redacted]E I WAS [redacted]LLING A PIECE [redacted]OF MYSELF[redacted]
HEY!
WAIT A SECOND!
TH-CHUNK
YOU [redacted] THOUG[redacted]
I DON'T FEEL BAD ABOUT PUTTING YOU TO YOUR END.
WHAT ARE YOU--
BEEP BEEP
--DOING?
AW...
BEEEEEEEP
WHRRRRRRRRRR
OKAY... OKAY...
RGGH
JOKE'S OVER, ALL RIGHT?!
RRRRRRRRRRRRRR
Y-YOU... RRGGH...CAN'T DO THIS TO ME!
GGRGH
YOU NEED ME!
I'M THE COMIC--
RRRRRRRRRRRRRR
--RREEGGHHGGGH
RRRRRRRRRRRRRR
SPLAT

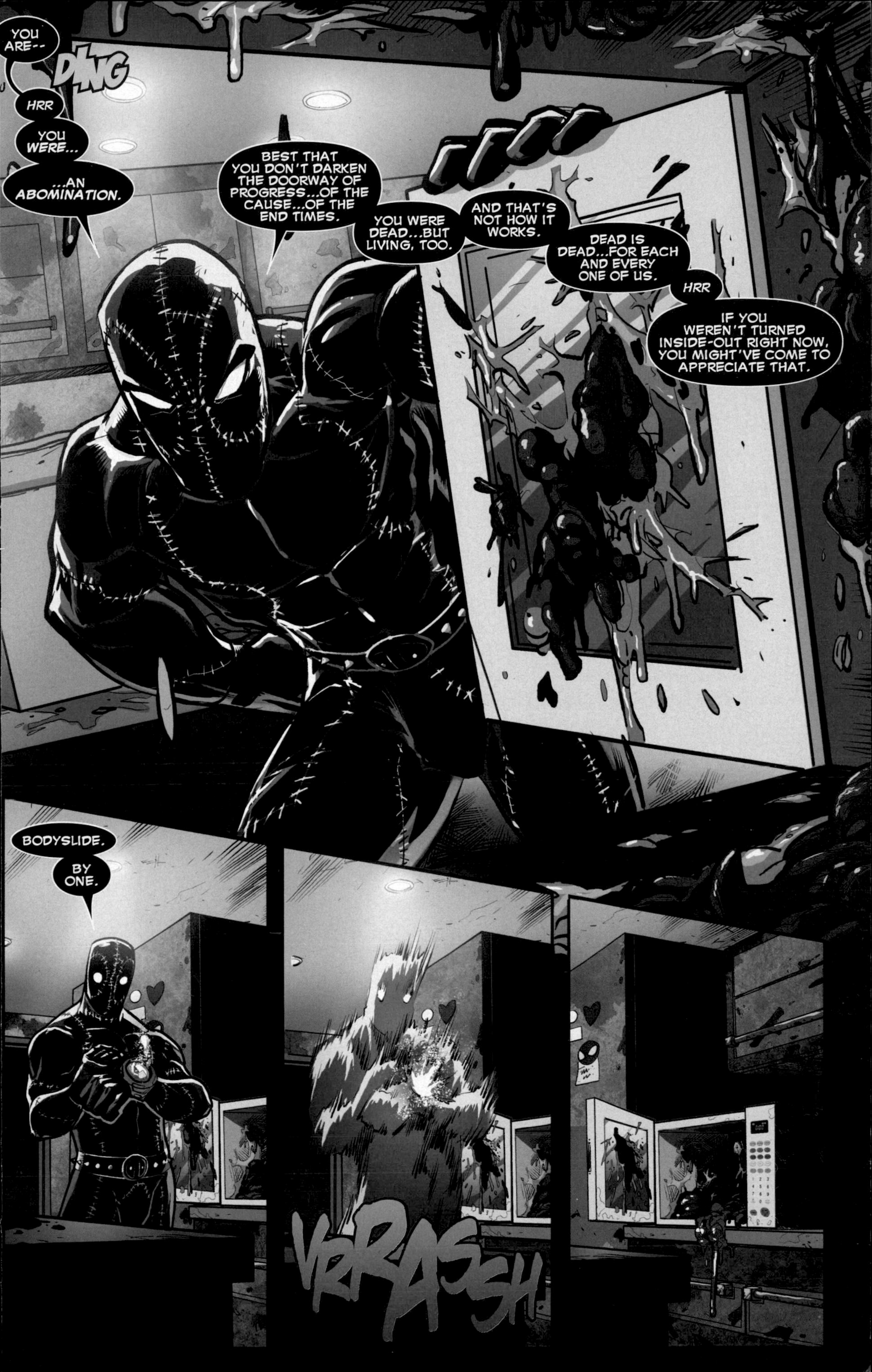
YOU ARE--
DING
HRR
YOU WERE...
...AN ABOMINATION.
BEST THAT YOU DON'T DARKEN THE DOORWAY OF PROGRESS...OF THE CAUSE...OF THE END TIMES.
YOU WERE DEAD...BUT LIVING, TOO.
AND THAT'S NOT HOW IT WORKS.
DEAD IS DEAD...FOR EACH AND EVERY ONE OF US.
HRR
IF YOU WEREN'T TURNED INSIDE-OUT RIGHT NOW, YOU MIGHT'VE COME TO APPRECIATE THAT.
BODYSLIDE.
BY ONE.
VRRASSH

DEADPOOL KILLS DEADPOOL

DEADPOOL. WADE WILSON. THE MERC WITH THE MOUTH.

POSSIBLY THE MOST SKILLED MERCENARY IN THE WORLD...AND DEFINITELY THE MOST ANNOYING. THE JOKE-CRACKING, REFERENCE-MAKING, FOURTH-WALL-BREAKING, TACO-EATING FUNNYMAN OF THE COLD-BLOODED KILLER SET, DEADPOOL HAS LONG SKIRTED THE LINE BETWEEN HERO AND VILLAIN, BETWEEN MANIAC AND GENIUS, BETWEEN UGLY AND SMELLY.

THE HEROES OF THE MARVEL UNIVERSE LOOK ON WADE AS A JOKE. THE OVERLY CAUTIOUS AMONG THEM SOMETIMES WORRY THAT THE JOKE MIGHT SOMEDAY TURN DARK, THAT DEADPOOL MIGHT BECOME TOO DANGEROUS TO BE ALLOWED TO RUN FREE. MOST DON'T GIVE HIM ENOUGH CREDIT FOR THAT. THEY SEE HIM AS SOMEONE TO BE AVOIDED FOR THE SAKE OF ONE'S SANITY AND DIGNITY, AND NOT MUCH MORE.

BUT THE UNIVERSE IS NOT ALL THERE IS. THERE EXISTS AN INFINITE MULTIVERSE OF WORLDS, EACH SLIGHTLY DIFFERENT FROM THE NEXT. ACROSS THAT ONGOING SPECTRUM EXISTS AN ENDLESS PANOPLY OF DEADPOOLS THAT COME IN EVERY SHAPE AND COLOR. DEADPOOLS OF DIFFERENT GENDERS, AGES, SPECIES, TIMES, BODY TYPES, STAR SIGNS, PREFERENCE OF GOLDEN GIRL... THE POSSIBILITIES GO ON AND ON.

AND THE POSSIBILITIES, TOO, TRAIL INTO THE DARKSIDE. THERE EXISTS ONE WORLD MUCH LIKE OUR OWN WHERE DEADPOOL SAW THE TRUTH...THAT HE, AND ALL THE OTHER HEROES OF HIS WORLD, WERE JUST WORKS OF FICTION CREATED FOR THE AMUSEMENT OF OTHERS. HE TOOK IT UPON HIMSELF TO SAVE THEM FROM THIS FATE...BY MURDERING THEM BRUTALLY. NOT STOPPING THERE, HE TRAVELED FROM WORLD TO WORLD, KILLING ALL THE HEROES HE FOUND, EVENTUALLY GOING INTO THE REALM OF IDEAS TO WIPE THE INSPIRATION FOR HEROES FROM THE VERY PAGES OF LITERATURE.

BUT THAT PROBABLY HAS NOTHING TO DO WITH THIS STORY, RIGHT? SO FORGET I MENTIONED IT.

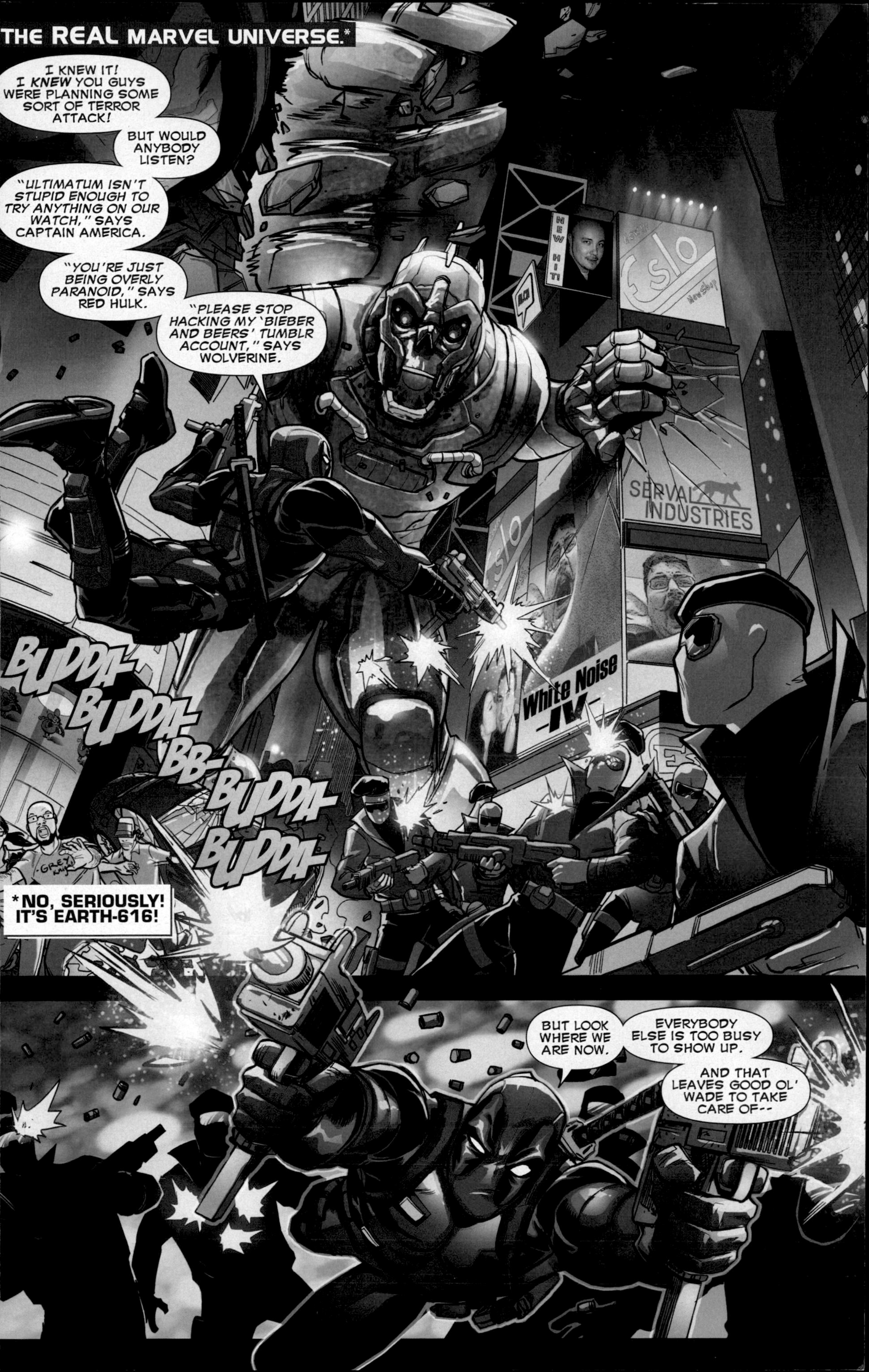
THE REAL MARVEL UNIVERSE.*
I KNEW IT! I KNEW YOU GUYS WERE PLANNING SOME SORT OF TERROR ATTACK!
BUT WOULD ANYBODY LISTEN?
"ULTIMATUM ISN'T STUPID ENOUGH TO TRY ANYTHING ON OUR WATCH," SAYS CAPTAIN AMERICA.
"YOU'RE JUST BEING OVERLY PARANOID," SAYS RED HULK.
"PLEASE STOP HACKING MY 'BIEBER AND BEERS' TUMBLR ACCOUNT," SAYS WOLVERINE.
NEW HIT!
SERVAL INDUSTRIES
White Noise IV
BUDDA-BUDDA-BB-BUDDA-BUDDA
*NO, SERIOUSLY! IT'S EARTH-616!
BUT LOOK WHERE WE ARE NOW.
EVERYBODY ELSE IS TOO BUSY TO SHOW UP.
AND THAT LEAVES GOOD OL' WADE TO TAKE CARE OF--

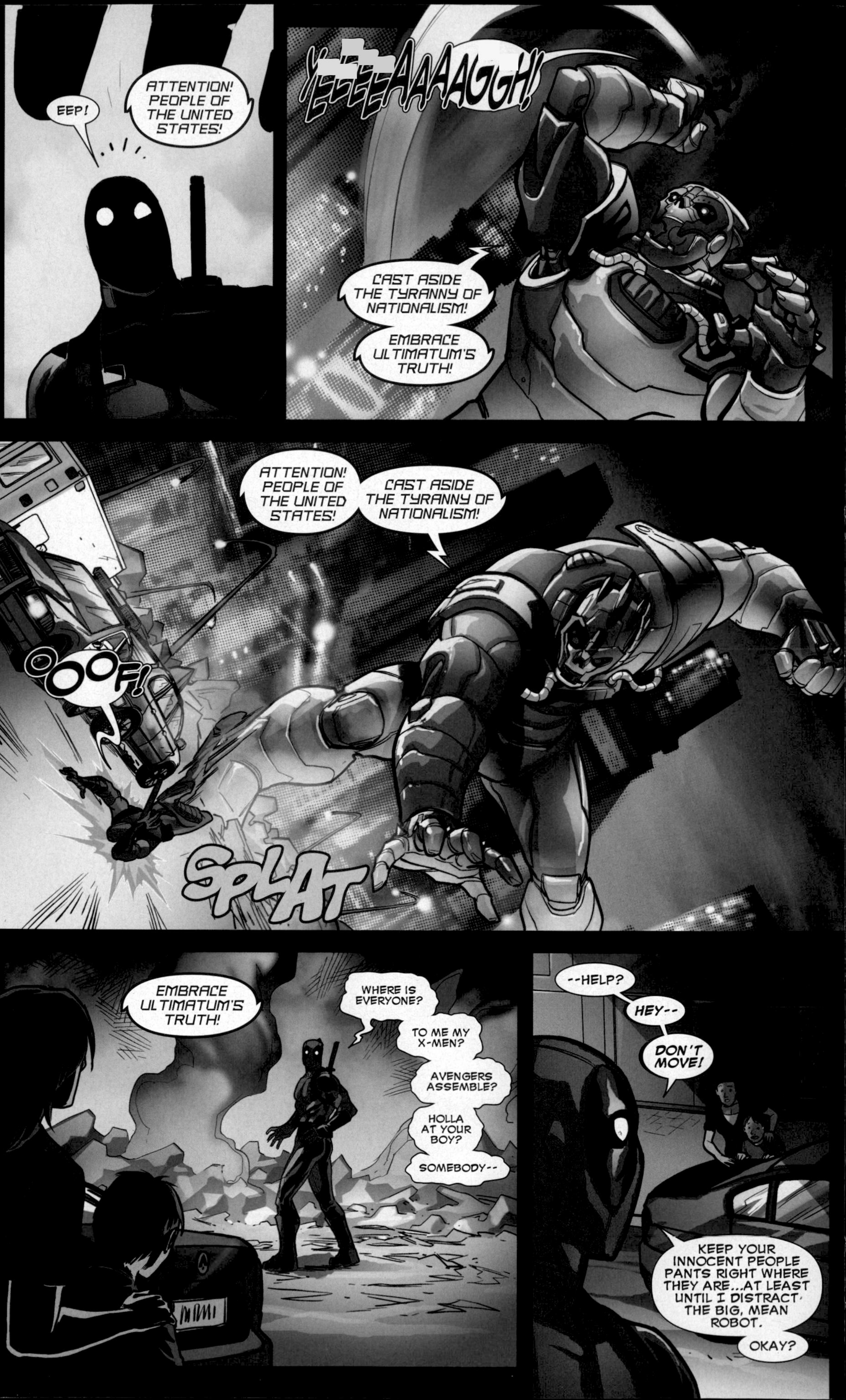

EEP!
ATTENTION! PEOPLE OF THE UNITED STATES!
YEEEEAAAAGGH!
CAST ASIDE THE TYRANNY OF NATIONALISM!
EMBRACE ULTIMATUM'S TRUTH!
ATTENTION! PEOPLE OF THE UNITED STATES!
CAST ASIDE THE TYRANNY OF NATIONALISM!
OOOF!
SPLAT
EMBRACE ULTIMATUM'S TRUTH!
WHERE IS EVERYONE?
TO ME MY X-MEN?
AVENGERS ASSEMBLE?
HOLLA AT YOUR BOY?
SOMEBODY--
--HELP?
HEY--
DON'T MOVE!
KEEP YOUR INNOCENT PEOPLE PANTS RIGHT WHERE THEY ARE...AT LEAST UNTIL I DISTRACT THE BIG, MEAN ROBOT.
OKAY?

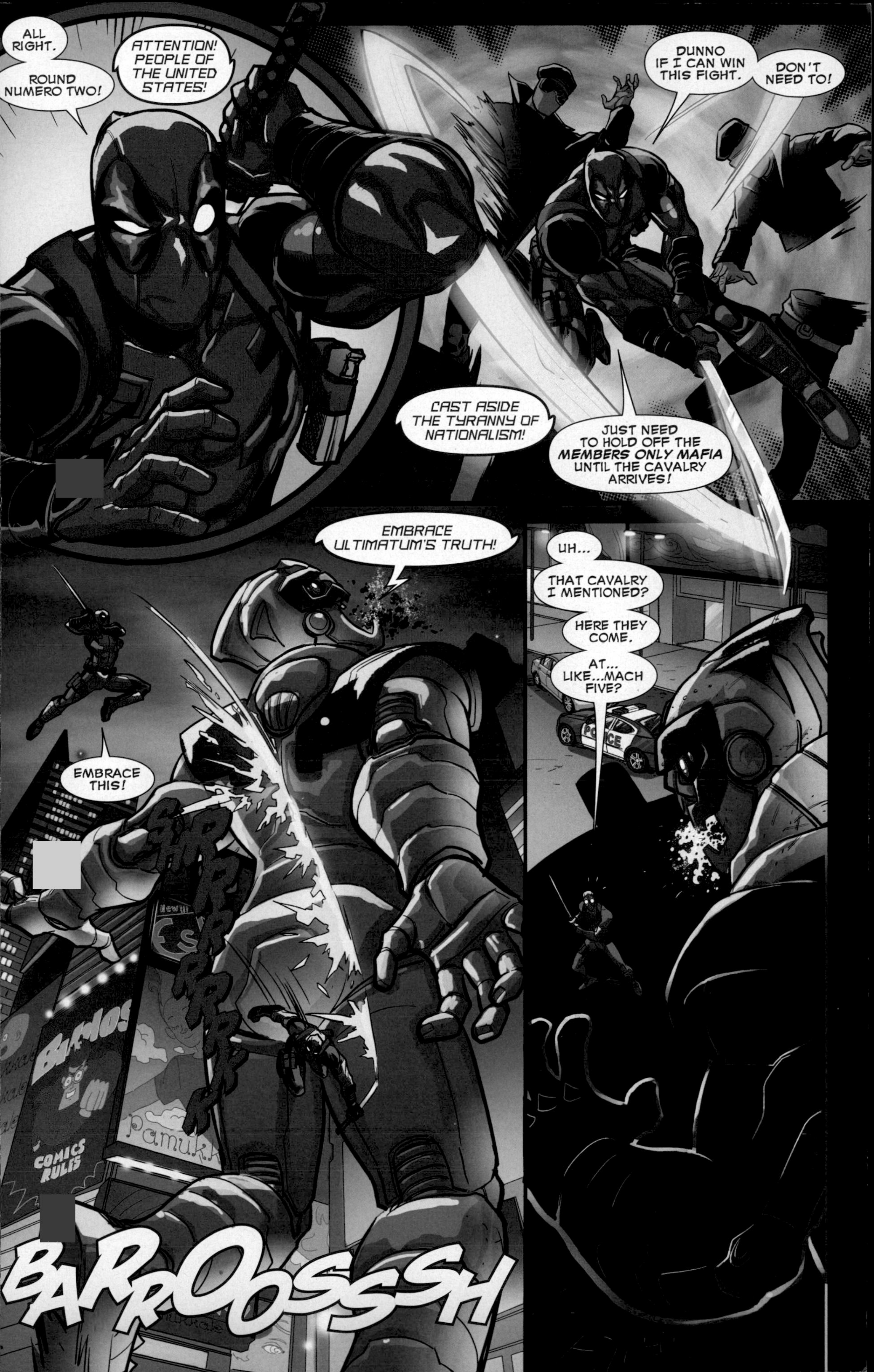
ALL RIGHT.
ROUND NUMERO TWO!
ATTENTION! PEOPLE OF THE UNITED STATES!
DUNNO IF I CAN WIN THIS FIGHT.
DON'T NEED TO!
CAST ASIDE THE TYRANNY OF NATIONALISM!
JUST NEED TO HOLD OFF THE **MEMBERS ONLY MAFIA** UNTIL THE CAVALRY ARRIVES!
EMBRACE ULTIMATUM'S TRUTH!
EMBRACE THIS!
BARROOSSSH
UH...
THAT CAVALRY I MENTIONED?
HERE THEY COME.
AT... LIKE...MACH FIVE?
POLICE

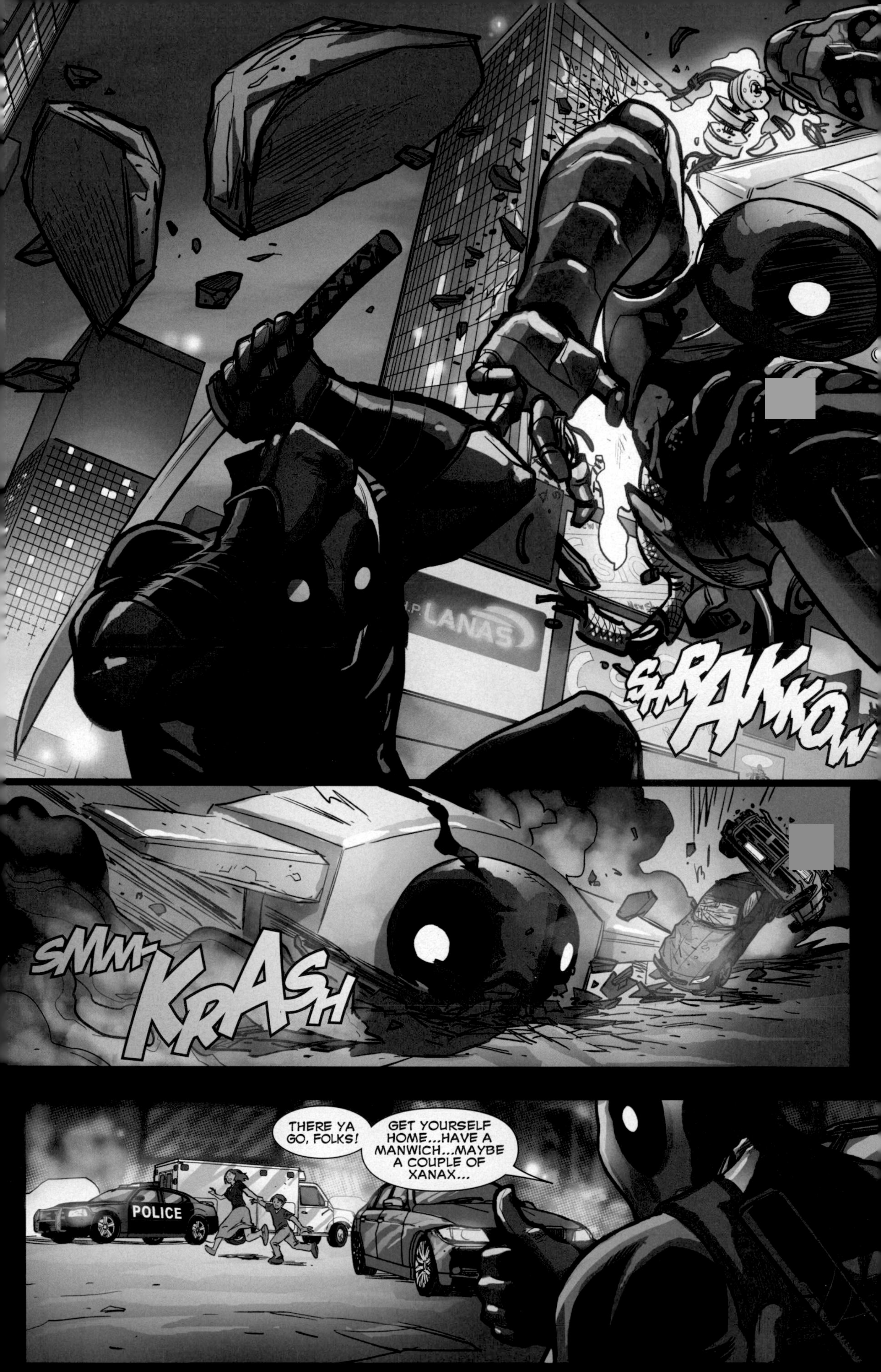
SHRAKKOW
SMM-KRASH
THERE YA GO, FOLKS!
GET YOURSELF HOME...HAVE A MANWICH...MAYBE A COUPLE OF XANAX...
POLICE
LANAS

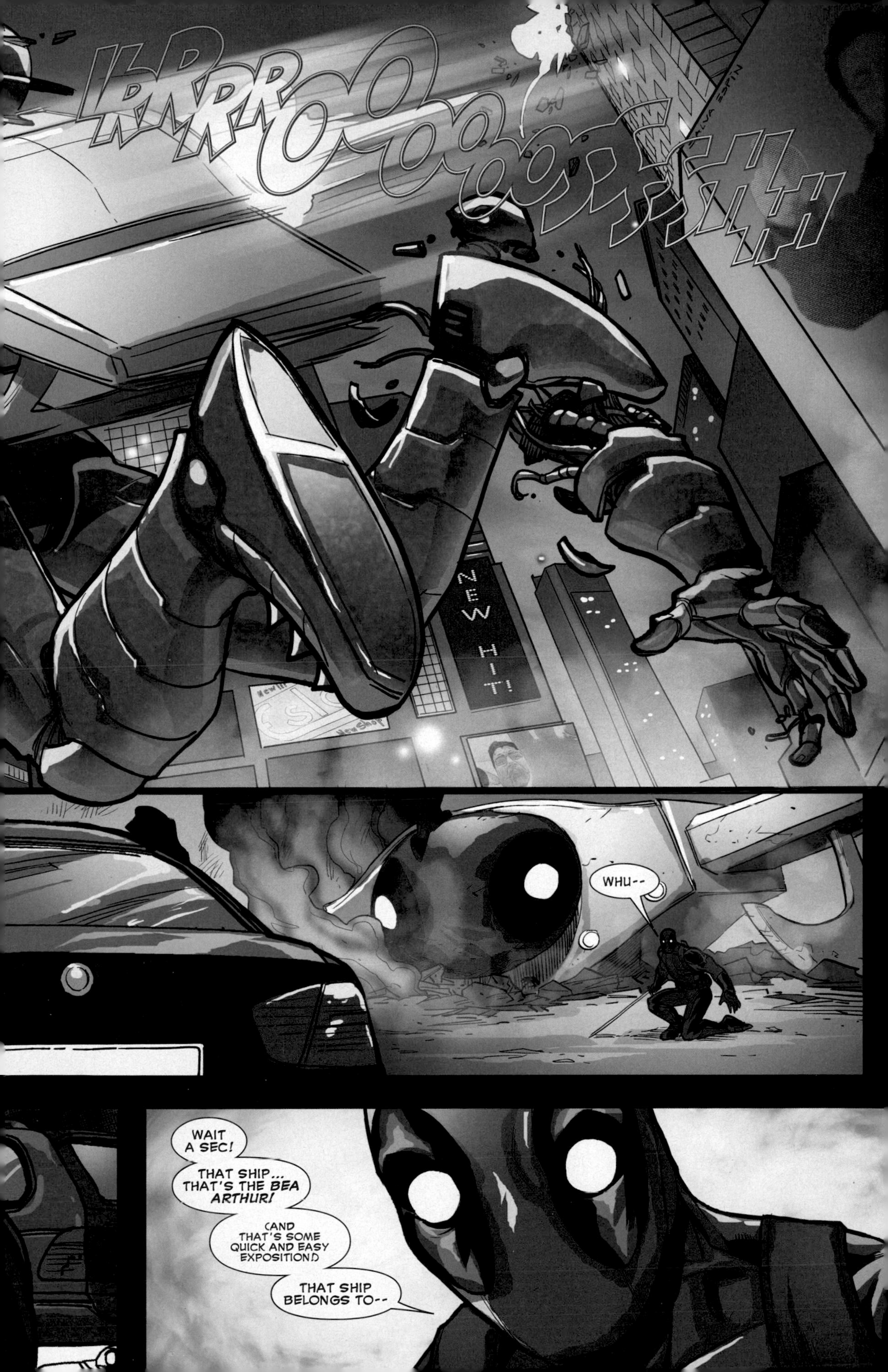
SALVA ESPIN
NEW HIT!
WHU--
WAIT A SEC!
THAT SHIP... THAT'S THE *BEA ARTHUR!*
(AND THAT'S SOME QUICK AND EASY EXPOSITION)
THAT SHIP BELONGS TO--

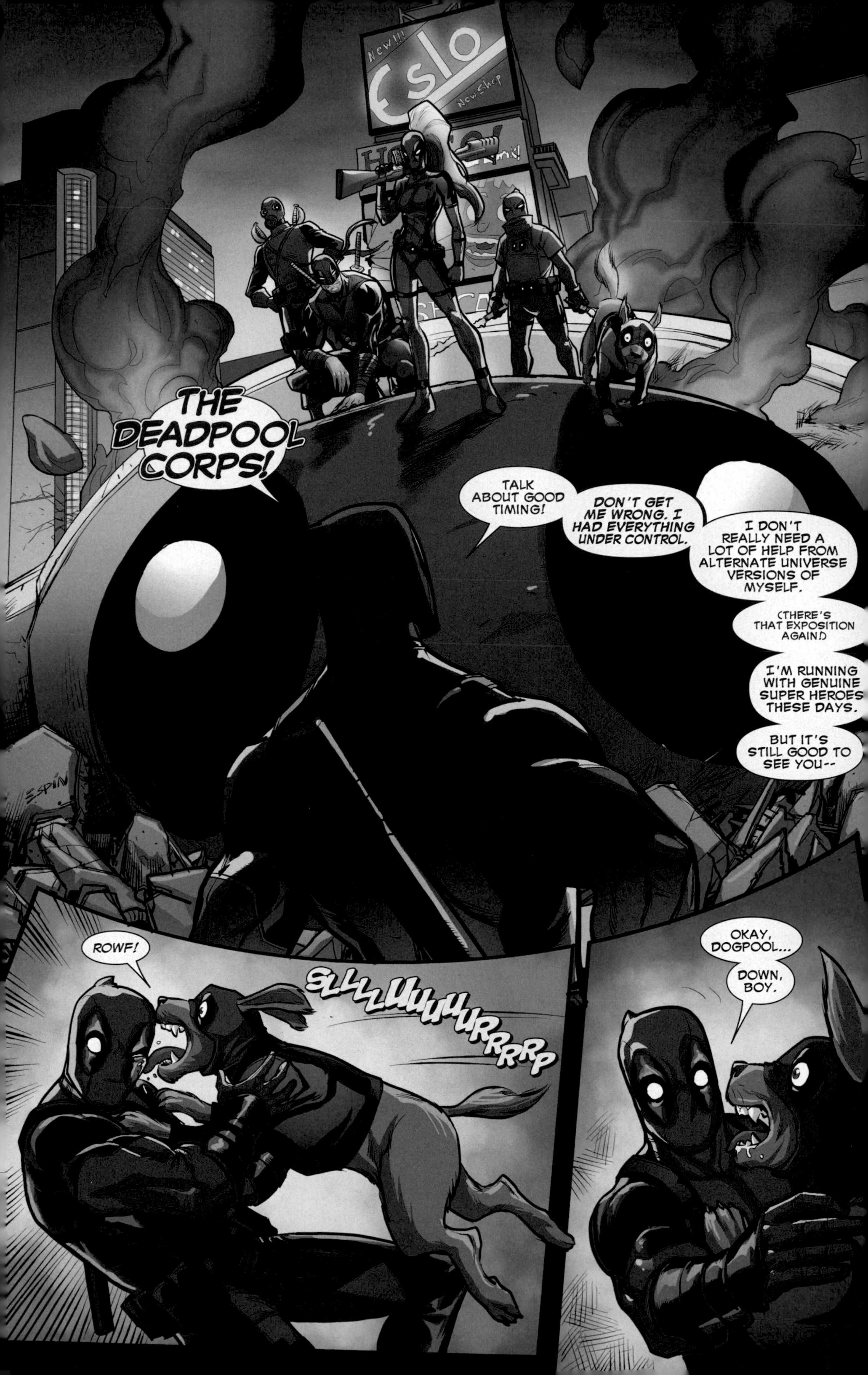

New!!!
Eslo
New Shop
THE DEADPOOL CORPS!
TALK ABOUT GOOD TIMING!
DON'T GET ME WRONG. I HAD EVERYTHING UNDER CONTROL.
I DON'T REALLY NEED A LOT OF HELP FROM ALTERNATE UNIVERSE VERSIONS OF MYSELF.
(THERE'S THAT EXPOSITION AGAIN.)
I'M RUNNING WITH GENUINE SUPER HEROES THESE DAYS.
BUT IT'S STILL GOOD TO SEE YOU--
ROWF!
SLLLLUUUUURRRRP
OKAY, DOGPOOL...
DOWN, BOY.

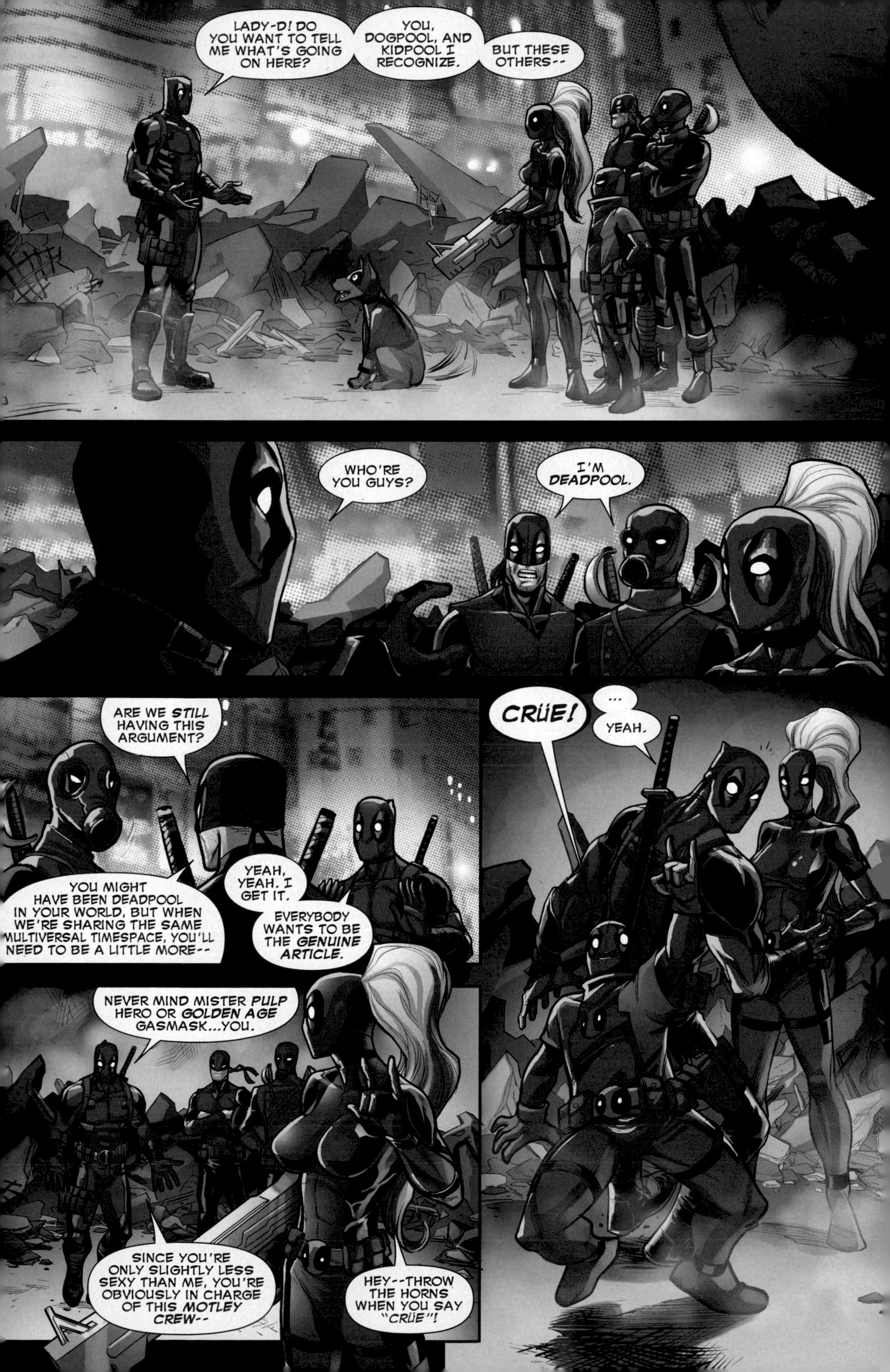

LADY-D! DO YOU WANT TO TELL ME WHAT'S GOING ON HERE?
YOU, DOGPOOL, AND KIDPOOL I RECOGNIZE.
BUT THESE OTHERS--
WHO'RE YOU GUYS?
I'M DEADPOOL.
ARE WE STILL HAVING THIS ARGUMENT?
YOU MIGHT HAVE BEEN DEADPOOL IN YOUR WORLD, BUT WHEN WE'RE SHARING THE SAME MULTIVERSAL TIMESPACE, YOU'LL NEED TO BE A LITTLE MORE--
YEAH, YEAH. I GET IT.
EVERYBODY WANTS TO BE THE GENUINE ARTICLE.
NEVER MIND MISTER PULP HERO OR GOLDEN AGE GASMASK...YOU.
SINCE YOU'RE ONLY SLIGHTLY LESS SEXY THAN ME, YOU'RE OBVIOUSLY IN CHARGE OF THIS MOTLEY CREW--
HEY--THROW THE HORNS WHEN YOU SAY "CRÜE"!
CRÜE!
...
YEAH.

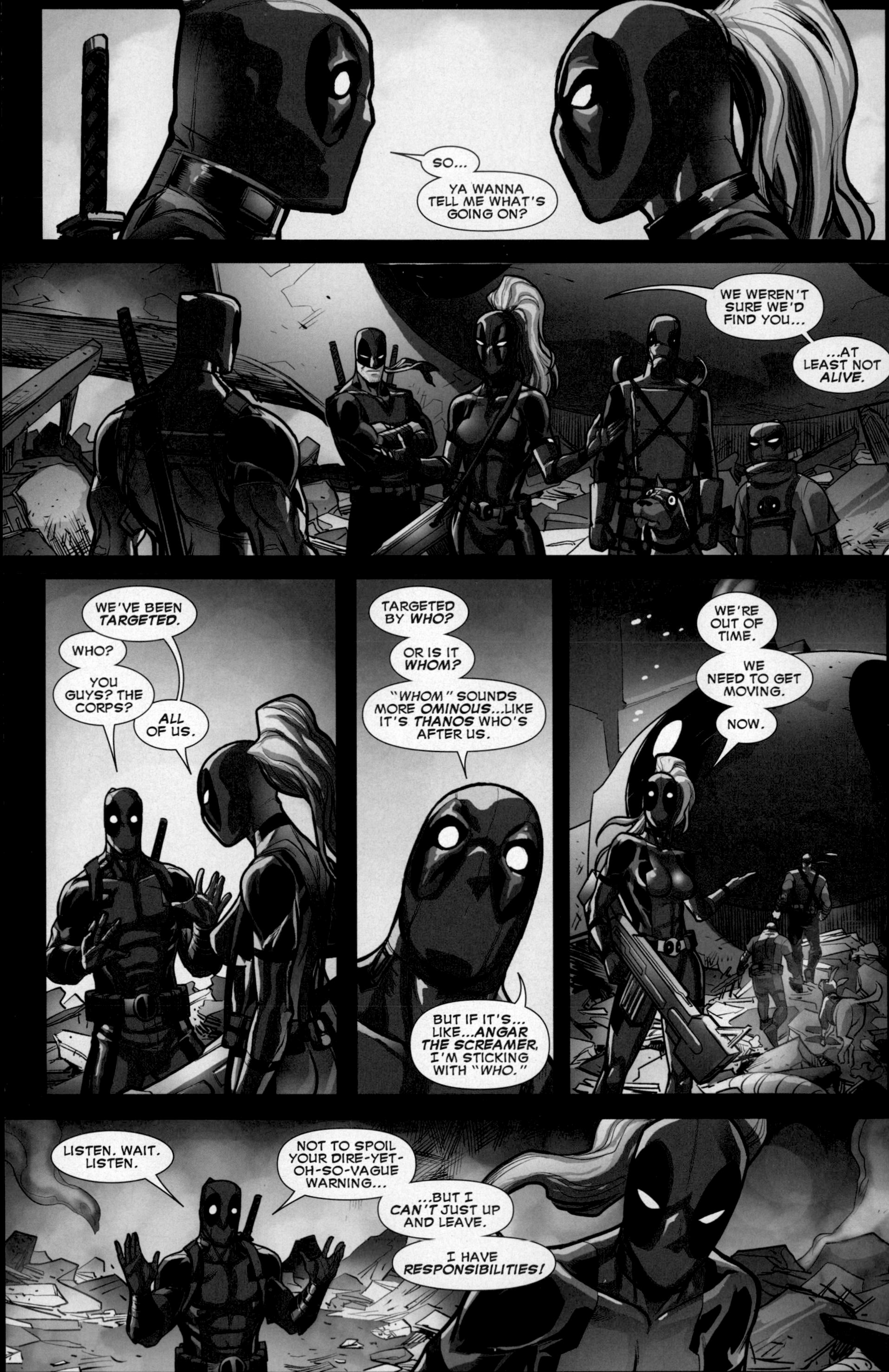

SO...
YA WANNA TELL ME WHAT'S GOING ON?
WE WEREN'T SURE WE'D FIND YOU...
...AT LEAST NOT ALIVE.
WE'VE BEEN TARGETED.
WHO?
YOU GUYS? THE CORPS?
ALL OF US.
TARGETED BY WHO?
OR IS IT WHOM?
"WHOM" SOUNDS MORE OMINOUS...LIKE IT'S THANOS WHO'S AFTER US.
BUT IF IT'S... LIKE...ANGAR THE SCREAMER, I'M STICKING WITH "WHO."
WE'RE OUT OF TIME.
WE NEED TO GET MOVING.
NOW.
LISTEN. WAIT. LISTEN.
NOT TO SPOIL YOUR DIRE-YET-OH-SO-VAGUE WARNING...
...BUT I CAN'T JUST UP AND LEAVE.
I HAVE RESPONSIBILITIES!

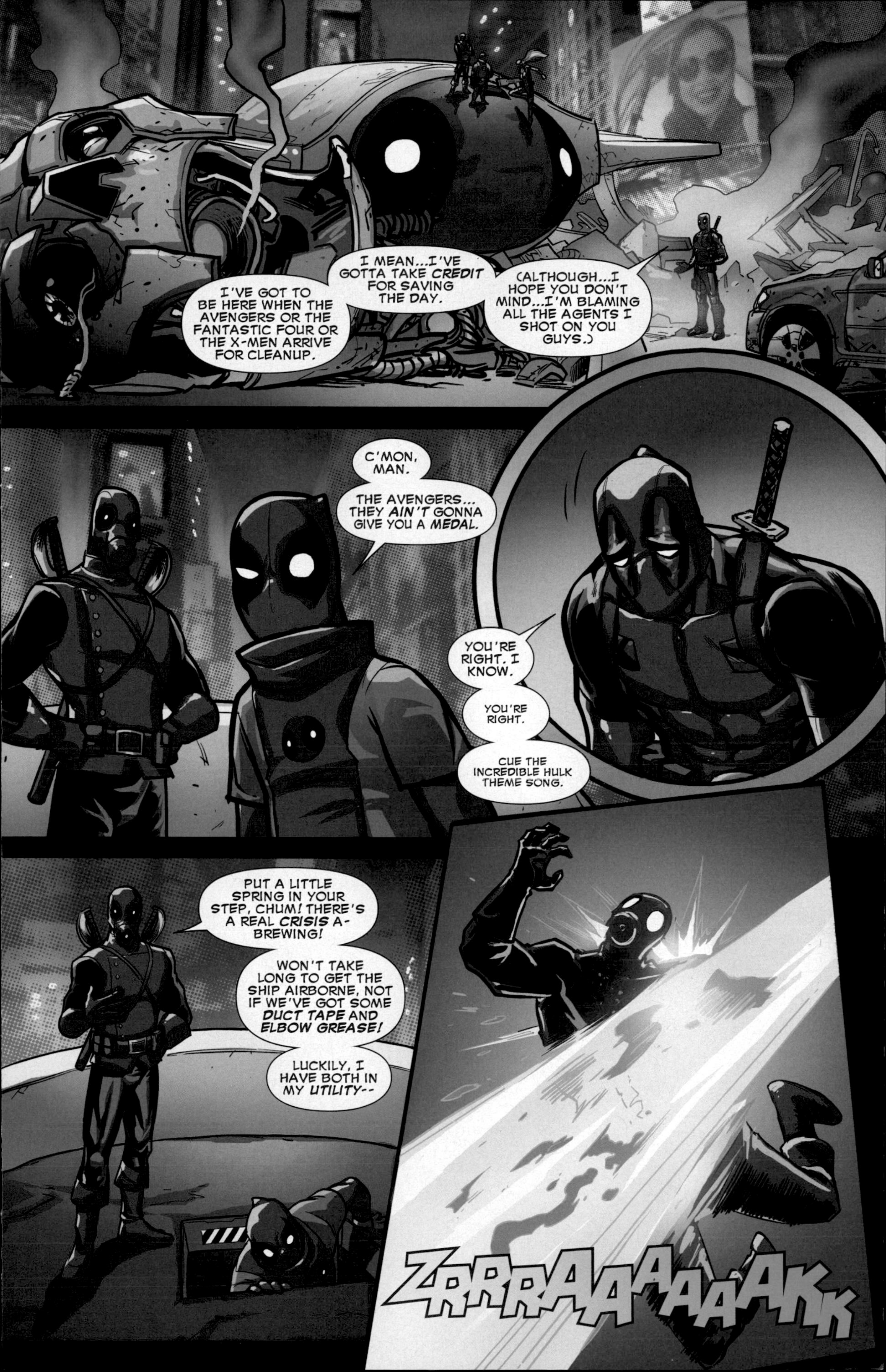
I'VE GOT TO BE HERE WHEN THE AVENGERS OR THE FANTASTIC FOUR OR THE X-MEN ARRIVE FOR CLEANUP.
I MEAN...I'VE GOTTA TAKE CREDIT FOR SAVING THE DAY.
(ALTHOUGH...I HOPE YOU DON'T MIND...I'M BLAMING ALL THE AGENTS I SHOT ON YOU GUYS.)
C'MON, MAN.
THE AVENGERS... THEY AIN'T GONNA GIVE YOU A MEDAL.
YOU'RE RIGHT. I KNOW.
YOU'RE RIGHT.
CUE THE INCREDIBLE HULK THEME SONG.
PUT A LITTLE SPRING IN YOUR STEP, CHUM! THERE'S A REAL CRISIS A-BREWING!
WON'T TAKE LONG TO GET THE SHIP AIRBORNE, NOT IF WE'VE GOT SOME DUCT TAPE AND ELBOW GREASE!
LUCKILY, I HAVE BOTH IN MY UTILITY--
ZRRRAAAAAAAKK

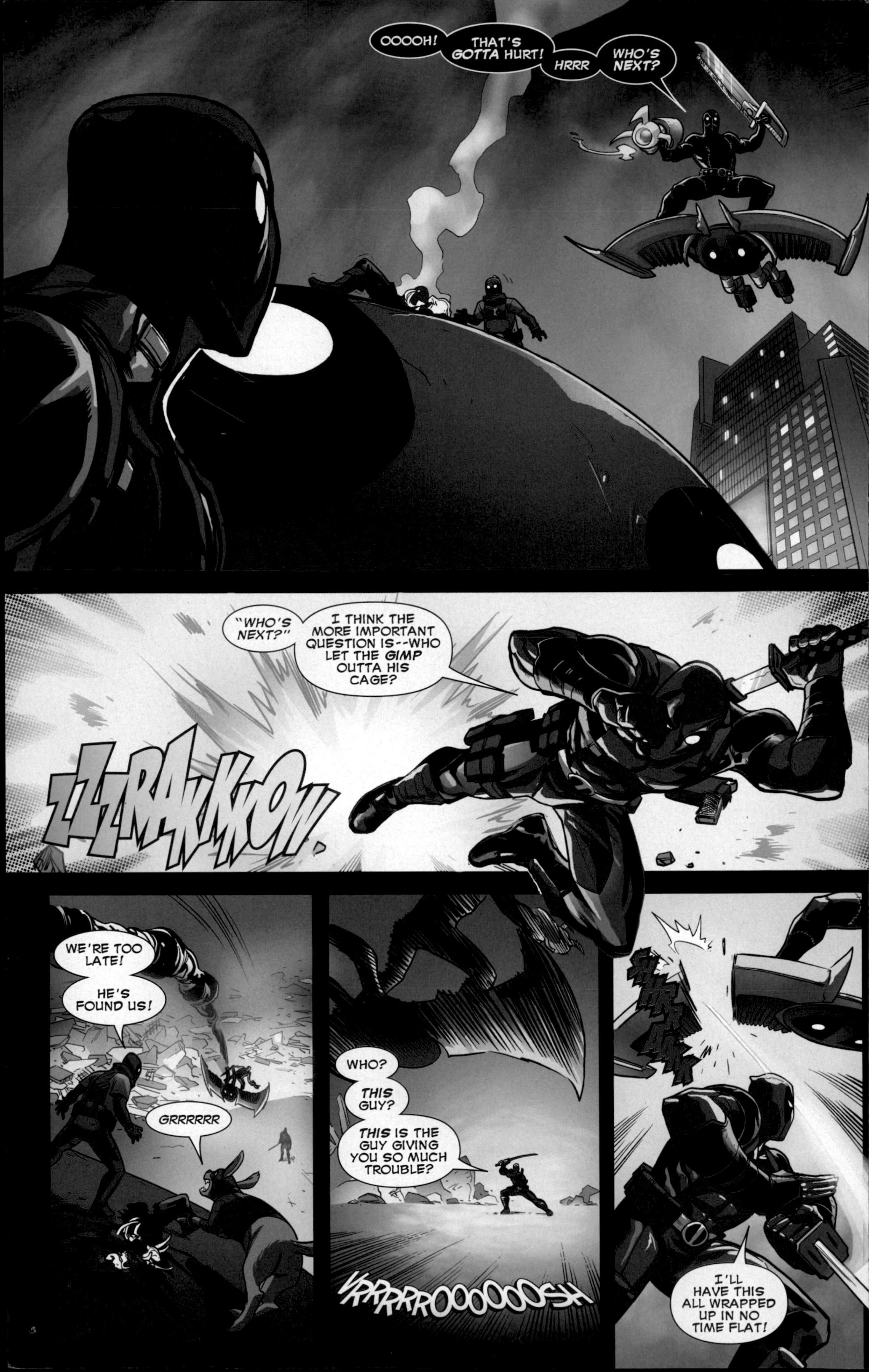
OOOOH!
THAT'S GOTTA HURT!
HRRR
WHO'S NEXT?
"WHO'S NEXT?"
I THINK THE MORE IMPORTANT QUESTION IS--WHO LET THE GIMP OUTTA HIS CAGE?
ZZZRAKKKOW
WE'RE TOO LATE!
HE'S FOUND US!
GRRRRRR
WHO?
THIS GUY?
THIS IS THE GUY GIVING YOU SO MUCH TROUBLE?
VRRRRROOOOOOOSH
I'LL HAVE THIS ALL WRAPPED UP IN NO TIME FLAT!

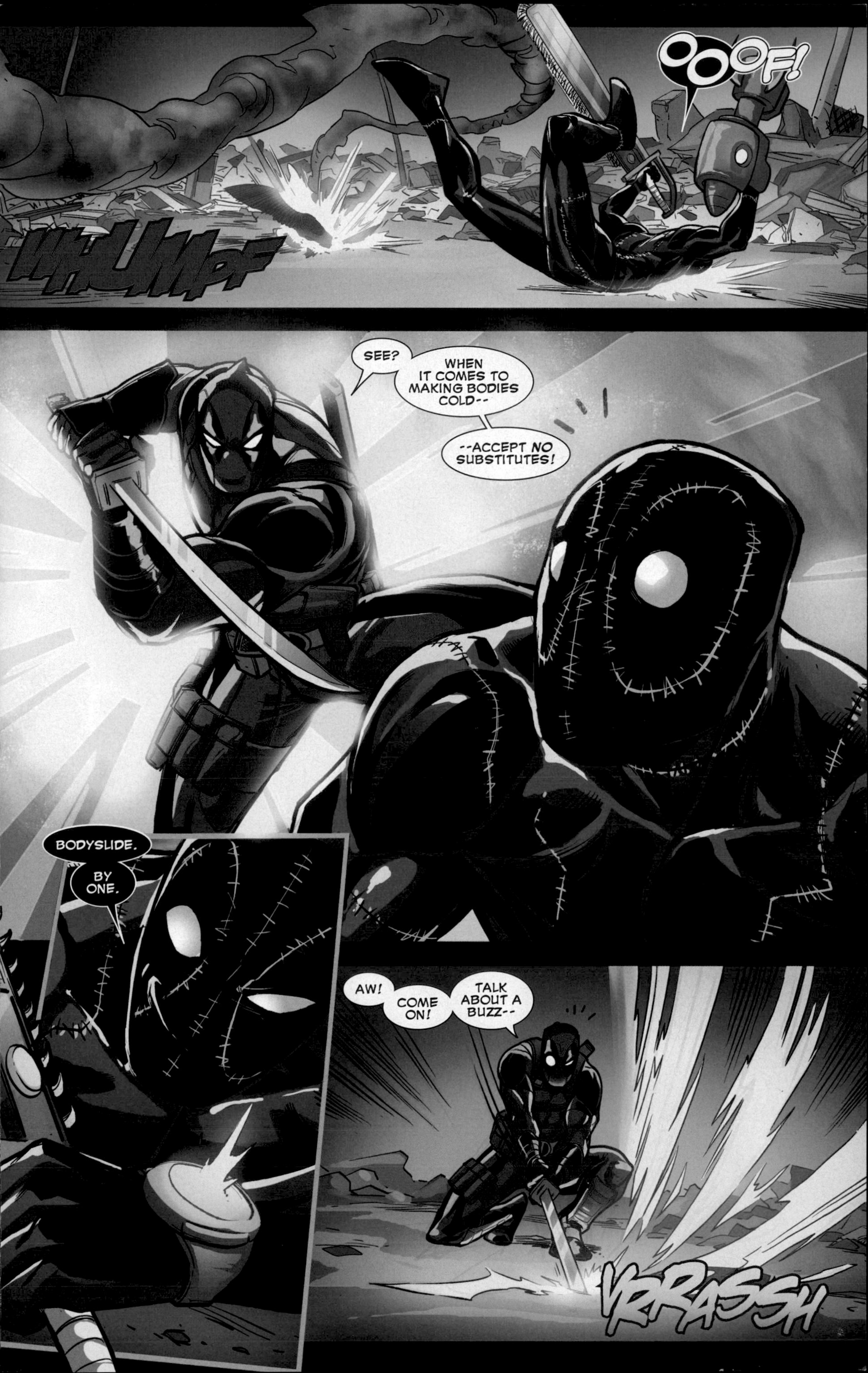
OOOF!
WHUMPF
SEE?
WHEN IT COMES TO MAKING BODIES COLD--
--ACCEPT NO SUBSTITUTES!
BODYSLIDE.
BY ONE.
AW!
COME ON!
TALK ABOUT A BUZZ--
VRRASSH

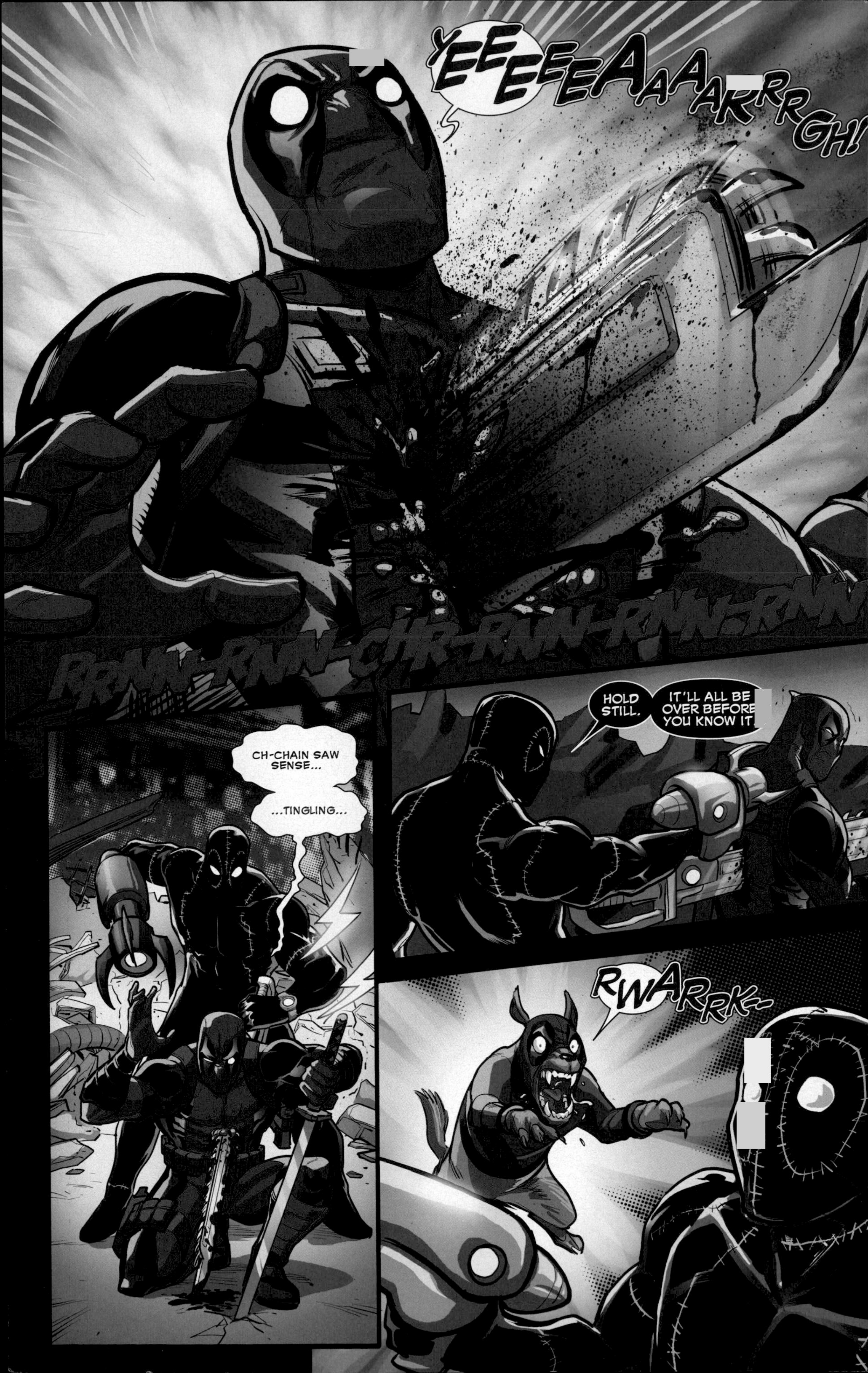
YEEEEEAAAARRRGH!
RRNN-RNN-CHR-RNN-RNN-RNN
CH-CHAIN SAW SENSE...
...TINGLING...
HOLD STILL.
IT'LL ALL BE OVER BEFORE YOU KNOW IT.
RWARRK--

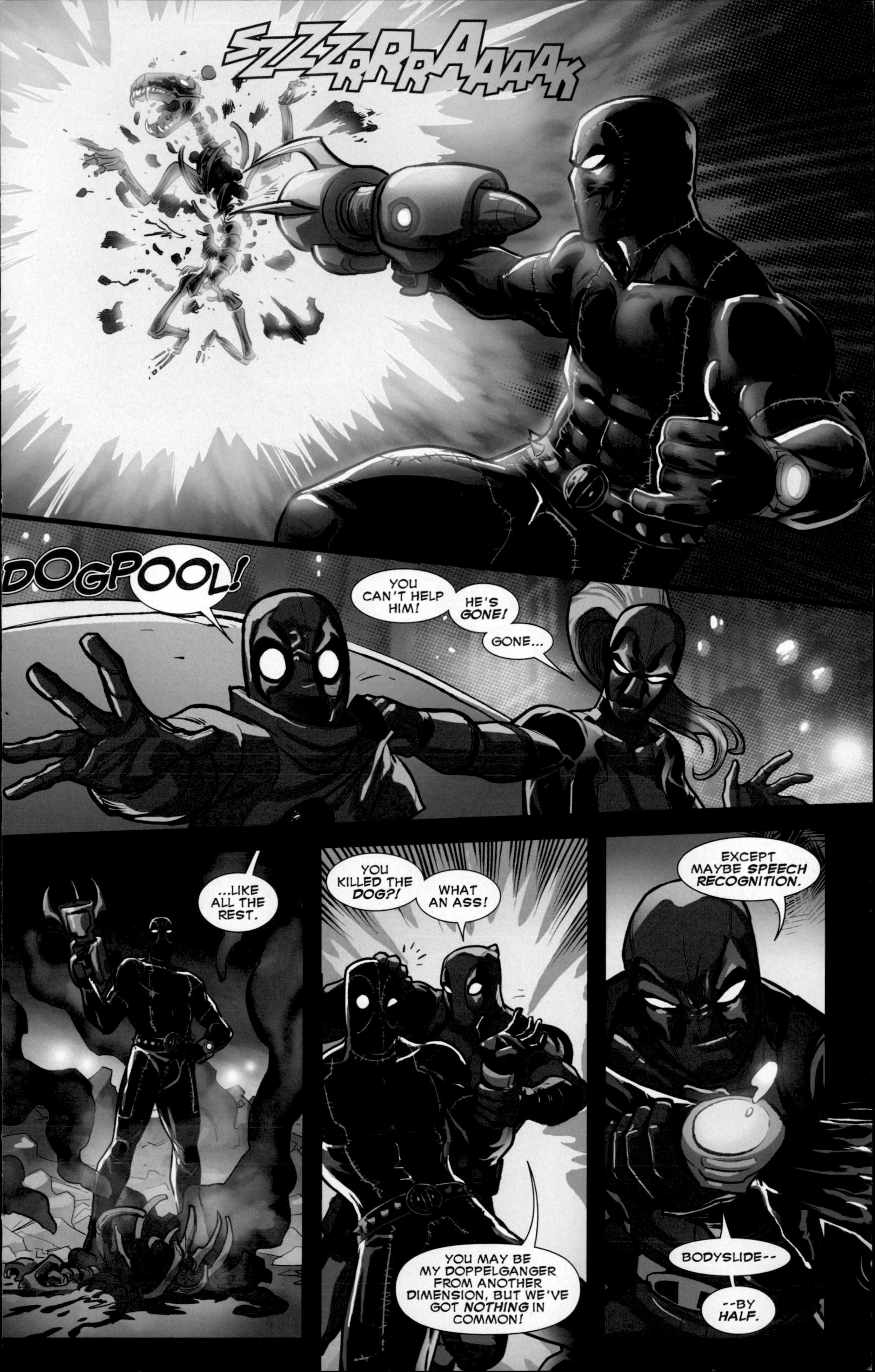
SZZZRRRAAAAK
DOGPOOL!
YOU CAN'T HELP HIM!
HE'S GONE!
GONE...
...LIKE ALL THE REST.
YOU KILLED THE DOG?!
WHAT AN ASS!
YOU MAY BE MY DOPPELGANGER FROM ANOTHER DIMENSION, BUT WE'VE GOT NOTHING IN COMMON!
EXCEPT MAYBE SPEECH RECOGNITION.
BODYSLIDE--
--BY HALF.

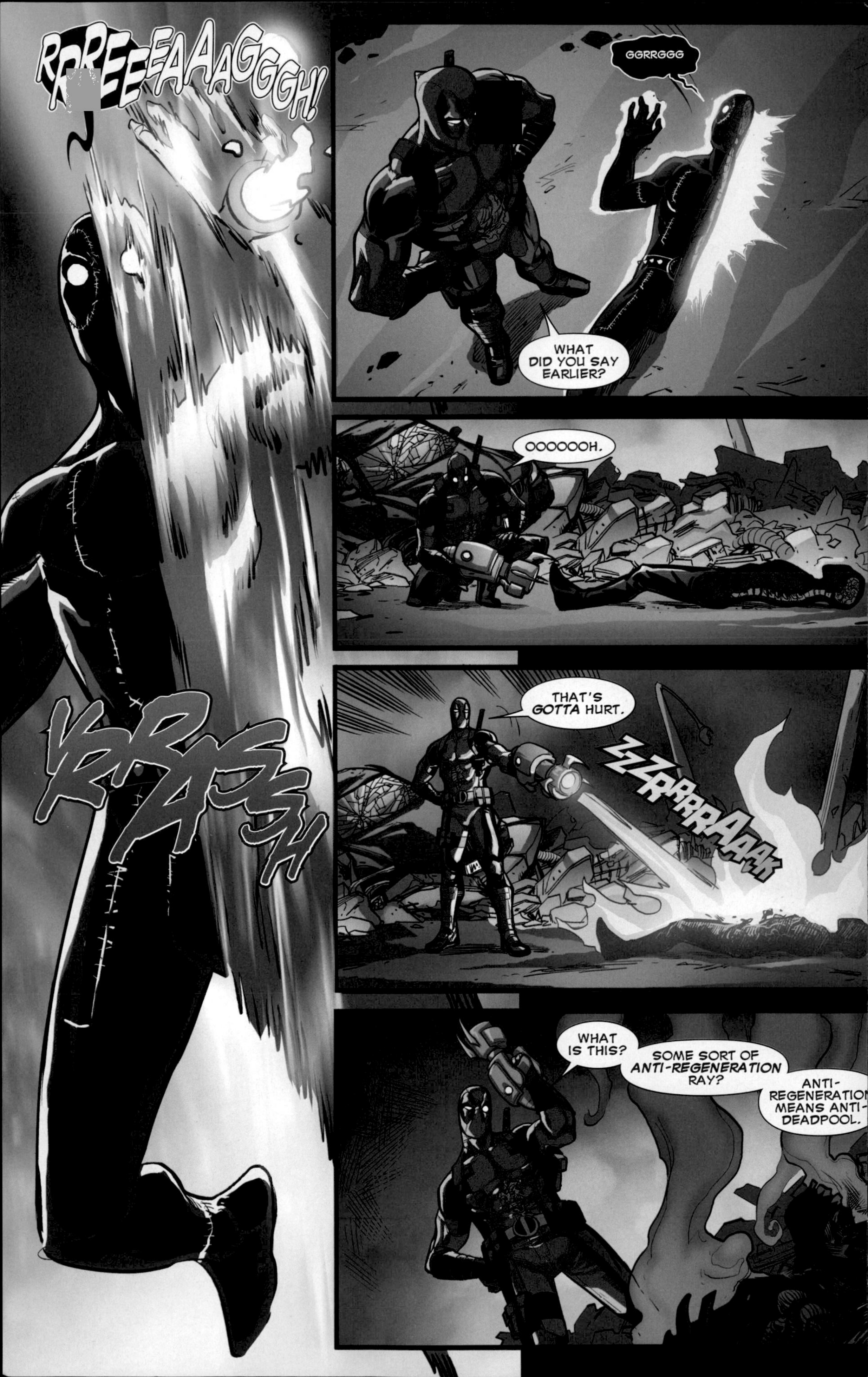
RRREEEAAAGGGGH!
KRASSH
GGRRGGG
WHAT DID YOU SAY EARLIER?
OOOOOOH.
THAT'S GOTTA HURT.
ZZZRRRRAAAK
WHAT IS THIS?
SOME SORT OF ANTI-REGENERATION RAY?
ANTI-REGENERATION MEANS ANTI-DEADPOOL.

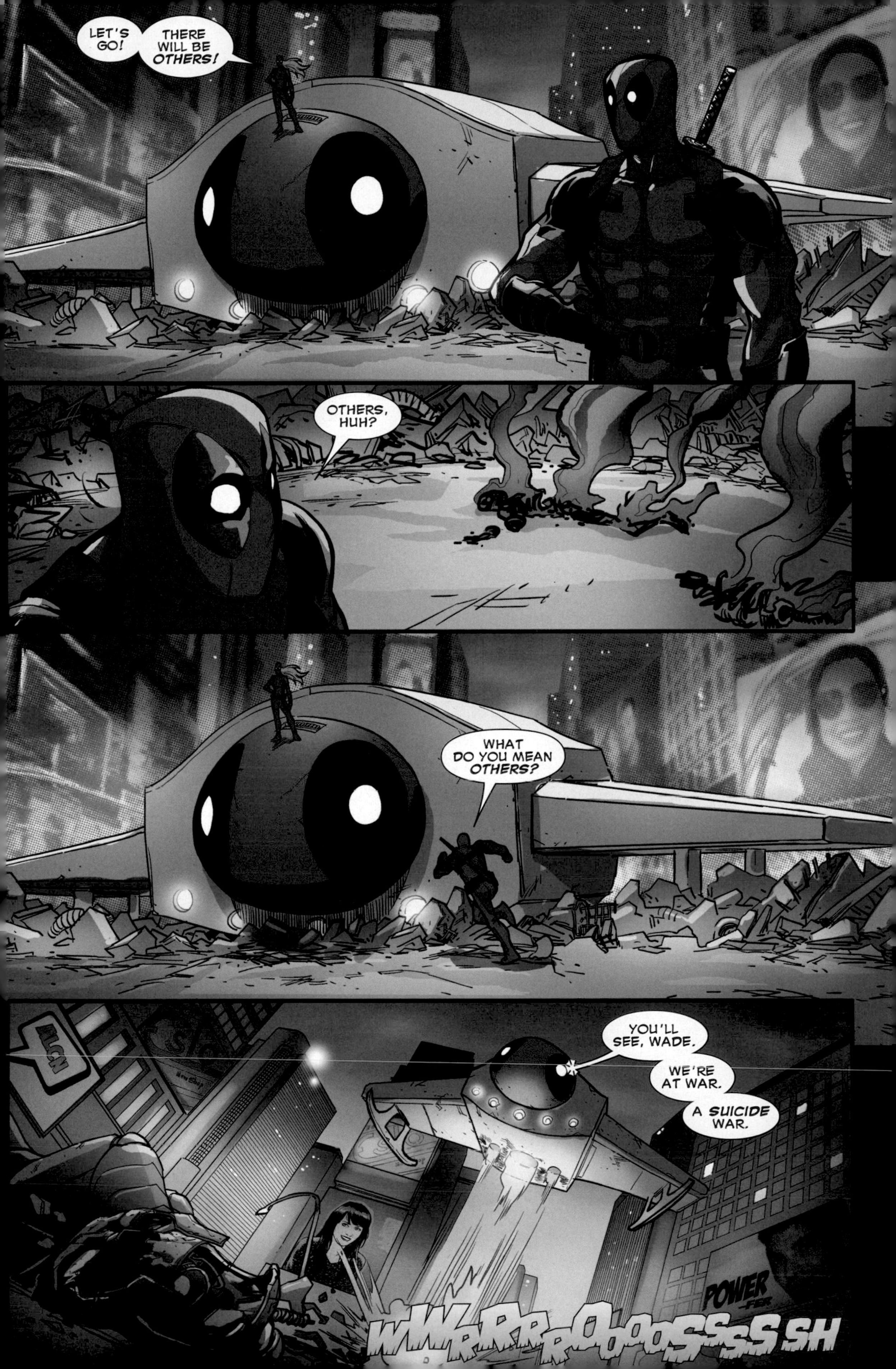
LET'S GO!
THERE WILL BE OTHERS!
OTHERS, HUH?
WHAT DO YOU MEAN OTHERS?
YOU'LL SEE, WADE.
WE'RE AT WAR.
A SUICIDE WAR.
POWER
WWRRRROOOOSSSSSH

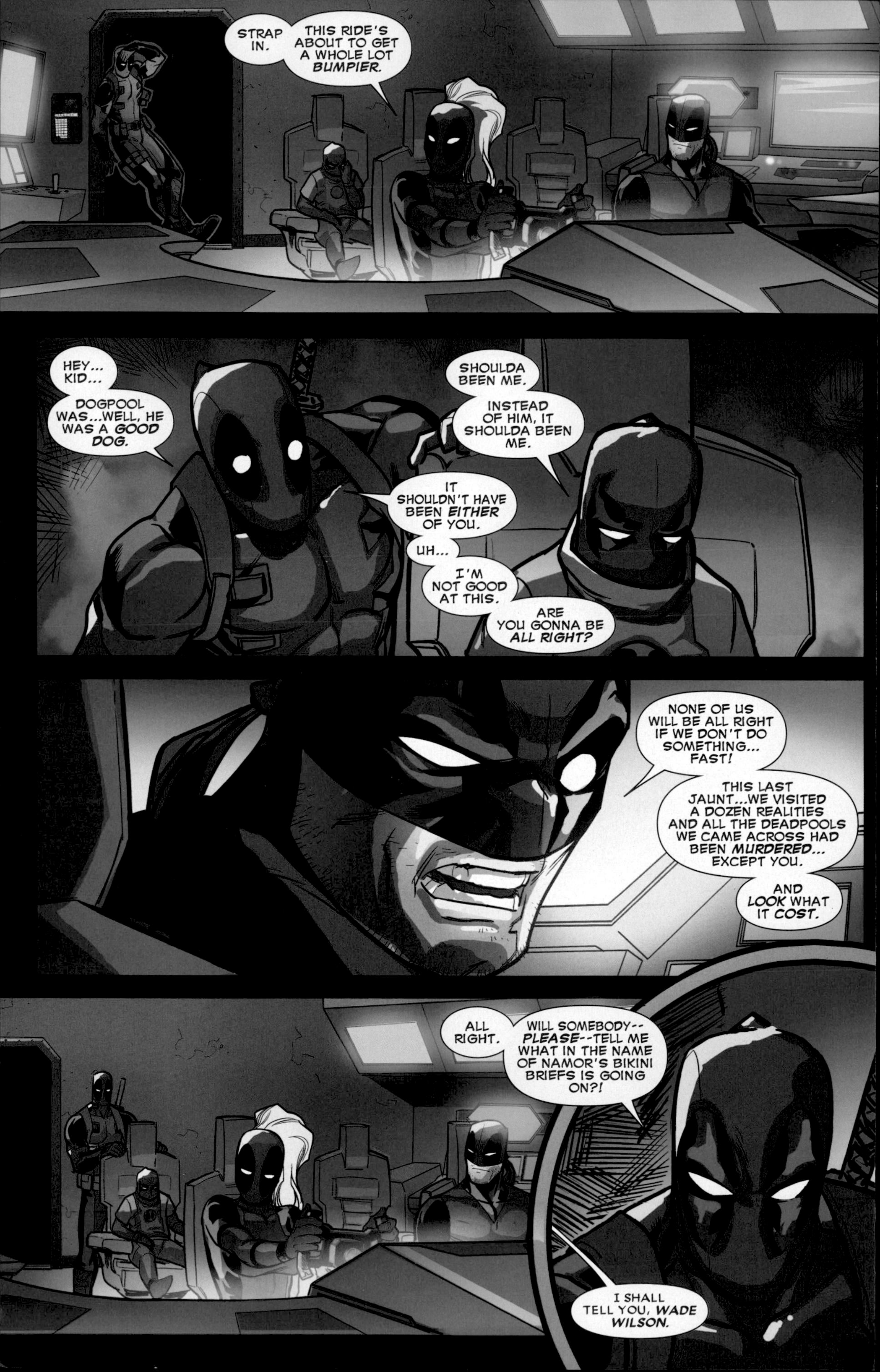
STRAP IN.
THIS RIDE'S ABOUT TO GET A WHOLE LOT BUMPIER.
HEY... KID...
DOGPOOL WAS...WELL, HE WAS A GOOD DOG.
SHOULDA BEEN ME.
INSTEAD OF HIM, IT SHOULDA BEEN ME.
IT SHOULDN'T HAVE BEEN EITHER OF YOU.
UH...
I'M NOT GOOD AT THIS.
ARE YOU GONNA BE ALL RIGHT?
NONE OF US WILL BE ALL RIGHT IF WE DON'T DO SOMETHING... FAST!
THIS LAST JAUNT...WE VISITED A DOZEN REALITIES AND ALL THE DEADPOOLS WE CAME ACROSS HAD BEEN MURDERED... EXCEPT YOU.
AND LOOK WHAT IT COST.
ALL RIGHT.
WILL SOMEBODY--PLEASE--TELL ME WHAT IN THE NAME OF NAMOR'S BIKINI BRIEFS IS GOING ON?!
I SHALL TELL YOU, WADE WILSON.

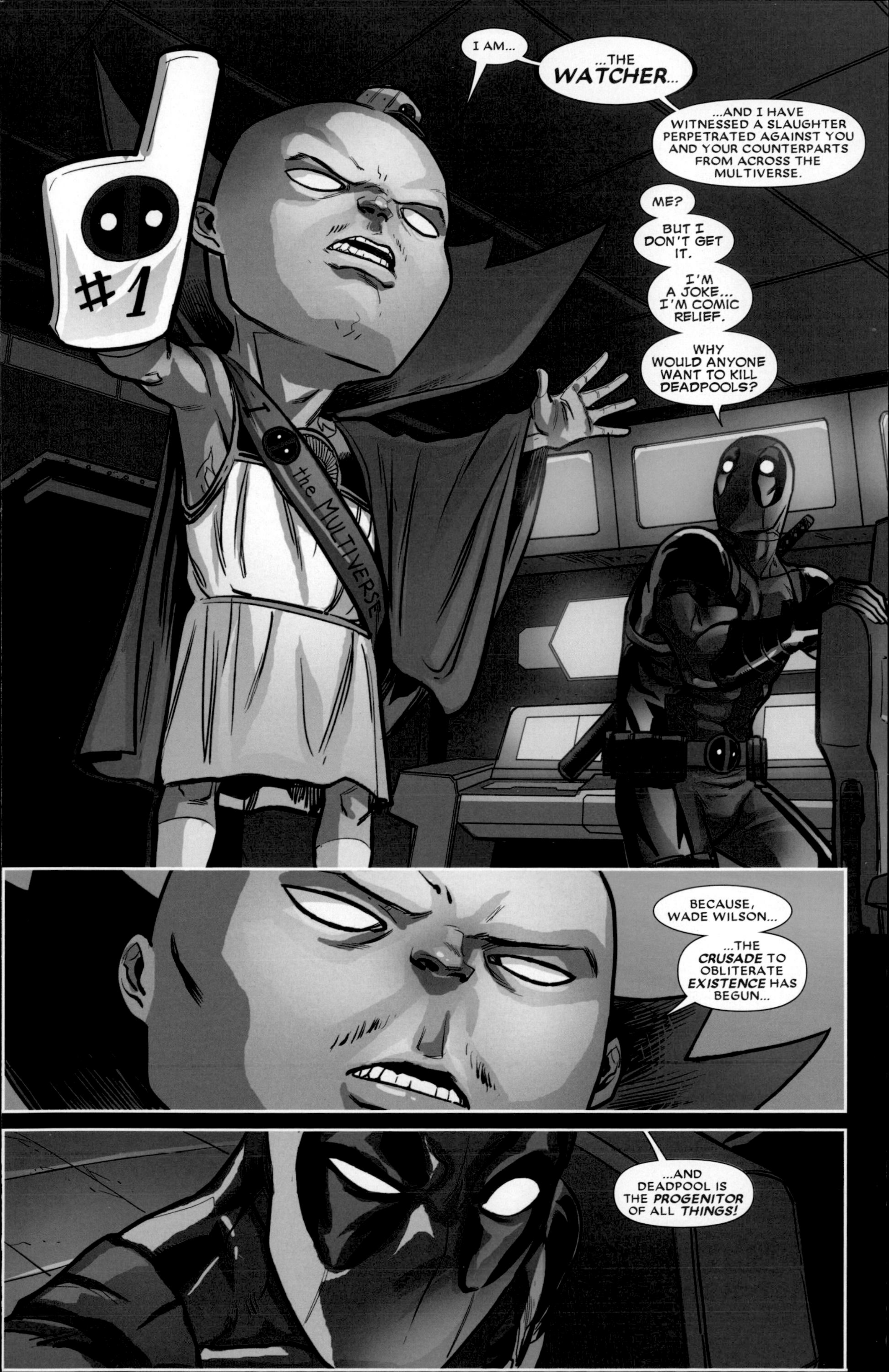
#1
I
the MULTIVERSE
I AM...
...THE WATCHER...
...AND I HAVE WITNESSED A SLAUGHTER PERPETRATED AGAINST YOU AND YOUR COUNTERPARTS FROM ACROSS THE MULTIVERSE.
ME?
BUT I DON'T GET IT.
I'M A JOKE... I'M COMIC RELIEF.
WHY WOULD ANYONE WANT TO KILL DEADPOOLS?
BECAUSE, WADE WILSON...
...THE CRUSADE TO OBLITERATE EXISTENCE HAS BEGUN...
...AND DEADPOOL IS THE PROGENITOR OF ALL THINGS!

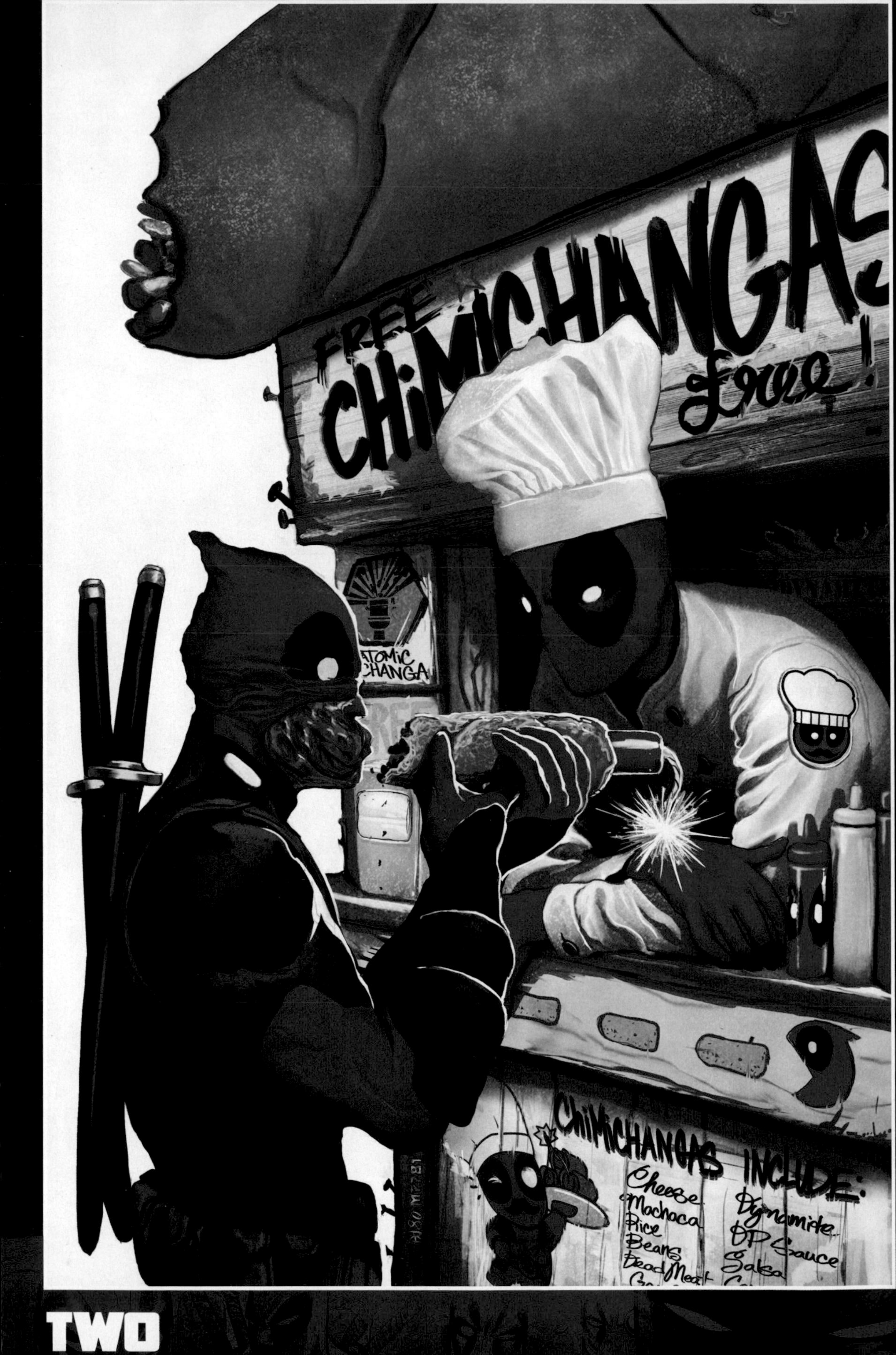
FREE
CHIMICHANGAS
Free!
ATOMIC CHANGA
CHIMICHANGAS INCLUDE:
Cheese
Machaca
Rice
Beans
Dead Meat
Dynamite
DP Sauce
Salsa

TWO

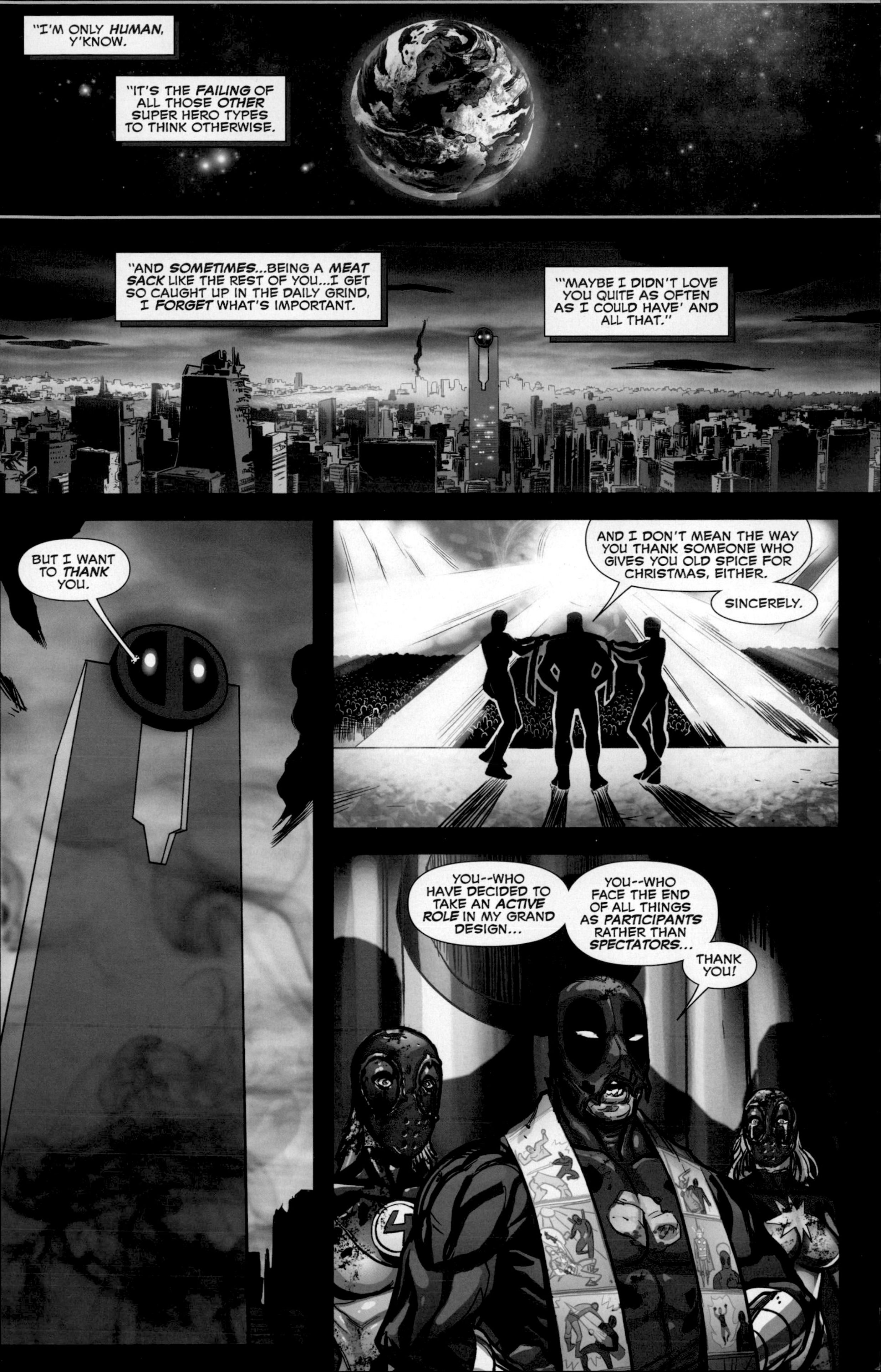
"I'M ONLY HUMAN, Y'KNOW.
"IT'S THE FAILING OF ALL THOSE OTHER SUPER HERO TYPES TO THINK OTHERWISE.
"AND SOMETIMES...BEING A MEAT SACK LIKE THE REST OF YOU...I GET SO CAUGHT UP IN THE DAILY GRIND, I FORGET WHAT'S IMPORTANT.
"'MAYBE I DIDN'T LOVE YOU QUITE AS OFTEN AS I COULD HAVE' AND ALL THAT."
BUT I WANT TO THANK YOU.
AND I DON'T MEAN THE WAY YOU THANK SOMEONE WHO GIVES YOU OLD SPICE FOR CHRISTMAS, EITHER.
SINCERELY.
YOU--WHO HAVE DECIDED TO TAKE AN ACTIVE ROLE IN MY GRAND DESIGN...
YOU--WHO FACE THE END OF ALL THINGS AS PARTICIPANTS RATHER THAN SPECTATORS...
THANK YOU!

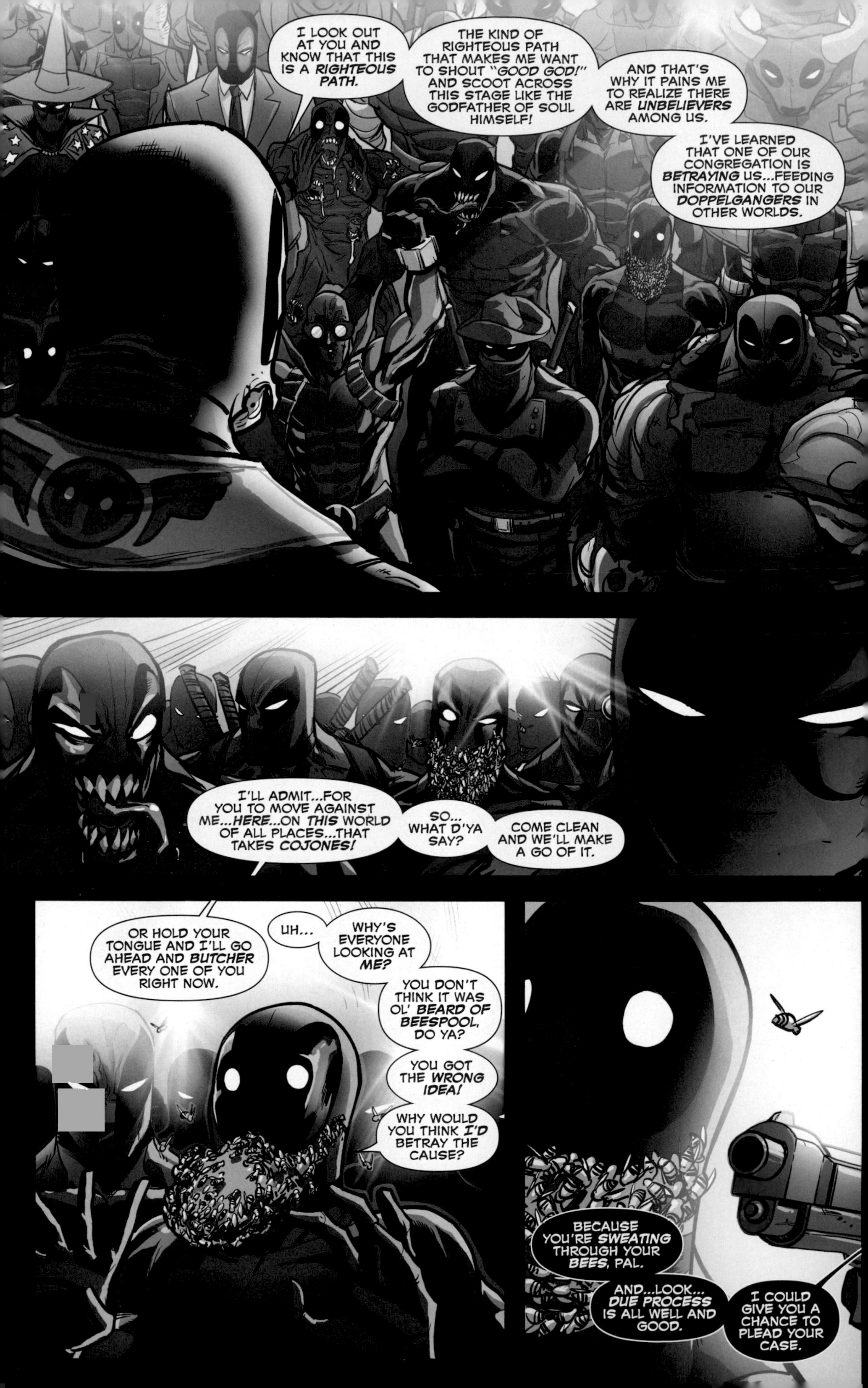
I LOOK OUT AT YOU AND KNOW THAT THIS IS A RIGHTEOUS PATH.
THE KIND OF RIGHTEOUS PATH THAT MAKES ME WANT TO SHOUT "GOOD GOD!" AND SCOOT ACROSS THIS STAGE LIKE THE GODFATHER OF SOUL HIMSELF!
AND THAT'S WHY IT PAINS ME TO REALIZE THERE ARE UNBELIEVERS AMONG US.
I'VE LEARNED THAT ONE OF OUR CONGREGATION IS BETRAYING US...FEEDING INFORMATION TO OUR DOPPELGANGERS IN OTHER WORLDS.
I'LL ADMIT...FOR YOU TO MOVE AGAINST ME...HERE...ON THIS WORLD OF ALL PLACES...THAT TAKES COJONES!
SO... WHAT D'YA SAY?
COME CLEAN AND WE'LL MAKE A GO OF IT.
OR HOLD YOUR TONGUE AND I'LL GO AHEAD AND BUTCHER EVERY ONE OF YOU RIGHT NOW.
UH...
WHY'S EVERYONE LOOKING AT ME?
YOU DON'T THINK IT WAS OL' BEARD OF BEESPOOL, DO YA?
YOU GOT THE WRONG IDEA!
WHY WOULD YOU THINK I'D BETRAY THE CAUSE?
BECAUSE YOU'RE SWEATING THROUGH YOUR BEES, PAL.
AND...LOOK... DUE PROCESS IS ALL WELL AND GOOD.
I COULD GIVE YOU A CHANCE TO PLEAD YOUR CASE.

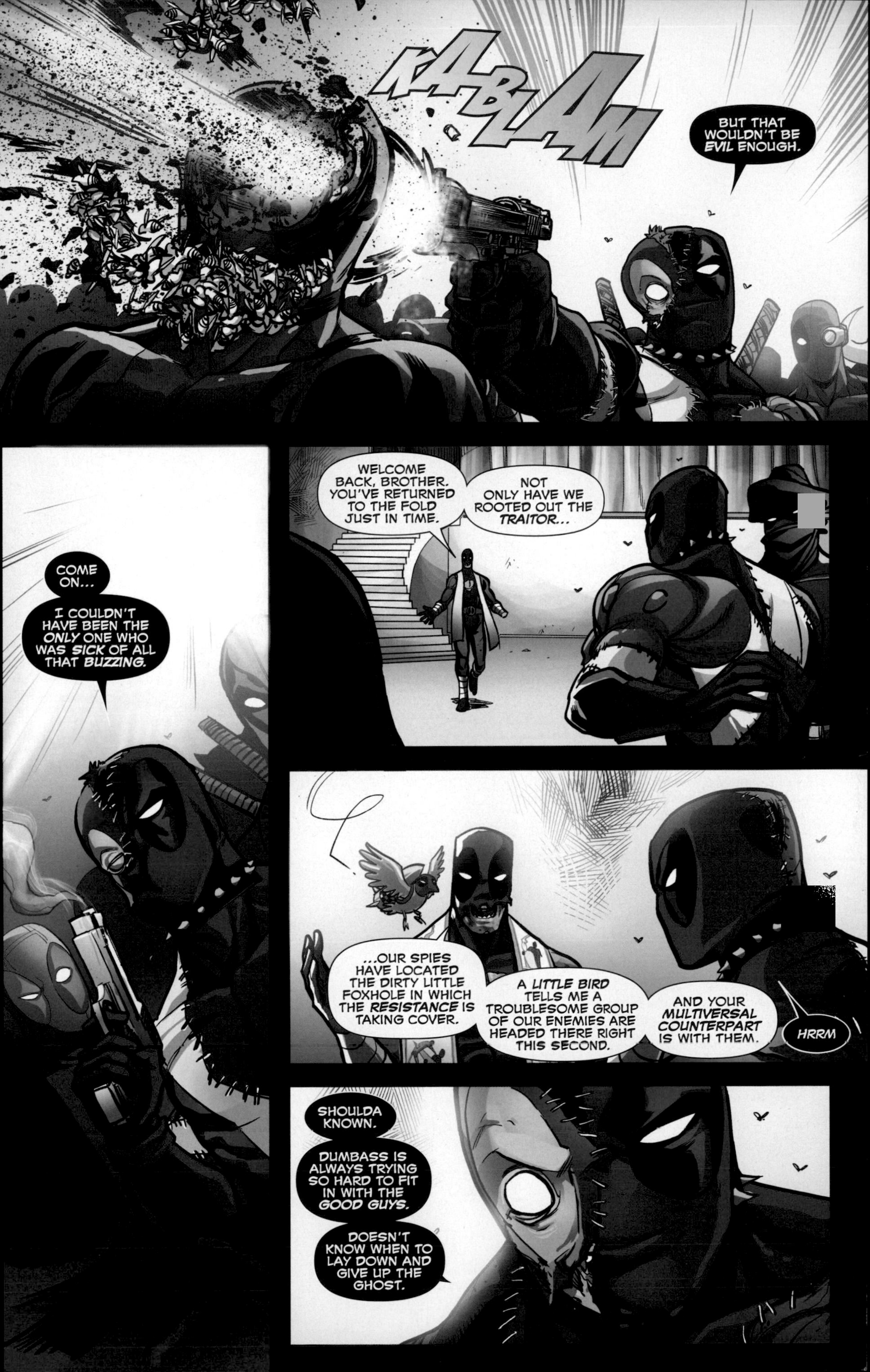
KABLAM
BUT THAT WOULDN'T BE EVIL ENOUGH.
COME ON...
I COULDN'T HAVE BEEN THE ONLY ONE WHO WAS SICK OF ALL THAT BUZZING.
WELCOME BACK, BROTHER. YOU'VE RETURNED TO THE FOLD JUST IN TIME.
NOT ONLY HAVE WE ROOTED OUT THE TRAITOR...
...OUR SPIES HAVE LOCATED THE DIRTY LITTLE FOXHOLE IN WHICH THE RESISTANCE IS TAKING COVER.
A LITTLE BIRD TELLS ME A TROUBLESOME GROUP OF OUR ENEMIES ARE HEADED THERE RIGHT THIS SECOND.
AND YOUR MULTIVERSAL COUNTERPART IS WITH THEM.
HRRM
SHOULDA KNOWN.
DUMBASS IS ALWAYS TRYING SO HARD TO FIT IN WITH THE GOOD GUYS.
DOESN'T KNOW WHEN TO LAY DOWN AND GIVE UP THE GHOST.

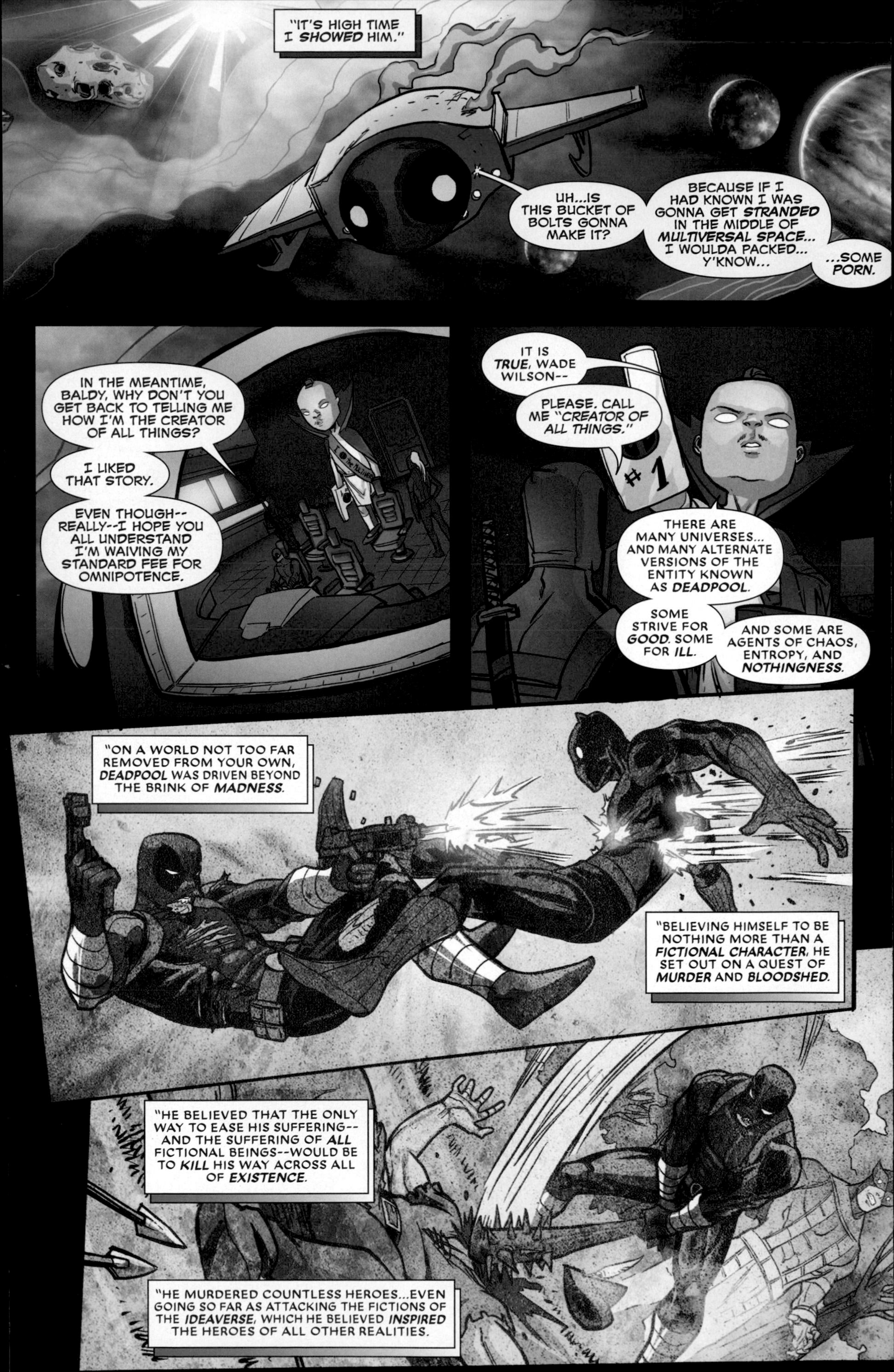
"IT'S HIGH TIME I SHOWED HIM."
UH...IS THIS BUCKET OF BOLTS GONNA MAKE IT?
BECAUSE IF I HAD KNOWN I WAS GONNA GET STRANDED IN THE MIDDLE OF MULTIVERSAL SPACE... I WOULDA PACKED... Y'KNOW...
...SOME PORN.
IN THE MEANTIME, BALDY, WHY DON'T YOU GET BACK TO TELLING ME HOW I'M THE CREATOR OF ALL THINGS?
I LIKED THAT STORY.
EVEN THOUGH-- REALLY--I HOPE YOU ALL UNDERSTAND I'M WAIVING MY STANDARD FEE FOR OMNIPOTENCE.
IT IS TRUE, WADE WILSON--
PLEASE. CALL ME "CREATOR OF ALL THINGS."
#1
THERE ARE MANY UNIVERSES... AND MANY ALTERNATE VERSIONS OF THE ENTITY KNOWN AS DEADPOOL.
SOME STRIVE FOR GOOD. SOME FOR ILL.
AND SOME ARE AGENTS OF CHAOS, ENTROPY, AND NOTHINGNESS.
"ON A WORLD NOT TOO FAR REMOVED FROM YOUR OWN, DEADPOOL WAS DRIVEN BEYOND THE BRINK OF MADNESS.
"BELIEVING HIMSELF TO BE NOTHING MORE THAN A FICTIONAL CHARACTER, HE SET OUT ON A QUEST OF MURDER AND BLOODSHED.
"HE BELIEVED THAT THE ONLY WAY TO EASE HIS SUFFERING-- AND THE SUFFERING OF ALL FICTIONAL BEINGS--WOULD BE TO KILL HIS WAY ACROSS ALL OF EXISTENCE.
"HE MURDERED COUNTLESS HEROES...EVEN GOING SO FAR AS ATTACKING THE FICTIONS OF THE IDEAVERSE, WHICH HE BELIEVED INSPIRED THE HEROES OF ALL OTHER REALITIES.

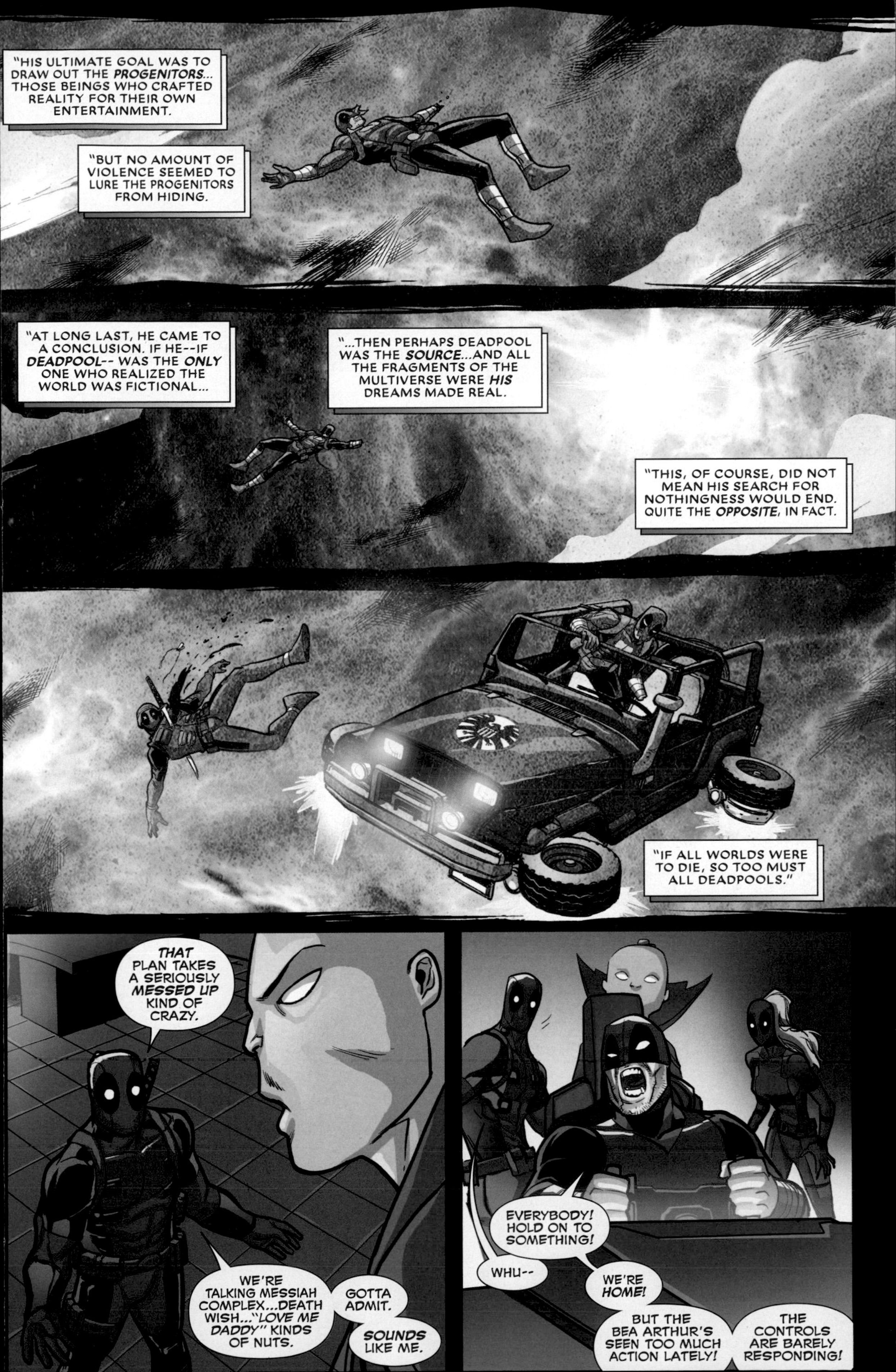
"HIS ULTIMATE GOAL WAS TO DRAW OUT THE PROGENITORS... THOSE BEINGS WHO CRAFTED REALITY FOR THEIR OWN ENTERTAINMENT.
"BUT NO AMOUNT OF VIOLENCE SEEMED TO LURE THE PROGENITORS FROM HIDING.
"AT LONG LAST, HE CAME TO A CONCLUSION. IF HE--IF DEADPOOL-- WAS THE ONLY ONE WHO REALIZED THE WORLD WAS FICTIONAL...
"...THEN PERHAPS DEADPOOL WAS THE SOURCE...AND ALL THE FRAGMENTS OF THE MULTIVERSE WERE HIS DREAMS MADE REAL.
"THIS, OF COURSE, DID NOT MEAN HIS SEARCH FOR NOTHINGNESS WOULD END. QUITE THE OPPOSITE, IN FACT.
"IF ALL WORLDS WERE TO DIE, SO TOO MUST ALL DEADPOOLS."
THAT PLAN TAKES A SERIOUSLY MESSED UP KIND OF CRAZY.
WE'RE TALKING MESSIAH COMPLEX...DEATH WISH..."LOVE ME DADDY" KINDS OF NUTS.
GOTTA ADMIT.
SOUNDS LIKE ME.
EVERYBODY! HOLD ON TO SOMETHING!
WHU--
WE'RE HOME!
BUT THE BEA ARTHUR'S SEEN TOO MUCH ACTION LATELY!
THE CONTROLS ARE BARELY RESPONDING!

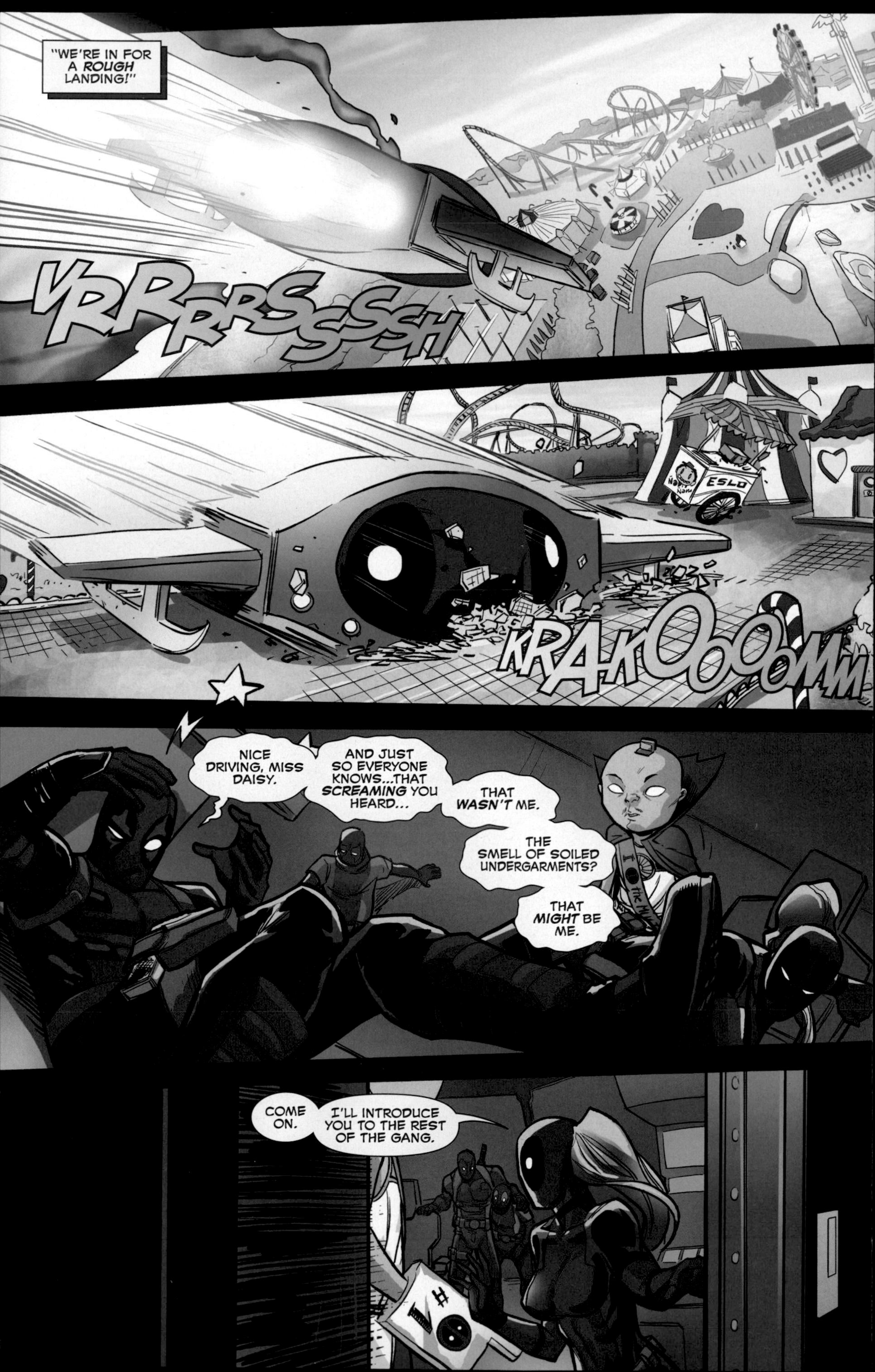
"WE'RE IN FOR A ROUGH LANDING!"
VRRRRSSSSH
ESLO
KRAKOOOOMM
NICE DRIVING, MISS DAISY.
AND JUST SO EVERYONE KNOWS...THAT SCREAMING YOU HEARD...
THAT WASN'T ME.
THE SMELL OF SOILED UNDERGARMENTS?
THAT MIGHT BE ME.
COME ON.
I'LL INTRODUCE YOU TO THE REST OF THE GANG.

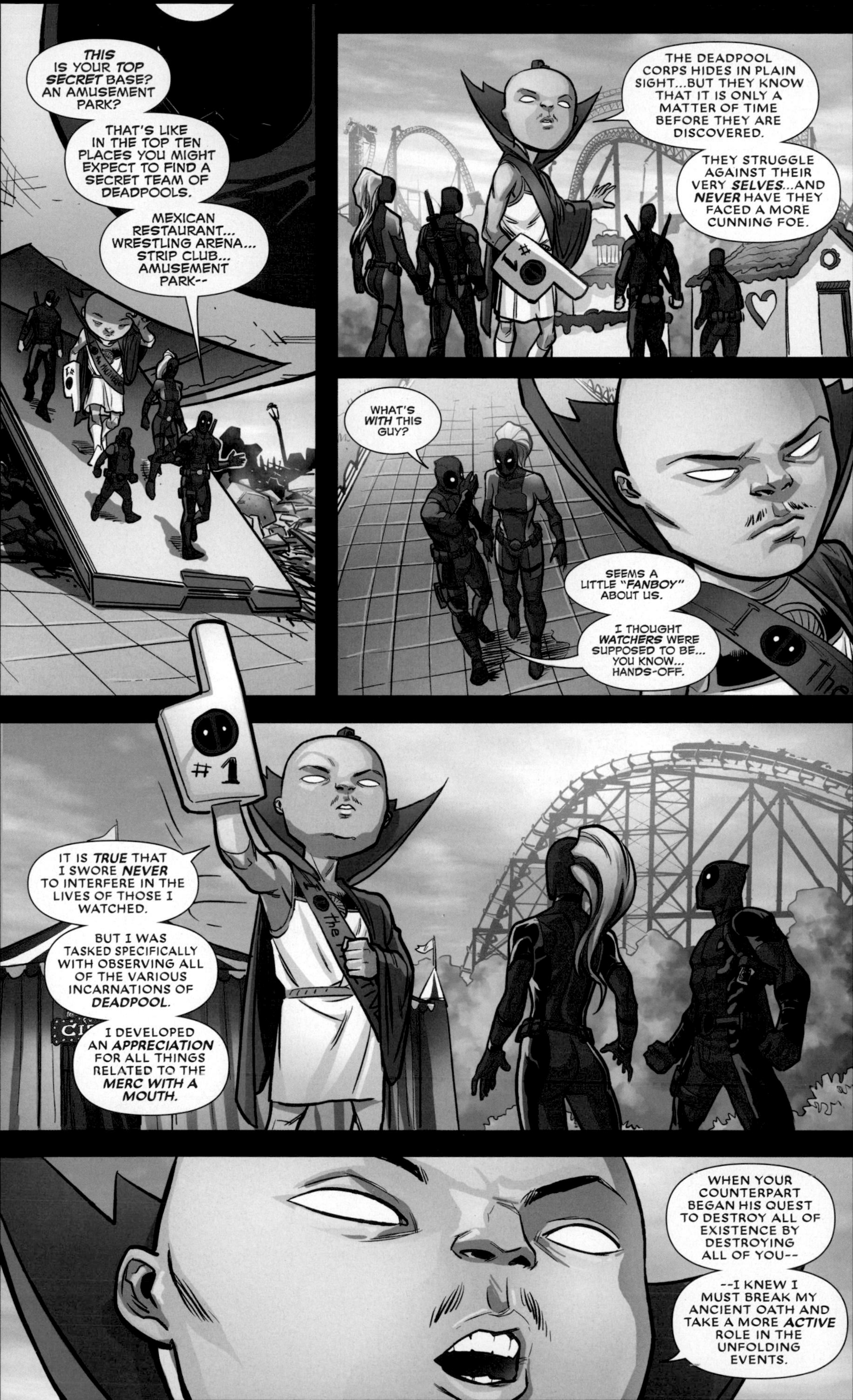
THIS IS YOUR TOP SECRET BASE? AN AMUSEMENT PARK?
THAT'S LIKE IN THE TOP TEN PLACES YOU MIGHT EXPECT TO FIND A SECRET TEAM OF DEADPOOLS.
MEXICAN RESTAURANT... WRESTLING ARENA... STRIP CLUB... AMUSEMENT PARK--
THE DEADPOOL CORPS HIDES IN PLAIN SIGHT...BUT THEY KNOW THAT IT IS ONLY A MATTER OF TIME BEFORE THEY ARE DISCOVERED.
THEY STRUGGLE AGAINST THEIR VERY SELVES...AND NEVER HAVE THEY FACED A MORE CUNNING FOE.
WHAT'S WITH THIS GUY?
SEEMS A LITTLE "FANBOY" ABOUT US.
I THOUGHT WATCHERS WERE SUPPOSED TO BE... YOU KNOW... HANDS-OFF.
#1
IT IS TRUE THAT I SWORE NEVER TO INTERFERE IN THE LIVES OF THOSE I WATCHED.
BUT I WAS TASKED SPECIFICALLY WITH OBSERVING ALL OF THE VARIOUS INCARNATIONS OF DEADPOOL.
I DEVELOPED AN APPRECIATION FOR ALL THINGS RELATED TO THE MERC WITH A MOUTH.
WHEN YOUR COUNTERPART BEGAN HIS QUEST TO DESTROY ALL OF EXISTENCE BY DESTROYING ALL OF YOU--
--I KNEW I MUST BREAK MY ANCIENT OATH AND TAKE A MORE ACTIVE ROLE IN THE UNFOLDING EVENTS.

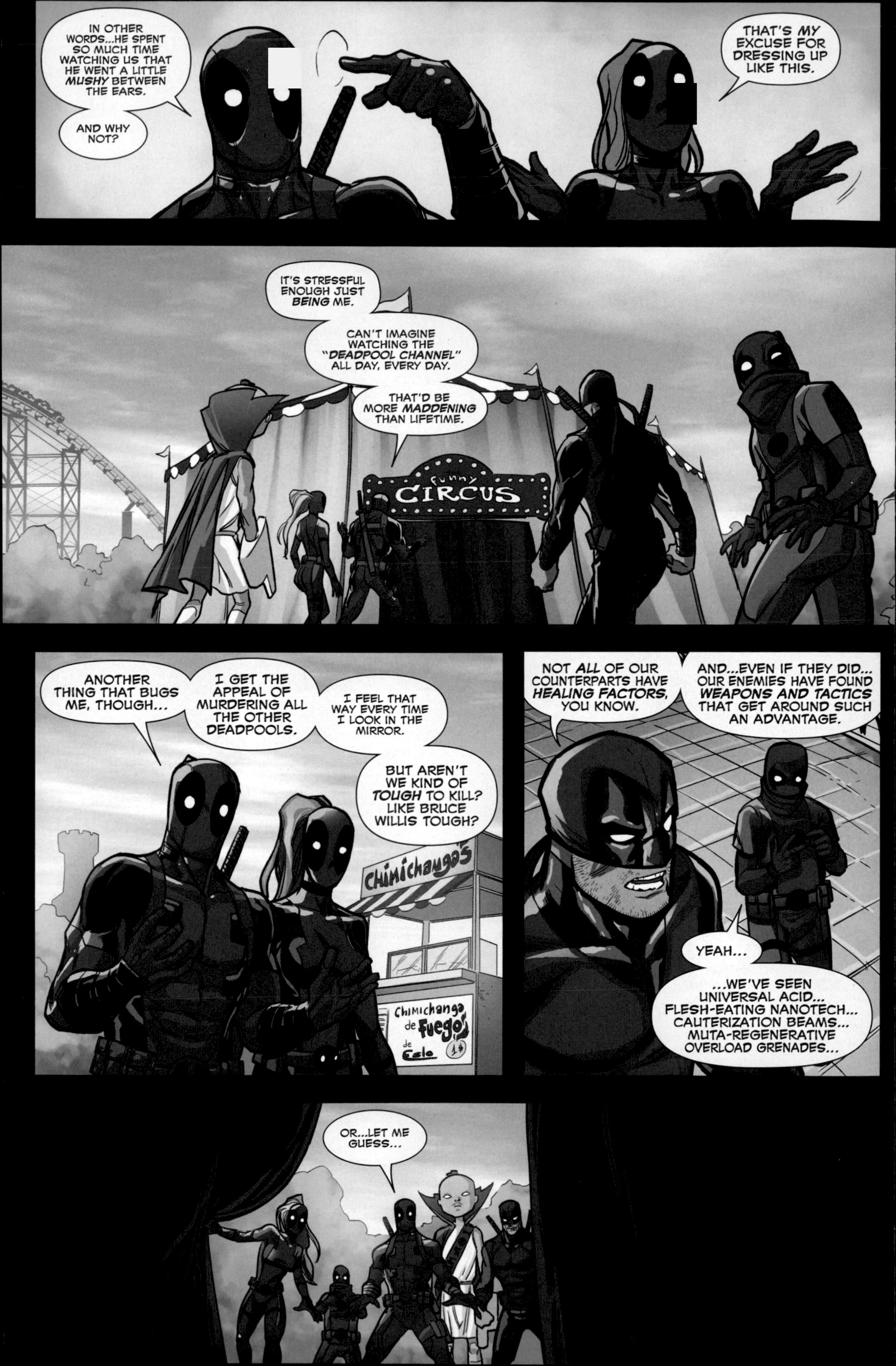
IN OTHER WORDS...HE SPENT SO MUCH TIME WATCHING US THAT HE WENT A LITTLE *MUSHY* BETWEEN THE EARS.
AND WHY NOT?
THAT'S *MY* EXCUSE FOR DRESSING UP LIKE THIS.
IT'S STRESSFUL ENOUGH JUST *BEING* ME.
CAN'T IMAGINE WATCHING THE *"DEADPOOL CHANNEL"* ALL DAY, EVERY DAY.
THAT'D BE MORE *MADDENING* THAN LIFETIME.
FUNNY CIRCUS
ANOTHER THING THAT BUGS ME, THOUGH...
I GET THE APPEAL OF MURDERING ALL THE OTHER DEADPOOLS.
I FEEL THAT WAY EVERY TIME I LOOK IN THE MIRROR.
BUT AREN'T WE KIND OF *TOUGH* TO KILL? LIKE BRUCE WILLIS TOUGH?
Chimichanga's
Chimichanga de Fuego de Eslo 1$
NOT *ALL* OF OUR COUNTERPARTS HAVE *HEALING FACTORS,* YOU KNOW.
AND...EVEN IF THEY DID... OUR ENEMIES HAVE FOUND *WEAPONS AND TACTICS* THAT GET AROUND SUCH AN ADVANTAGE.
YEAH...
...WE'VE SEEN UNIVERSAL ACID... FLESH-EATING NANOTECH... CAUTERIZATION BEAMS... MUTA-REGENERATIVE OVERLOAD GRENADES...
OR...LET ME GUESS...

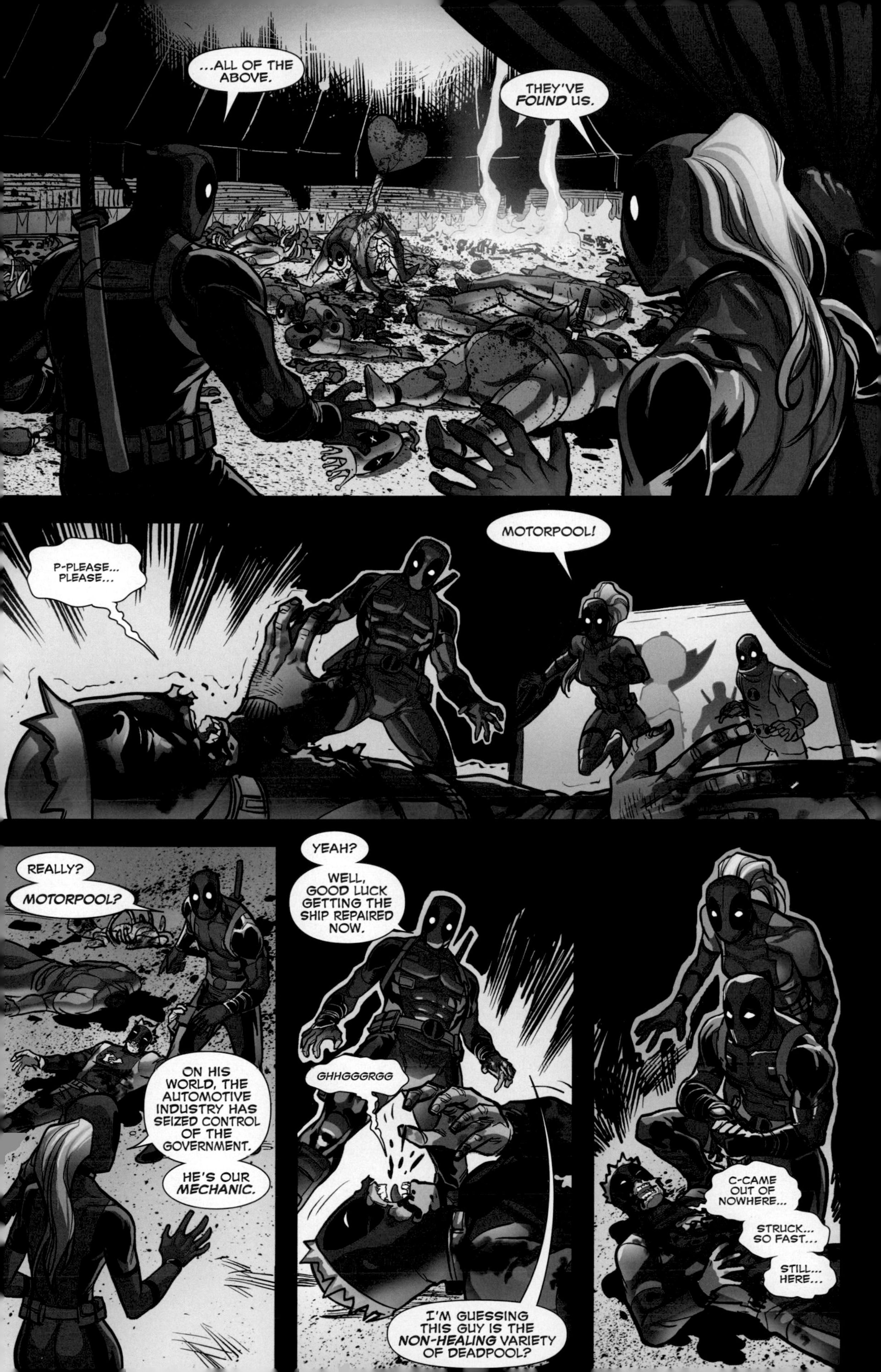
...ALL OF THE ABOVE.
THEY'VE FOUND US.
P-PLEASE... PLEASE...
MOTORPOOL!
REALLY?
MOTORPOOL?
ON HIS WORLD, THE AUTOMOTIVE INDUSTRY HAS SEIZED CONTROL OF THE GOVERNMENT.
HE'S OUR MECHANIC.
YEAH?
WELL, GOOD LUCK GETTING THE SHIP REPAIRED NOW.
GHHGGGRGG
I'M GUESSING THIS GUY IS THE NON-HEALING VARIETY OF DEADPOOL?
C-CAME OUT OF NOWHERE...
STRUCK... SO FAST...
STILL... HERE...

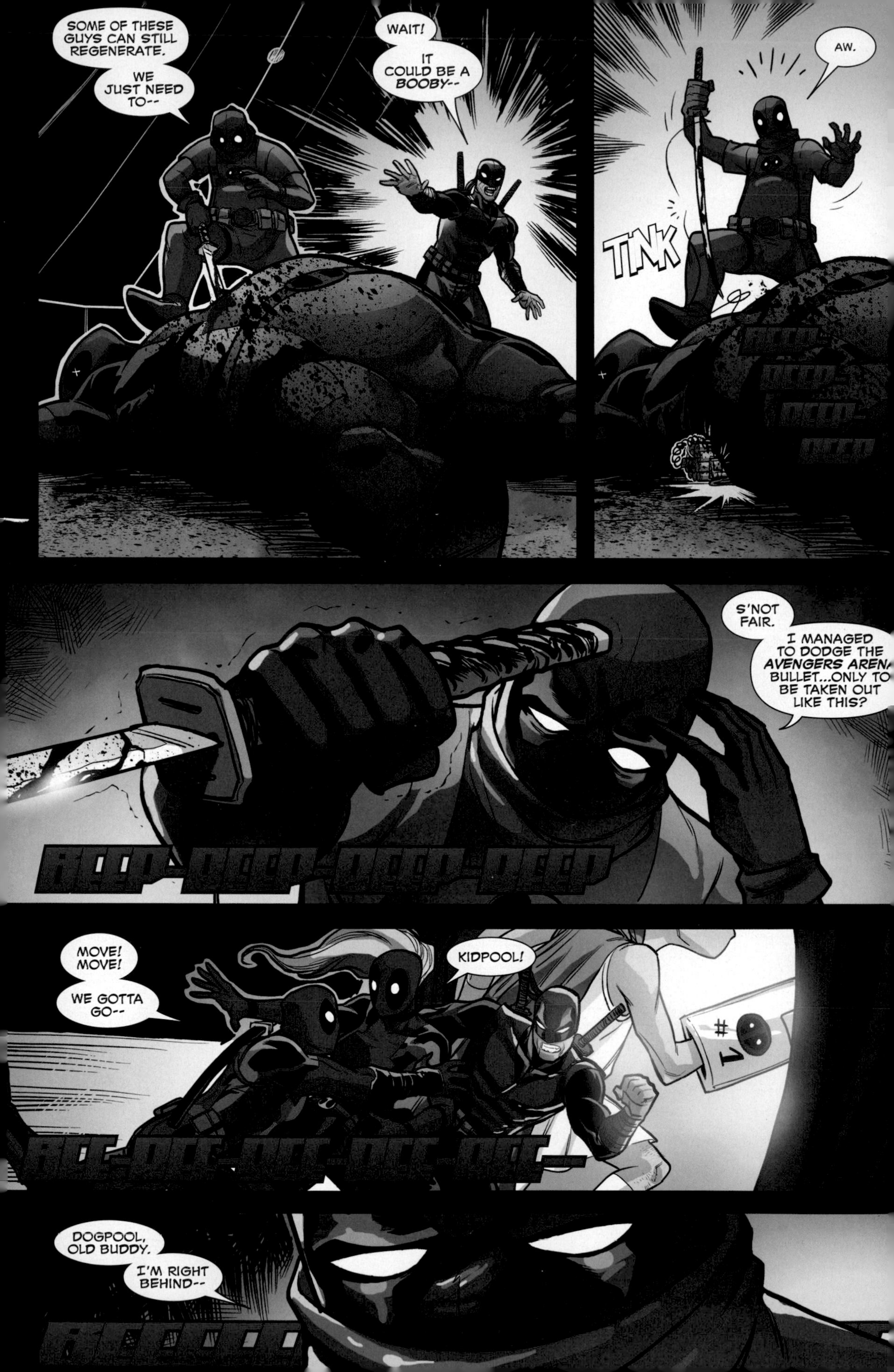
SOME OF THESE GUYS CAN STILL REGENERATE.
WE JUST NEED TO--
WAIT!
IT COULD BE A *BOOBY*--
AW.
TINK
S'NOT FAIR.
I MANAGED TO DODGE THE *AVENGERS ARENA* BULLET...ONLY TO BE TAKEN OUT LIKE THIS?
MOVE! MOVE!
WE GOTTA GO--
KIDPOOL!
DOGPOOL, OLD BUDDY.
I'M RIGHT BEHIND--

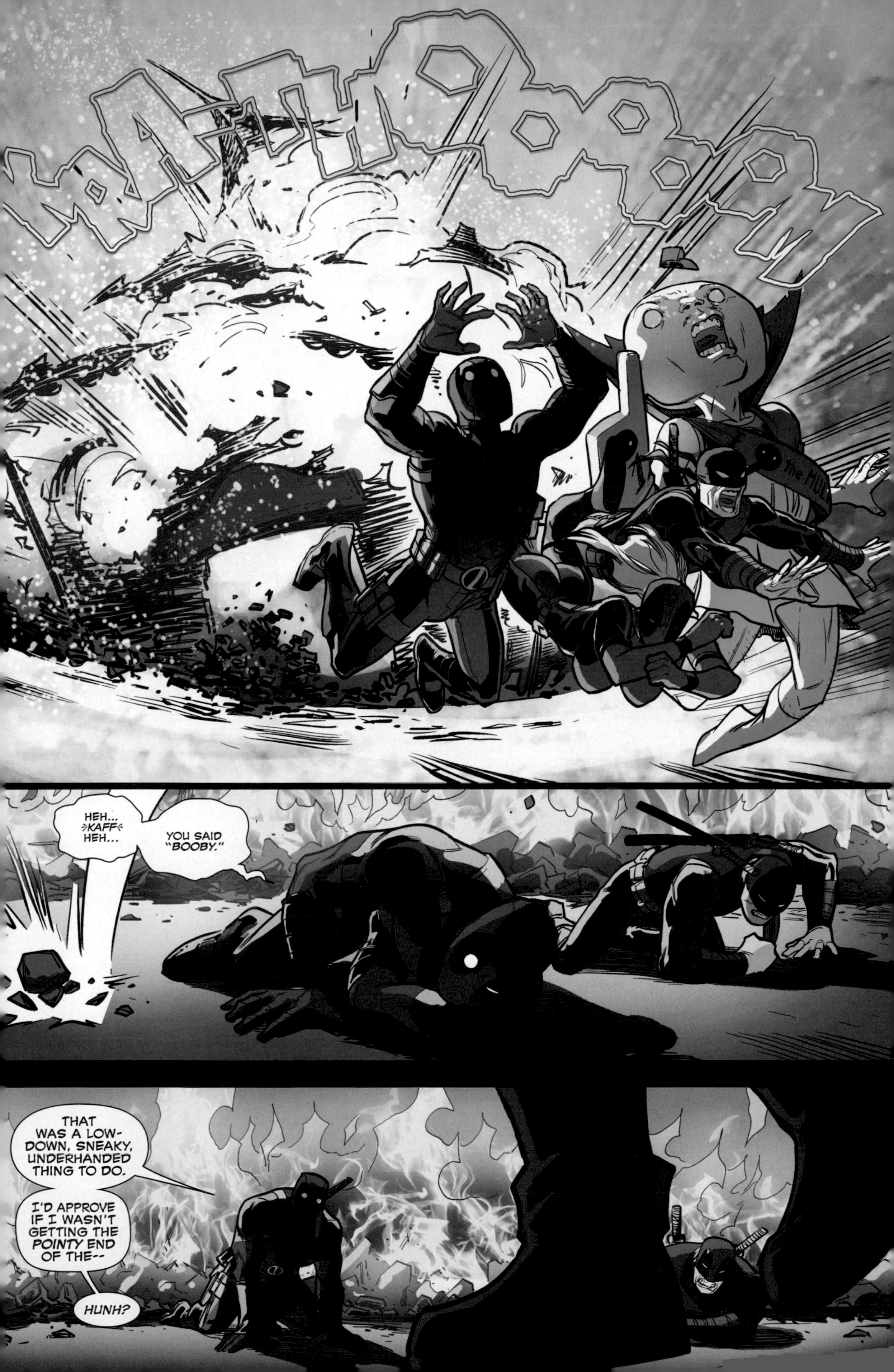
KRA-THOOOOM
HEH... *KAFF* HEH...
YOU SAID "BOOBY."
THAT WAS A LOW-DOWN, SNEAKY, UNDERHANDED THING TO DO.
I'D APPROVE IF I WASN'T GETTING THE POINTY END OF THE--
HUNH?

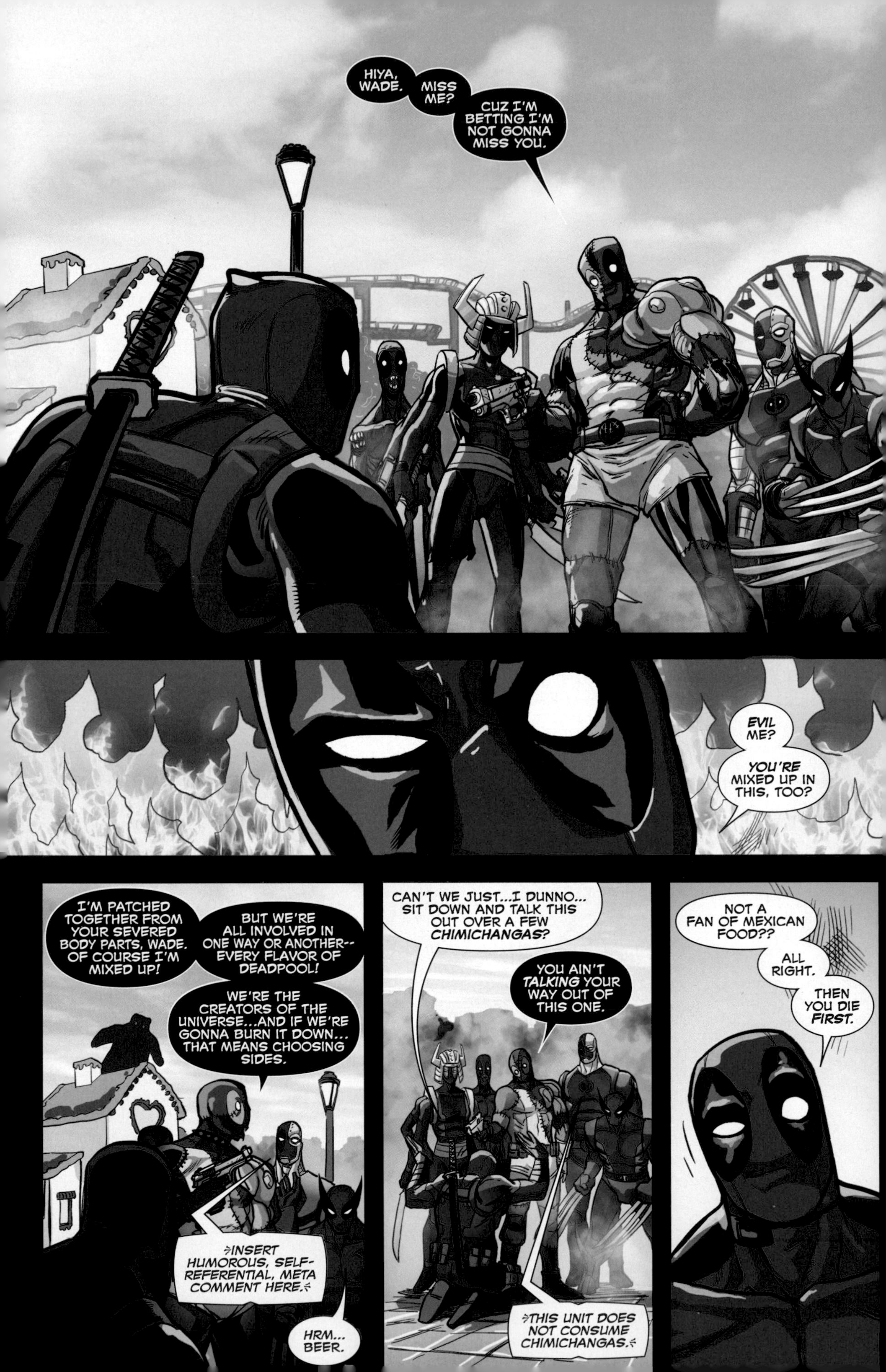
HIYA, WADE.
MISS ME?
CUZ I'M BETTING I'M NOT GONNA MISS YOU.
EVIL ME?
YOU'RE MIXED UP IN THIS, TOO?
I'M PATCHED TOGETHER FROM YOUR SEVERED BODY PARTS, WADE. OF COURSE I'M MIXED UP!
BUT WE'RE ALL INVOLVED IN ONE WAY OR ANOTHER-- EVERY FLAVOR OF DEADPOOL!
WE'RE THE CREATORS OF THE UNIVERSE...AND IF WE'RE GONNA BURN IT DOWN... THAT MEANS CHOOSING SIDES.
INSERT HUMOROUS, SELF-REFERENTIAL, META COMMENT HERE.
HRM... BEER.
CAN'T WE JUST...I DUNNO... SIT DOWN AND TALK THIS OUT OVER A FEW CHIMICHANGAS?
YOU AIN'T TALKING YOUR WAY OUT OF THIS ONE.
THIS UNIT DOES NOT CONSUME CHIMICHANGAS.
NOT A FAN OF MEXICAN FOOD??
ALL RIGHT.
THEN YOU DIE FIRST.

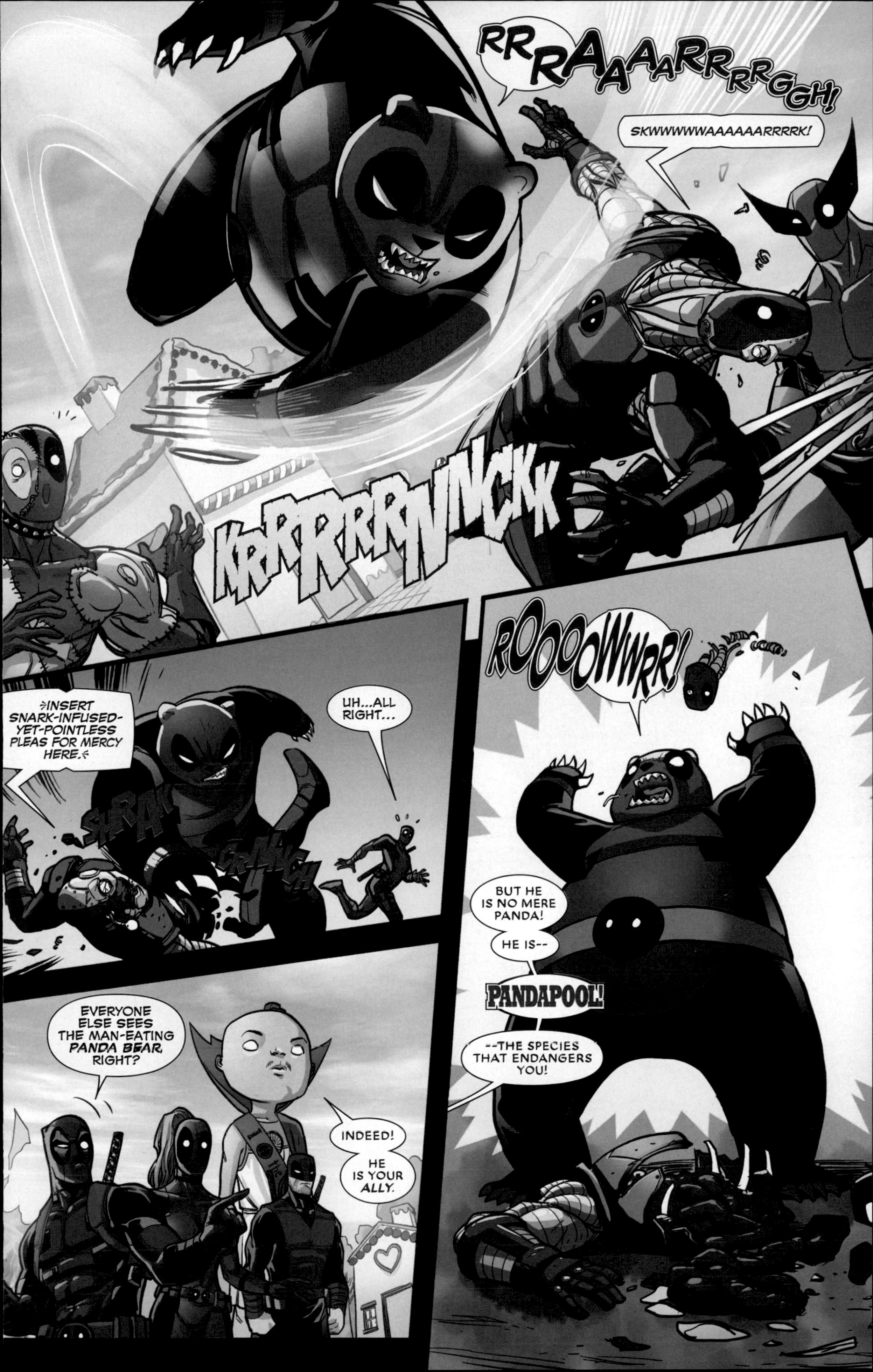
RRRAAAARRRRGGH!
SKWWWWWAAAAAARRRRK!
KRRRRRRNNCKK
⇉INSERT SNARK-INFUSED-YET-POINTLESS PLEAS FOR MERCY HERE.⇇
UH...ALL RIGHT...
ROOOOWWRR!
BUT HE IS NO MERE PANDA!
HE IS--
PANDAPOOL!
--THE SPECIES THAT ENDANGERS YOU!
EVERYONE ELSE SEES THE MAN-EATING PANDA BEAR, RIGHT?
INDEED!
HE IS YOUR ALLY.

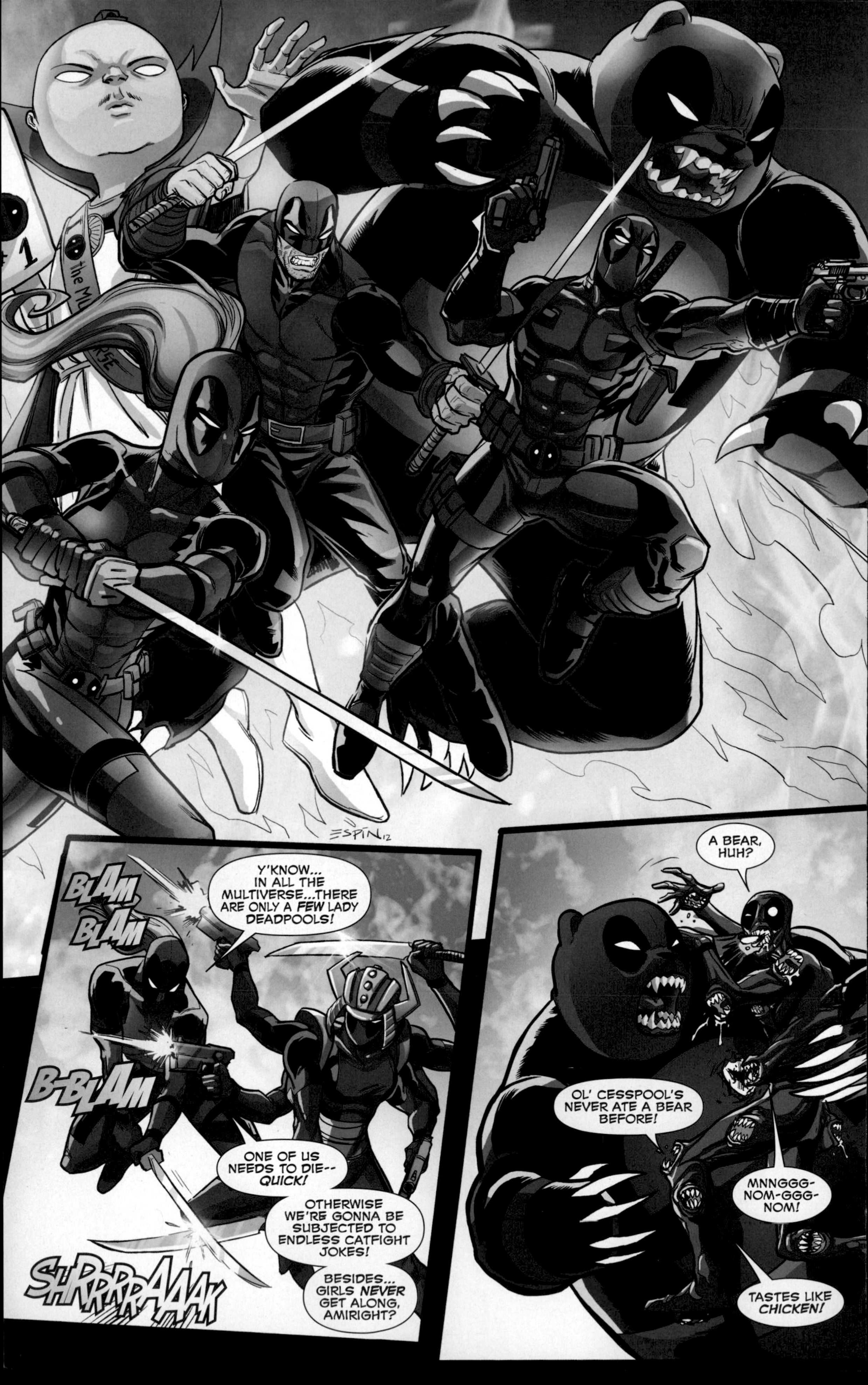
BLAM
BLAM
Y'KNOW... IN ALL THE MULTIVERSE...THERE ARE ONLY A FEW LADY DEADPOOLS!
B-BLAM
ONE OF US NEEDS TO DIE-- QUICK!
OTHERWISE WE'RE GONNA BE SUBJECTED TO ENDLESS CATFIGHT JOKES!
BESIDES... GIRLS NEVER GET ALONG, AMIRIGHT?
SHRRRRAAAK
A BEAR, HUH?
OL' CESSPOOL'S NEVER ATE A BEAR BEFORE!
MNNGGG-NOM-GGG-NOM!
TASTES LIKE CHICKEN!

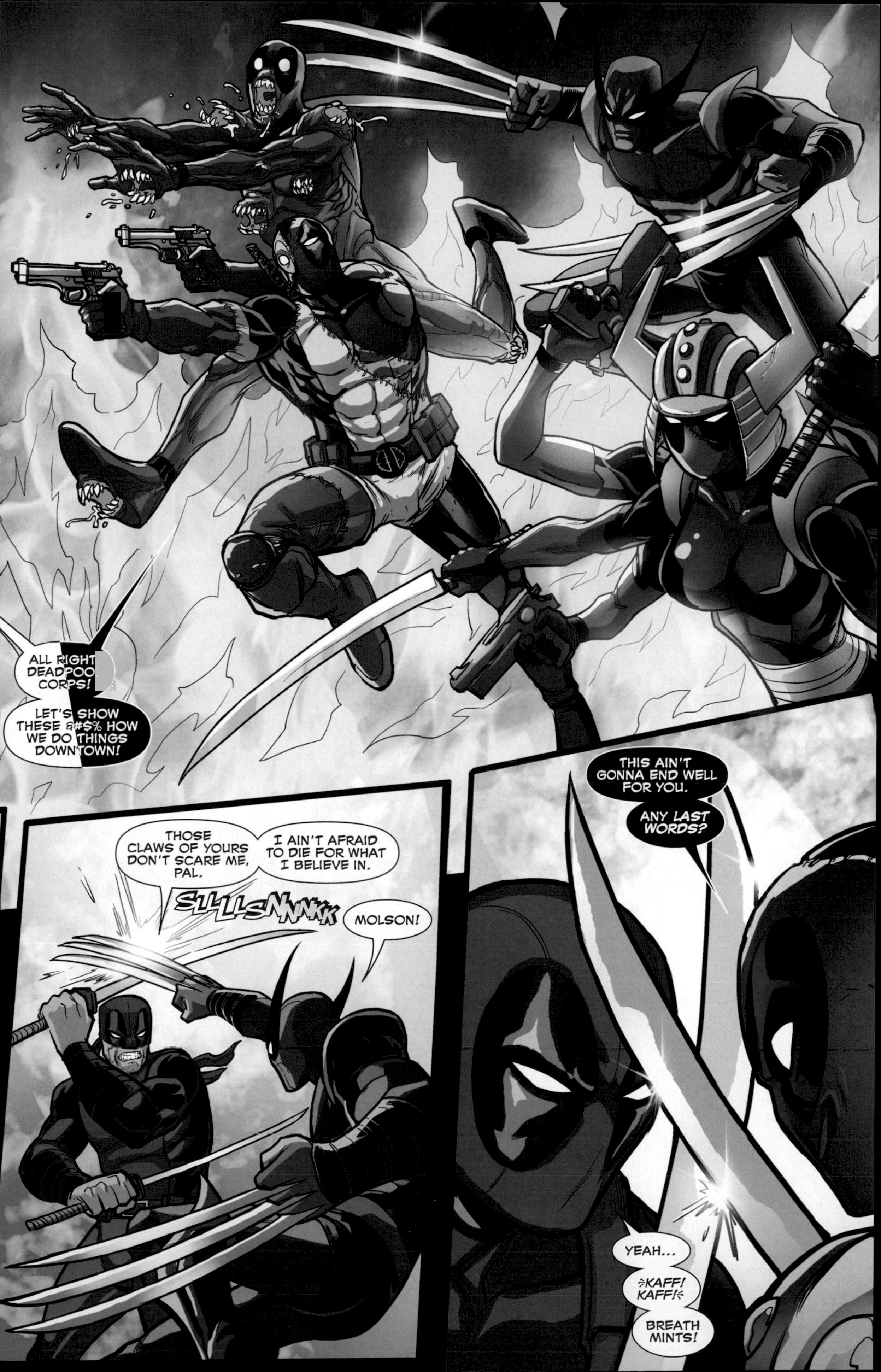

ALL RIGHT DEADPOO CORPS!
LET'S SHOW THESE &#$% HOW WE DO THINGS DOWNTOWN!
THOSE CLAWS OF YOURS DON'T SCARE ME, PAL.
I AIN'T AFRAID TO DIE FOR WHAT I BELIEVE IN.
SLLLLSNNNKK
MOLSON!
THIS AIN'T GONNA END WELL FOR YOU.
ANY *LAST* WORDS?
YEAH...
KAFF! KAFF!
BREATH MINTS!

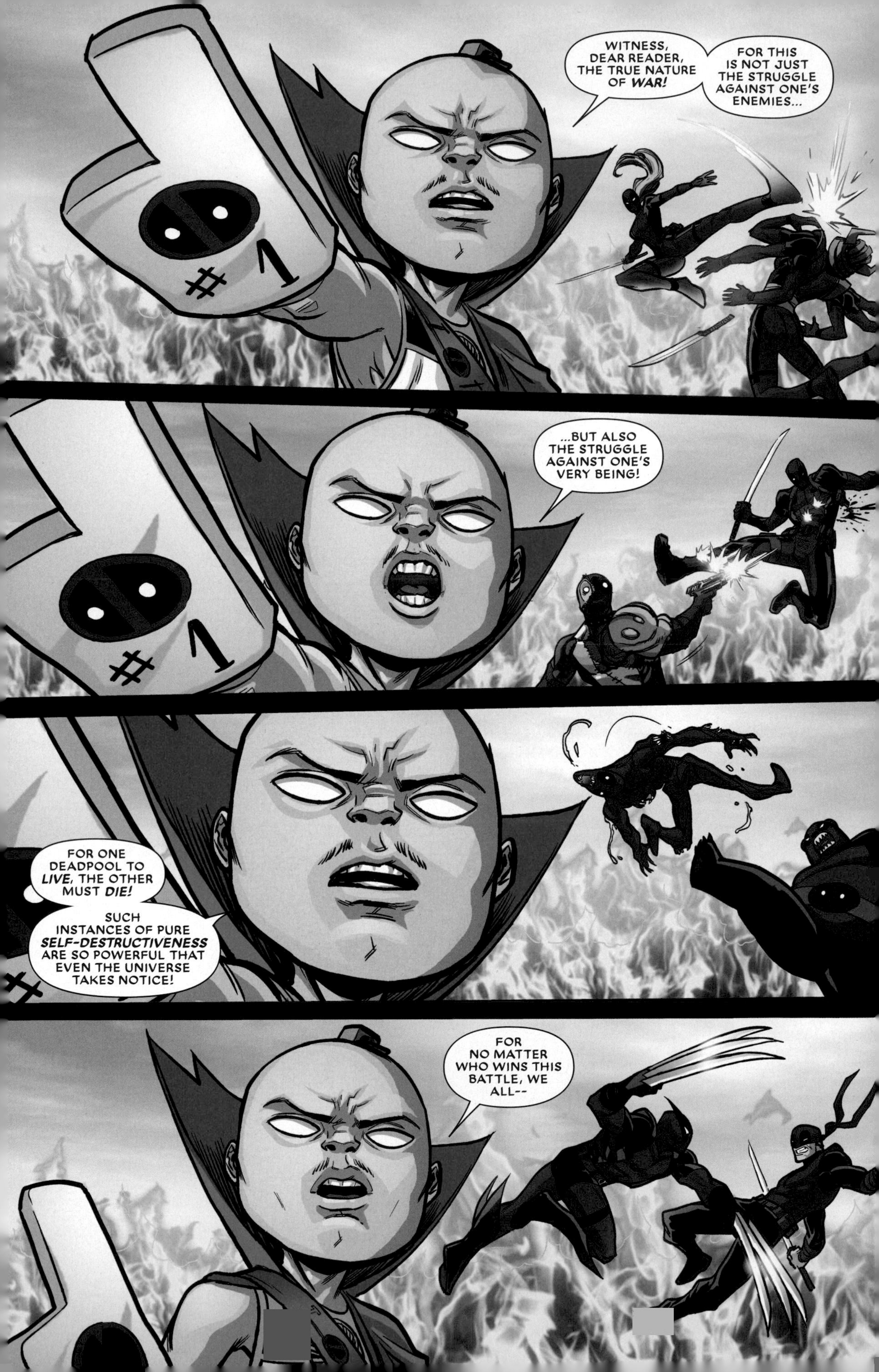

WITNESS, DEAR READER, THE TRUE NATURE OF ***WAR!***
FOR THIS IS NOT JUST THE STRUGGLE AGAINST ONE'S ENEMIES...
...BUT ALSO THE STRUGGLE AGAINST ONE'S VERY BEING!
FOR ONE DEADPOOL TO ***LIVE,*** THE OTHER MUST ***DIE!***
SUCH INSTANCES OF PURE ***SELF-DESTRUCTIVENESS*** ARE SO POWERFUL THAT EVEN THE UNIVERSE TAKES NOTICE!
FOR NO MATTER WHO WINS THIS BATTLE, WE ALL--

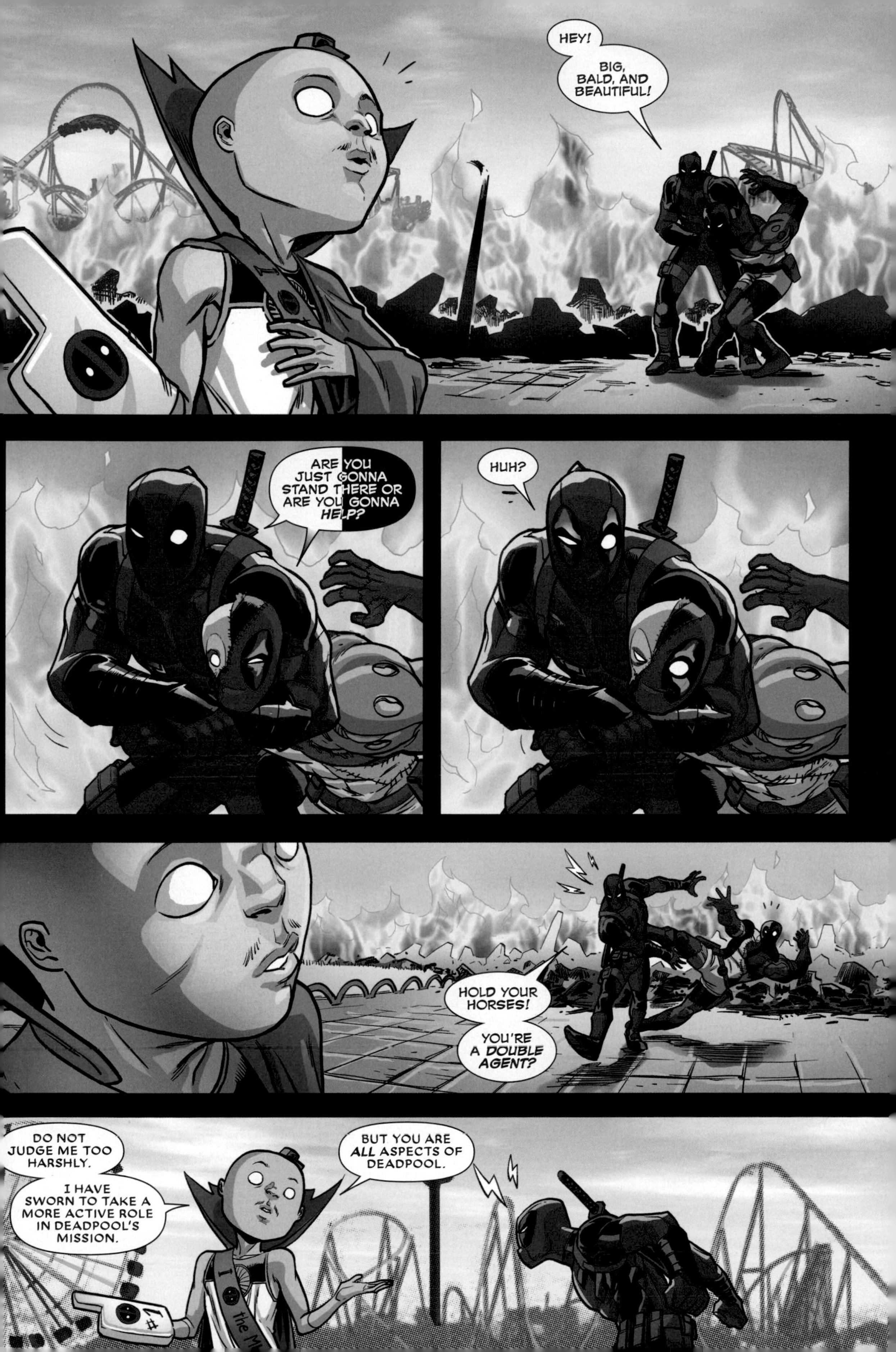
HEY!
BIG, BALD, AND BEAUTIFUL!
ARE YOU JUST GONNA STAND THERE OR ARE YOU GONNA HELP?
HUH?
HOLD YOUR HORSES!
YOU'RE A DOUBLE AGENT?
DO NOT JUDGE ME TOO HARSHLY.
I HAVE SWORN TO TAKE A MORE ACTIVE ROLE IN DEADPOOL'S MISSION.
BUT YOU ARE ALL ASPECTS OF DEADPOOL.

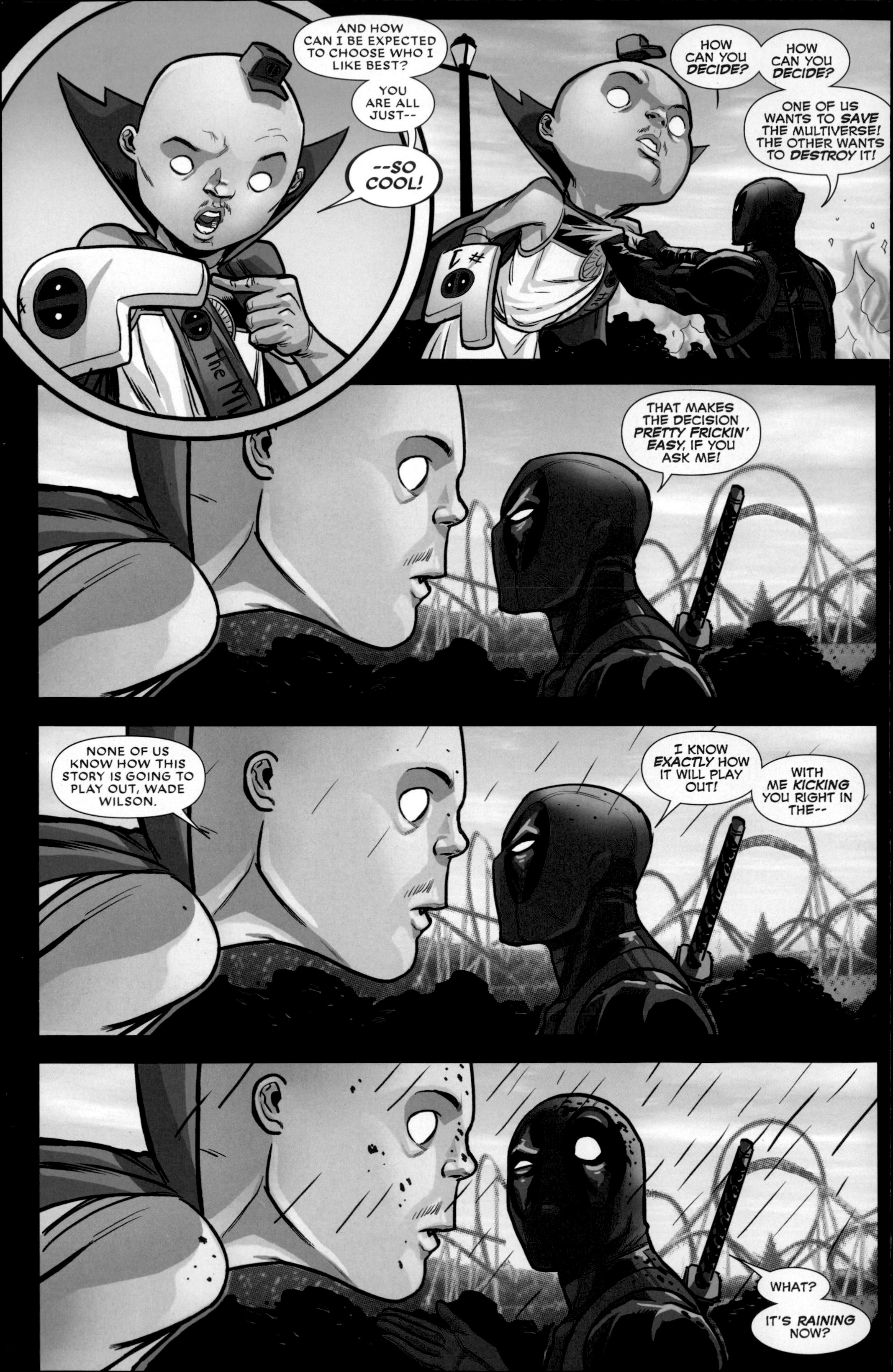
AND HOW CAN I BE EXPECTED TO CHOOSE WHO I LIKE BEST?
YOU ARE ALL JUST--
--SO COOL!
HOW CAN YOU DECIDE?
HOW CAN YOU DECIDE?
ONE OF US WANTS TO SAVE THE MULTIVERSE! THE OTHER WANTS TO DESTROY IT!
THAT MAKES THE DECISION PRETTY FRICKIN' EASY, IF YOU ASK ME!
NONE OF US KNOW HOW THIS STORY IS GOING TO PLAY OUT, WADE WILSON.
I KNOW EXACTLY HOW IT WILL PLAY OUT!
WITH ME KICKING YOU RIGHT IN THE--
WHAT?
IT'S RAINING NOW?

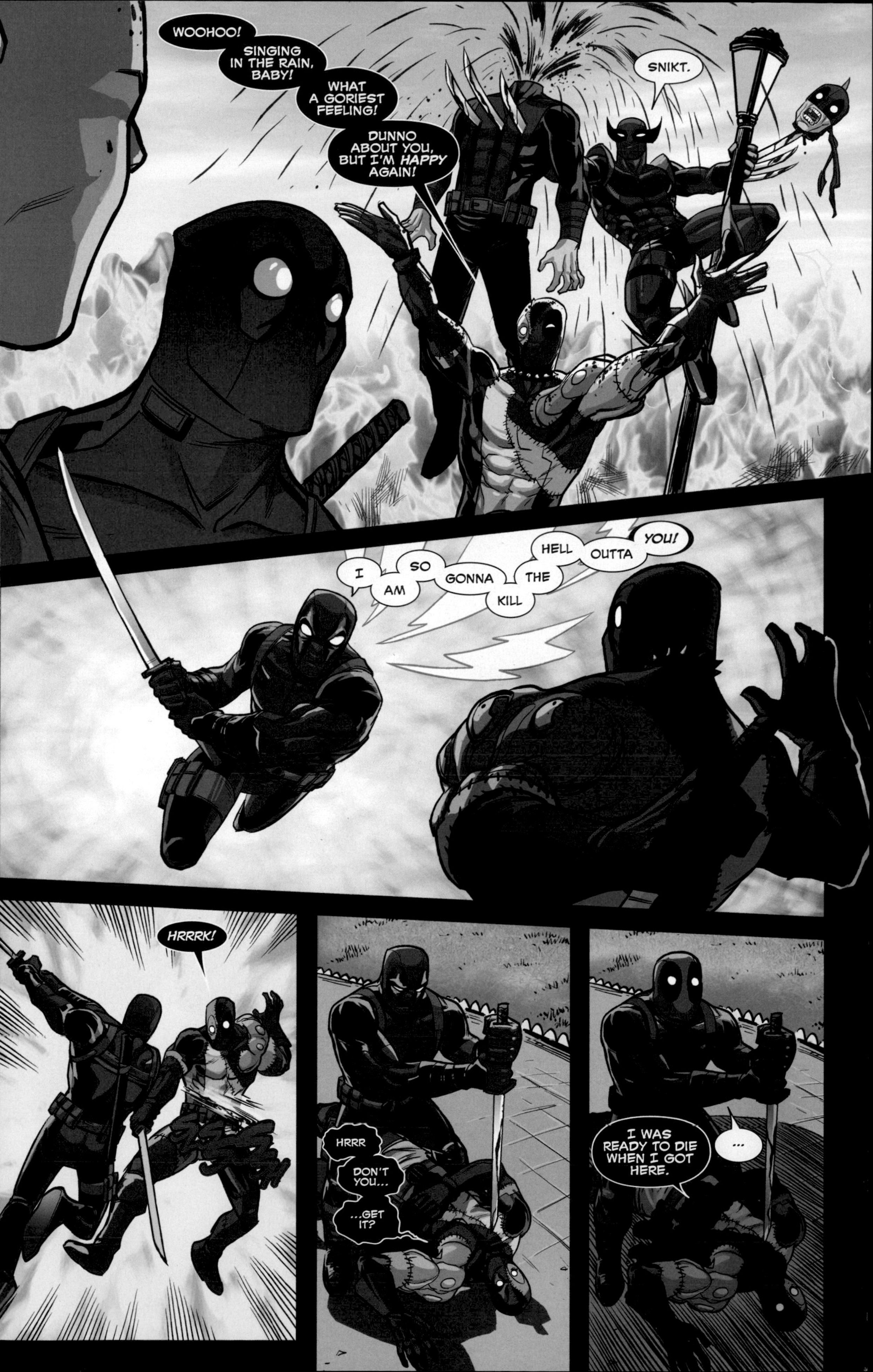
WOOHOO!
SINGING IN THE RAIN, BABY!
WHAT A GORIEST FEELING!
DUNNO ABOUT YOU, BUT I'M *HAPPY* AGAIN!
SNIKT.
I
AM
SO
GONNA
KILL
THE
HELL
OUTTA
YOU!
HRRRK!
HRRR
DON'T YOU...
...GET IT?
I WAS READY TO DIE WHEN I GOT HERE.
...

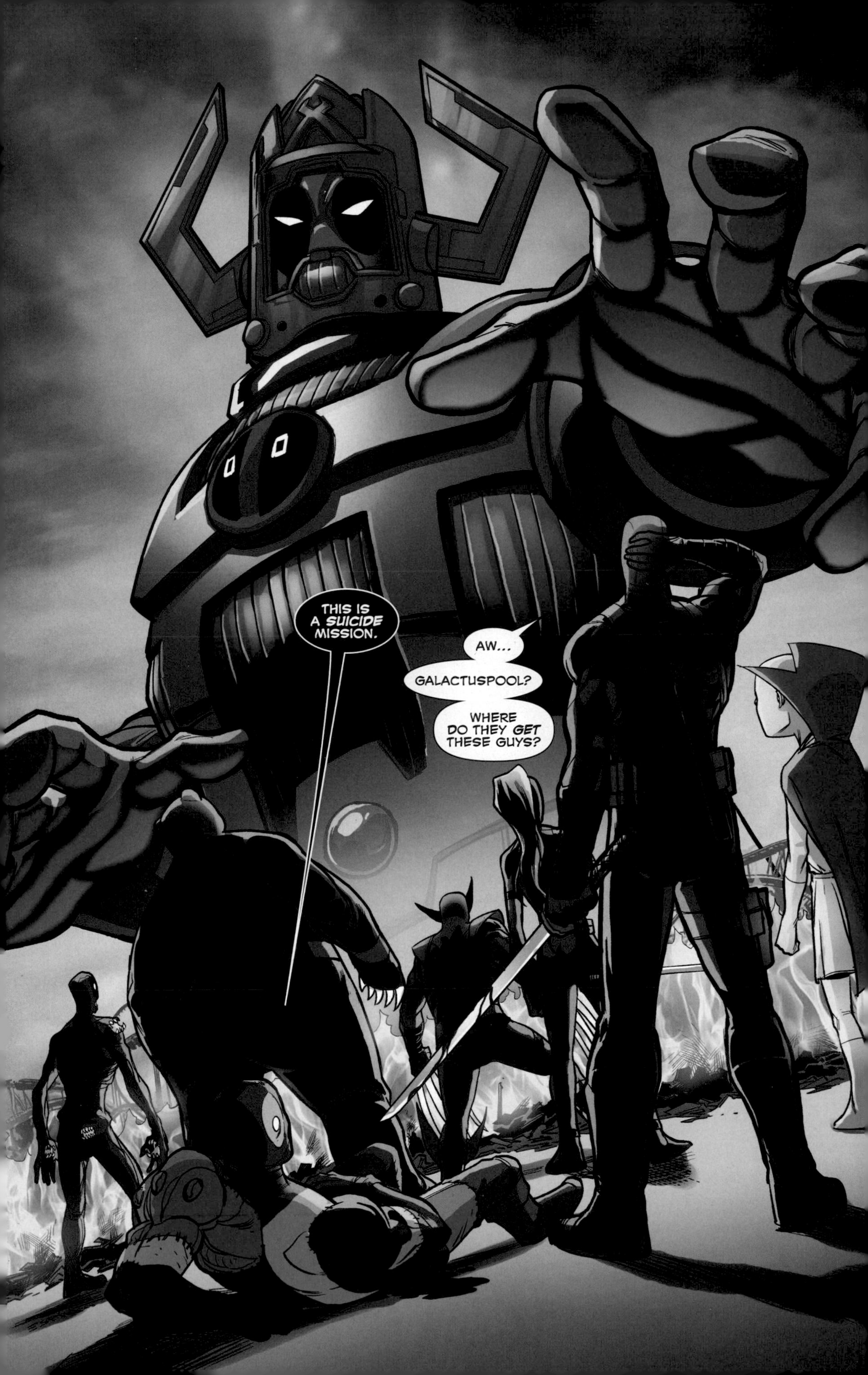
THIS IS A SUICIDE MISSION.
AW...
GALACTUSPOOL?
WHERE DO THEY GET THESE GUYS?

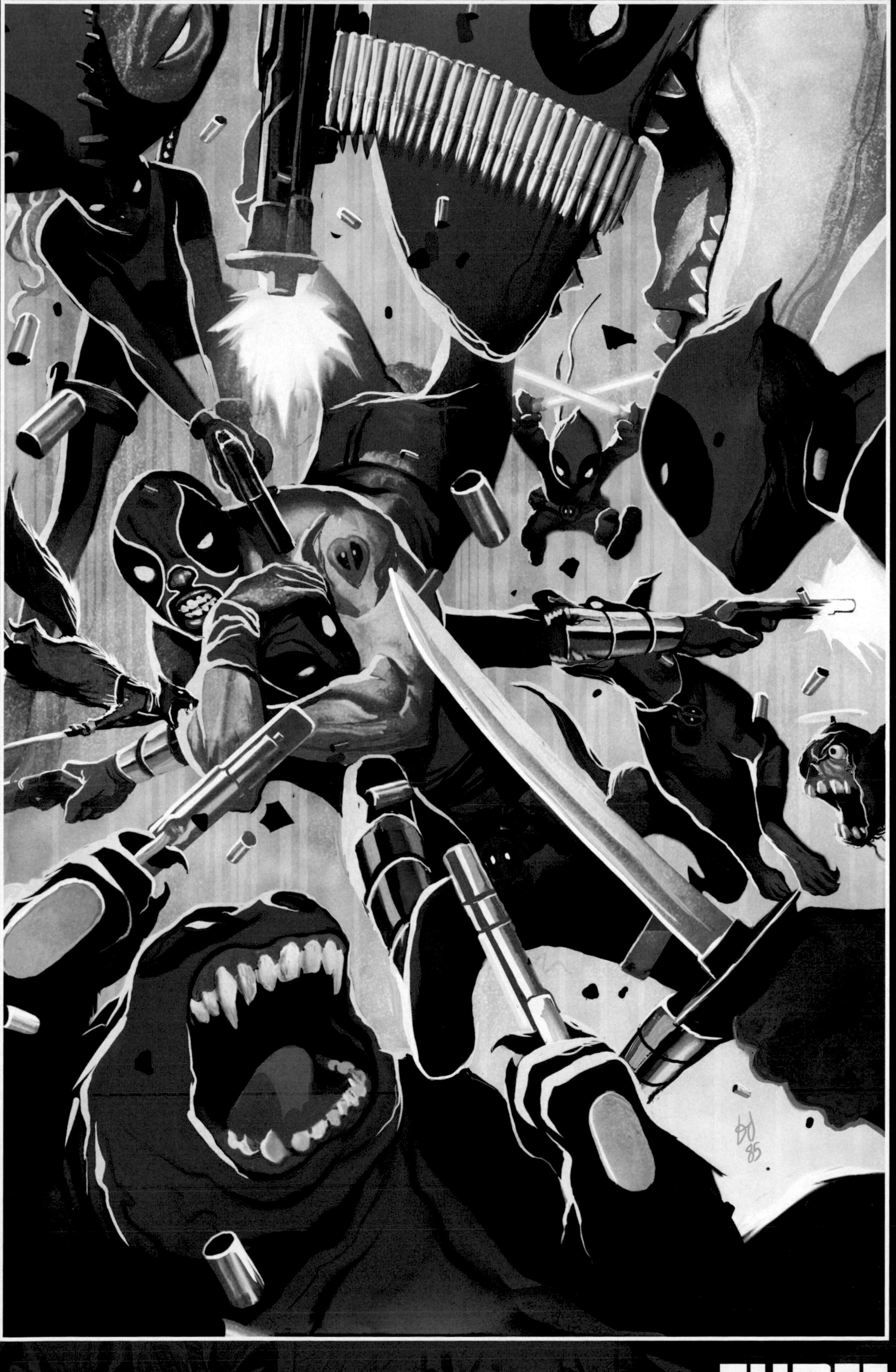

THREE

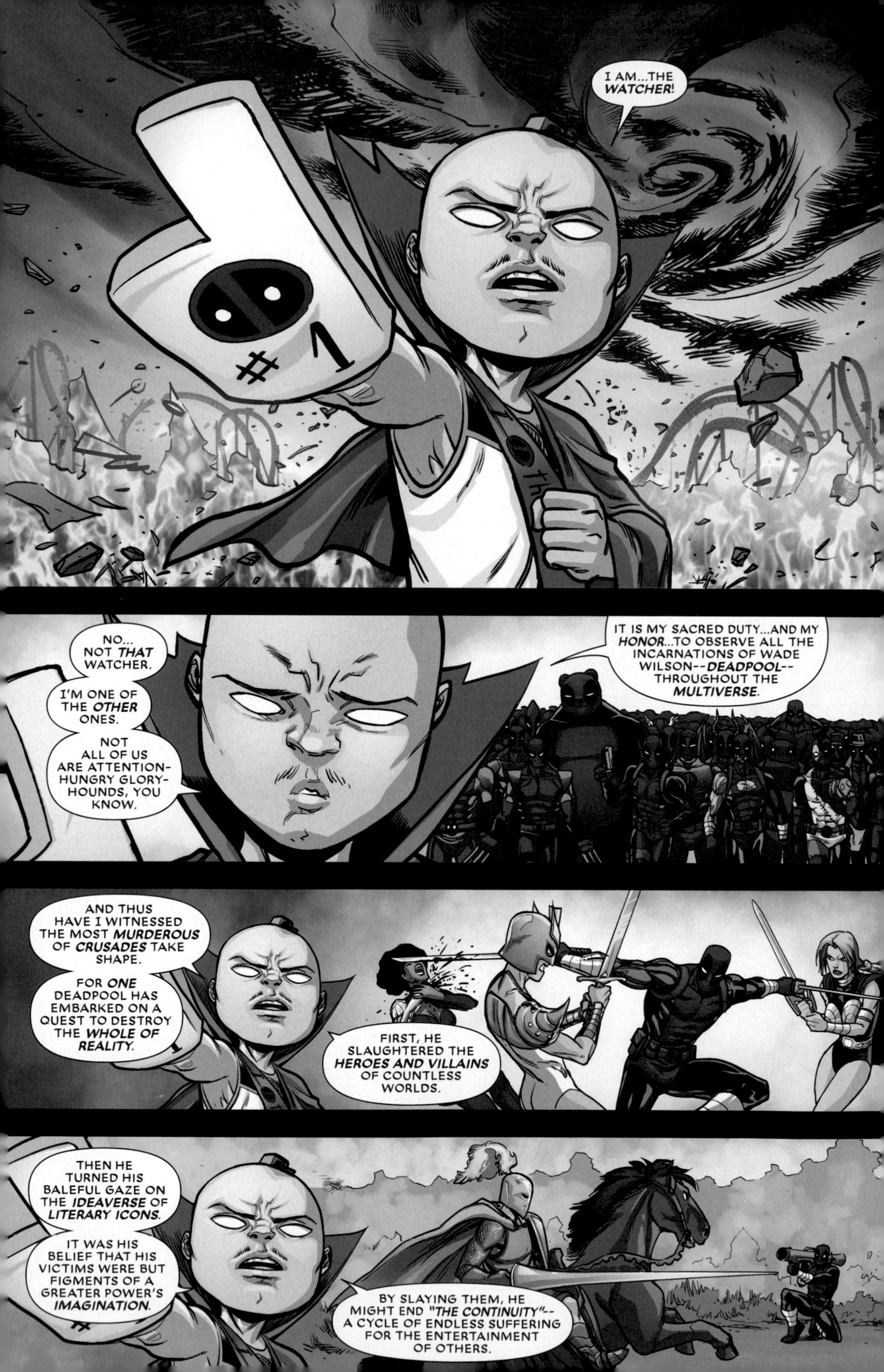

I AM...THE *WATCHER*!
NO... NOT *THAT* WATCHER.
I'M ONE OF THE *OTHER* ONES.
NOT ALL OF US ARE ATTENTION-HUNGRY GLORY-HOUNDS, YOU KNOW.
IT IS MY SACRED DUTY...AND MY *HONOR*...TO OBSERVE ALL THE INCARNATIONS OF WADE WILSON--*DEADPOOL*--THROUGHOUT THE *MULTIVERSE*.
AND THUS HAVE I WITNESSED THE MOST *MURDEROUS* OF *CRUSADES* TAKE SHAPE.
FOR *ONE* DEADPOOL HAS EMBARKED ON A QUEST TO DESTROY THE *WHOLE OF REALITY*.
FIRST, HE SLAUGHTERED THE *HEROES AND VILLAINS* OF COUNTLESS WORLDS.
THEN HE TURNED HIS BALEFUL GAZE ON THE *IDEAVERSE* OF *LITERARY ICONS*.
IT WAS HIS BELIEF THAT HIS VICTIMS WERE BUT FIGMENTS OF A GREATER POWER'S *IMAGINATION*.
BY SLAYING THEM, HE MIGHT END *"THE CONTINUITY"*--A CYCLE OF ENDLESS SUFFERING FOR THE ENTERTAINMENT OF OTHERS.

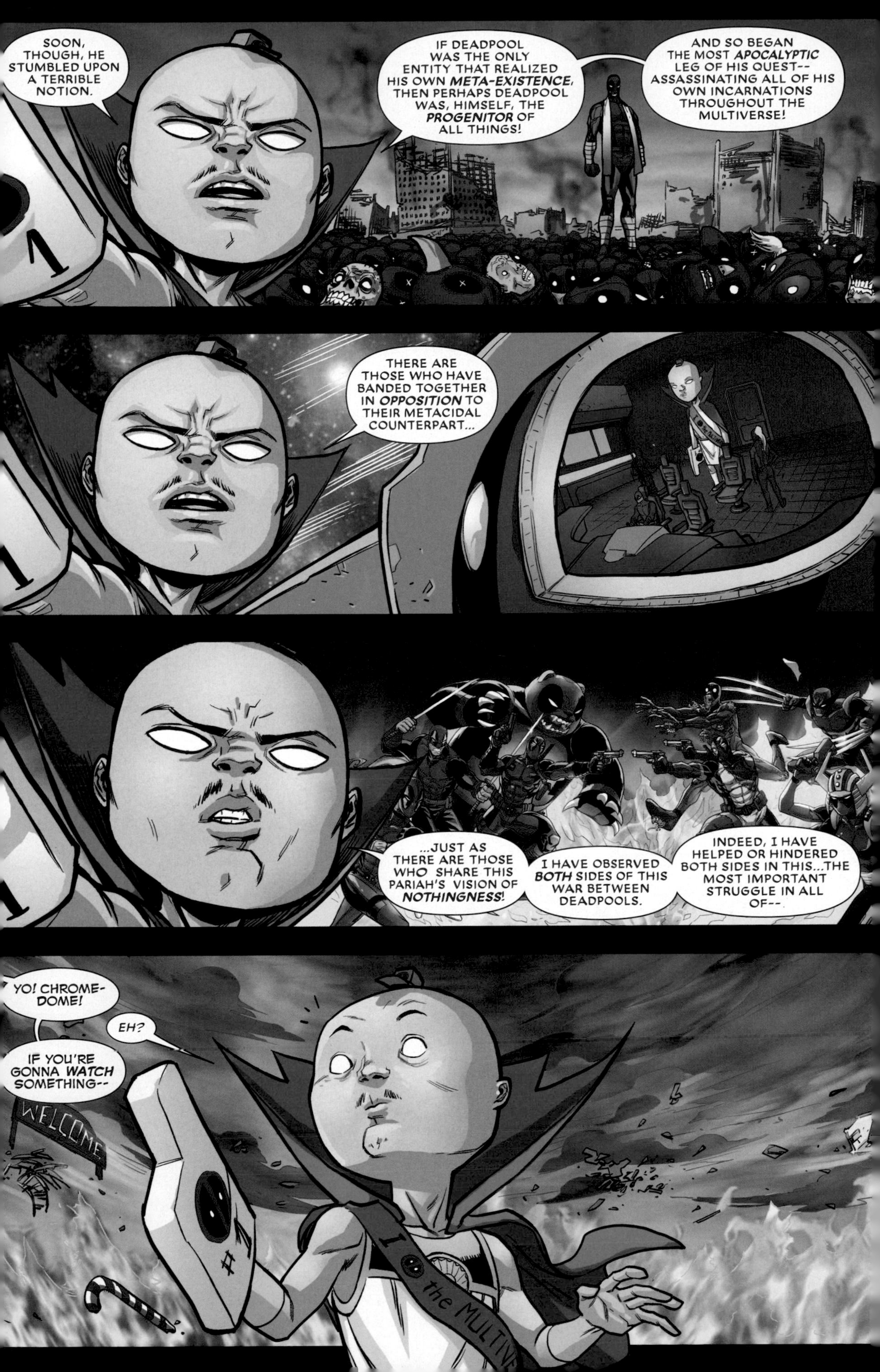
SOON, THOUGH, HE STUMBLED UPON A TERRIBLE NOTION.
IF DEADPOOL WAS THE ONLY ENTITY THAT REALIZED HIS OWN *META-EXISTENCE*, THEN PERHAPS DEADPOOL WAS, HIMSELF, THE *PROGENITOR* OF ALL THINGS!
AND SO BEGAN THE MOST *APOCALYPTIC* LEG OF HIS QUEST-- ASSASSINATING ALL OF HIS OWN INCARNATIONS THROUGHOUT THE MULTIVERSE!
THERE ARE THOSE WHO HAVE BANDED TOGETHER IN *OPPOSITION* TO THEIR METACIDAL COUNTERPART...
...JUST AS THERE ARE THOSE WHO SHARE THIS PARIAH'S VISION OF *NOTHINGNESS*!
I HAVE OBSERVED *BOTH* SIDES OF THIS WAR BETWEEN DEADPOOLS.
INDEED, I HAVE HELPED OR HINDERED BOTH SIDES IN THIS...THE MOST IMPORTANT STRUGGLE IN ALL OF--
YO! CHROME-DOME!
EH?
IF YOU'RE GONNA *WATCH* SOMETHING--
WELCOME

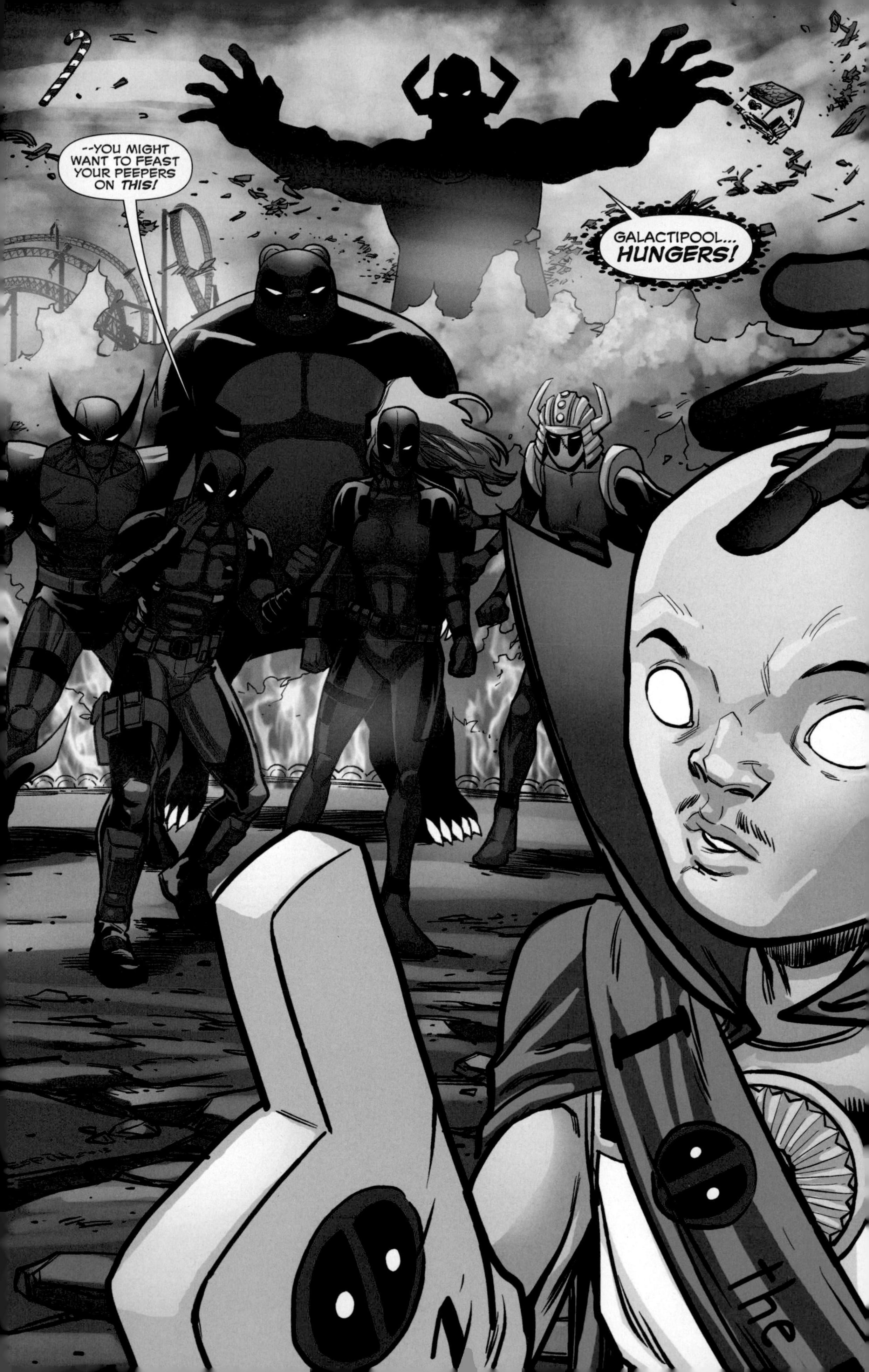
--YOU MIGHT WANT TO FEAST YOUR PEEPERS ON THIS!
GALACTIPOOL... HUNGERS!
the

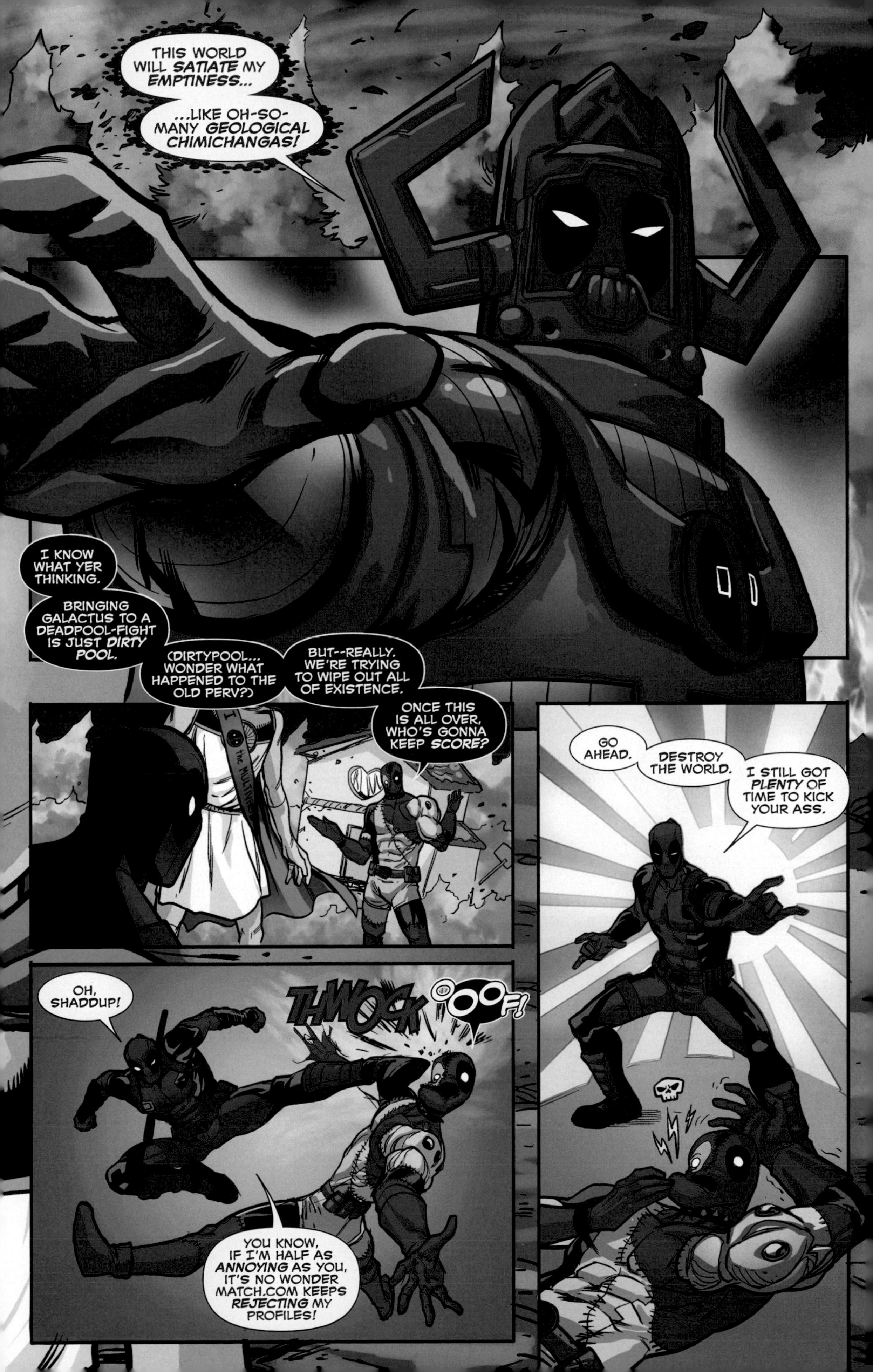
THIS WORLD WILL SATIATE MY EMPTINESS...
...LIKE OH-SO-MANY GEOLOGICAL CHIMICHANGAS!
I KNOW WHAT YER THINKING.
BRINGING GALACTUS TO A DEADPOOL-FIGHT IS JUST DIRTY POOL.
(DIRTYPOOL... WONDER WHAT HAPPENED TO THE OLD PERV?)
BUT--REALLY. WE'RE TRYING TO WIPE OUT ALL OF EXISTENCE.
ONCE THIS IS ALL OVER, WHO'S GONNA KEEP SCORE?
GO AHEAD.
DESTROY THE WORLD.
I STILL GOT PLENTY OF TIME TO KICK YOUR ASS.
OH, SHADDUP!
THWOCK
OOOF!
YOU KNOW, IF I'M HALF AS ANNOYING AS YOU, IT'S NO WONDER MATCH.COM KEEPS REJECTING MY PROFILES!

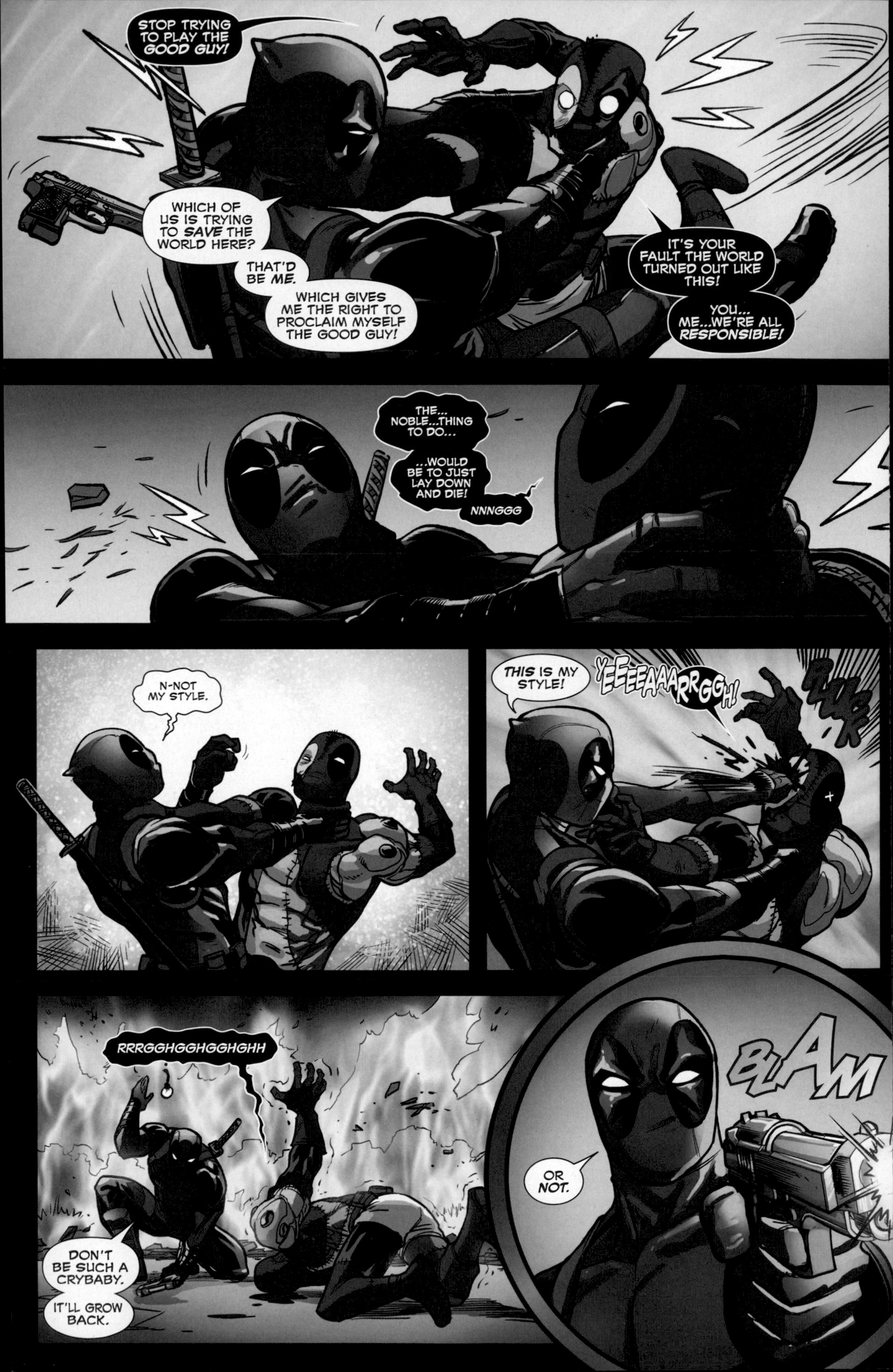
STOP TRYING TO PLAY THE GOOD GUY!
WHICH OF US IS TRYING TO SAVE THE WORLD HERE?
THAT'D BE ME.
WHICH GIVES ME THE RIGHT TO PROCLAIM MYSELF THE GOOD GUY!
IT'S YOUR FAULT THE WORLD TURNED OUT LIKE THIS!
YOU... ME...WE'RE ALL RESPONSIBLE!
THE... NOBLE...THING TO DO...
...WOULD BE TO JUST LAY DOWN AND DIE!
NNNGGG
N-NOT MY STYLE.
THIS IS MY STYLE!
YEEEEAAARRGGH!
RRRGGHGGHGGHGHH
DON'T BE SUCH A CRYBABY.
IT'LL GROW BACK.
BLAM
OR NOT.

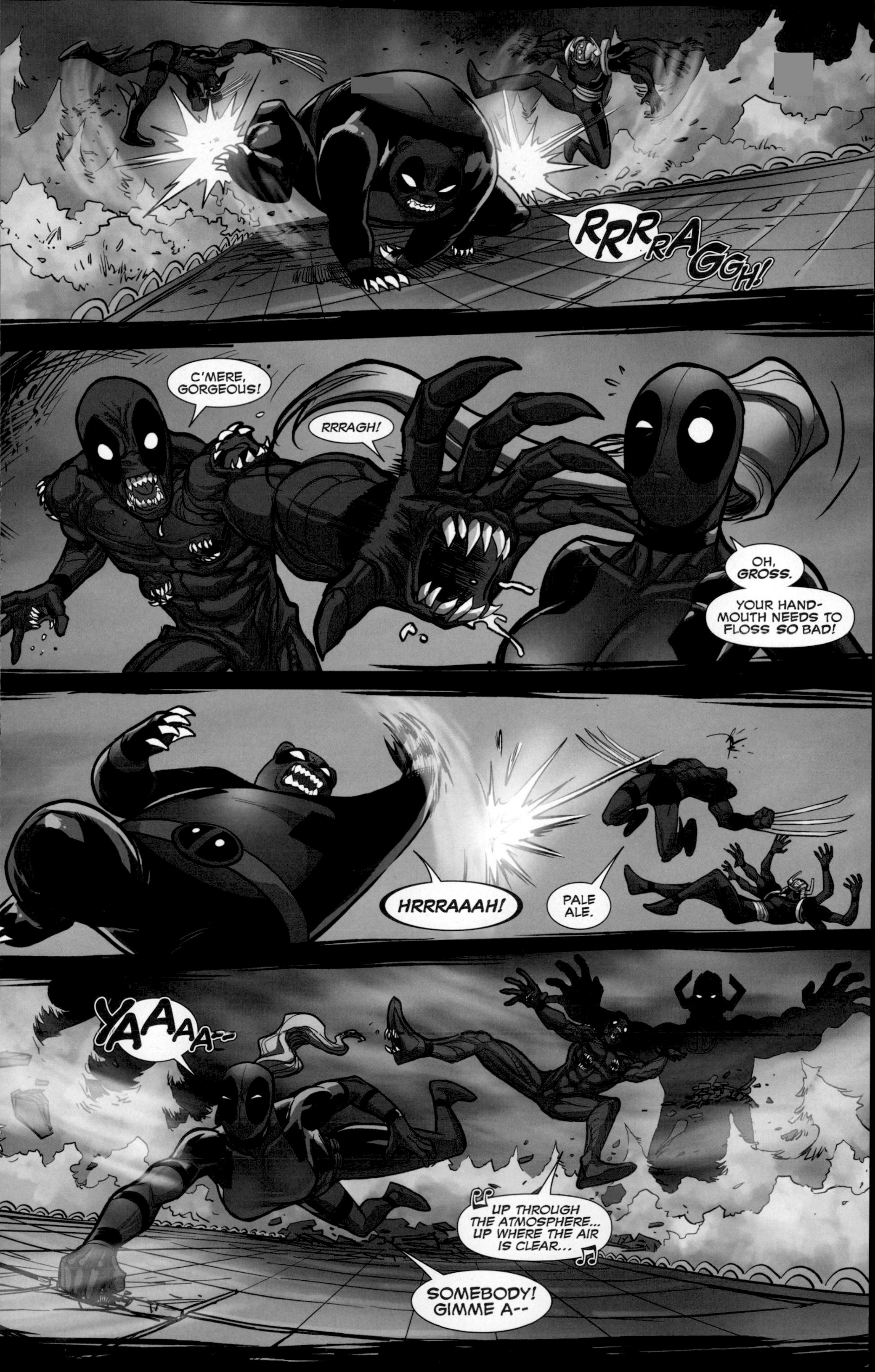
RRRRAGGH!
C'MERE, GORGEOUS!
RRRAGH!
OH, GROSS.
YOUR HAND-MOUTH NEEDS TO FLOSS SO BAD!
HRRRAAAH!
PALE ALE.
YAAAA--
UP THROUGH THE ATMOSPHERE... UP WHERE THE AIR IS CLEAR...
SOMEBODY! GIMME A--

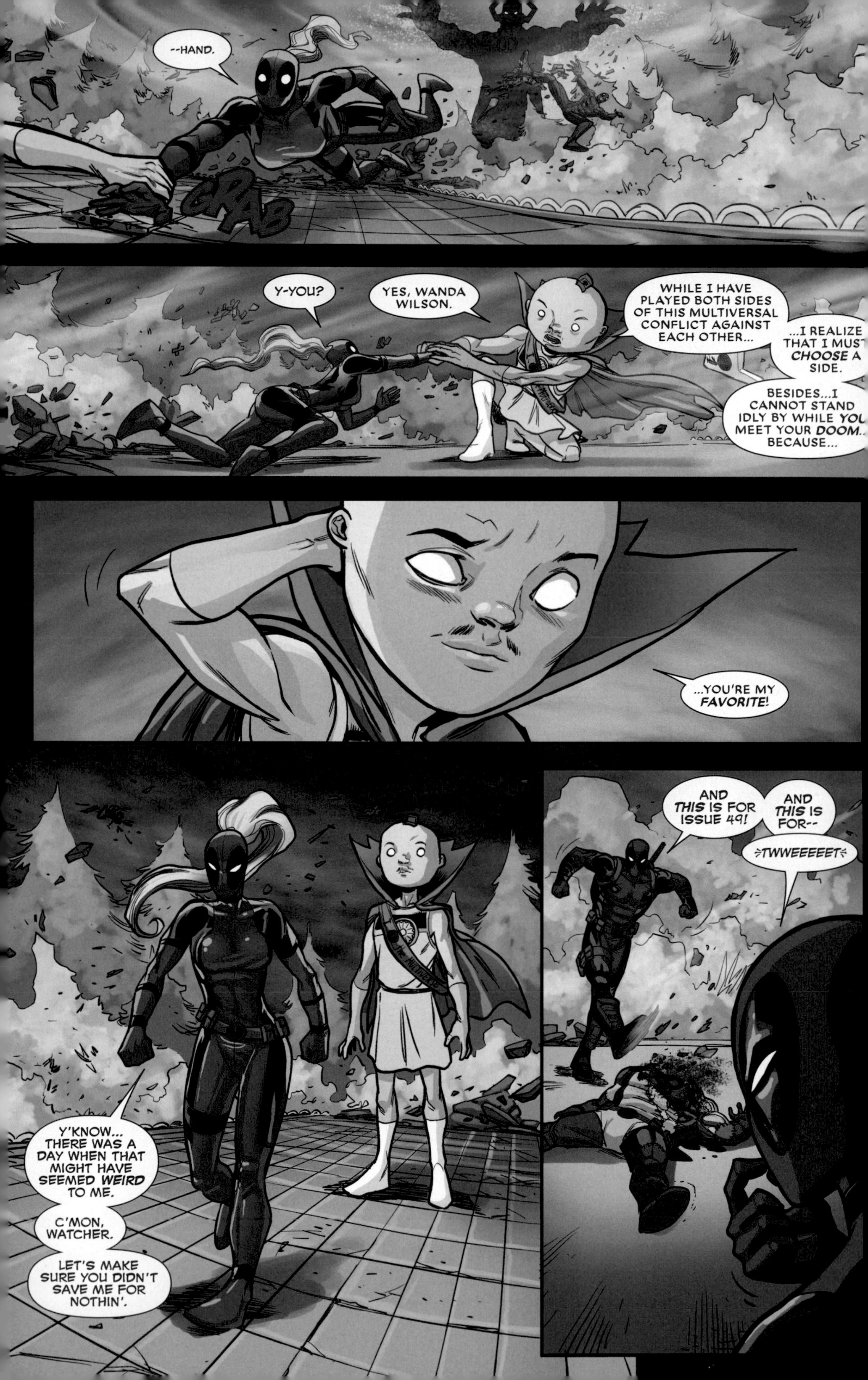
--HAND.
GRAB
Y-YOU?
YES, WANDA WILSON.
WHILE I HAVE PLAYED BOTH SIDES OF THIS MULTIVERSAL CONFLICT AGAINST EACH OTHER...
...I REALIZE THAT I MUST *CHOOSE* A SIDE.
BESIDES...I CANNOT STAND IDLY BY WHILE *YOU* MEET YOUR *DOOM*... BECAUSE...
...YOU'RE MY *FAVORITE!*
Y'KNOW... THERE WAS A DAY WHEN THAT MIGHT HAVE SEEMED *WEIRD* TO ME.
C'MON, WATCHER.
LET'S MAKE SURE YOU DIDN'T SAVE ME FOR NOTHIN'.
AND *THIS* IS FOR ISSUE 49!
AND *THIS* IS FOR--
TWWEEEEET

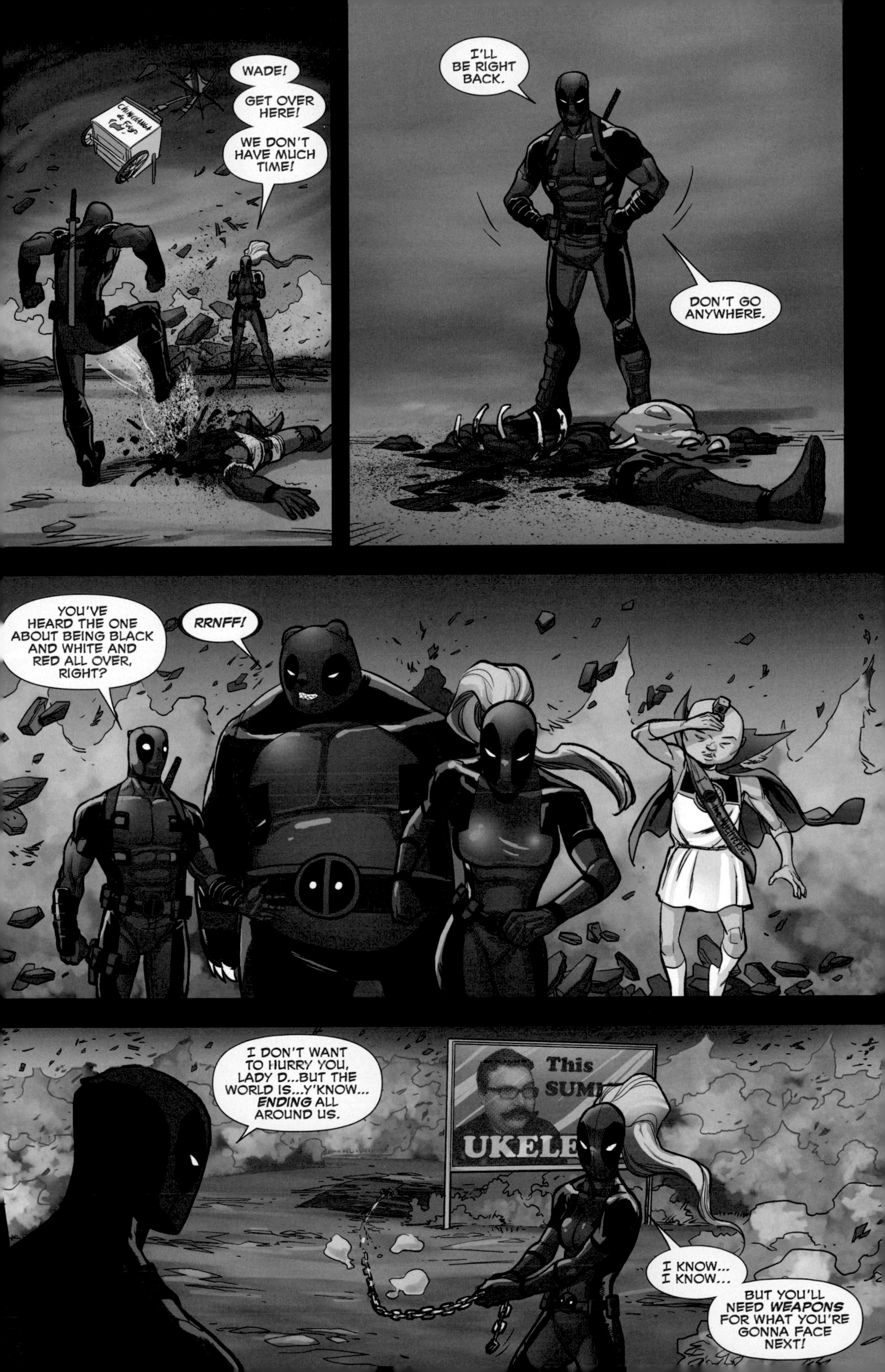
WADE!
GET OVER HERE!
WE DON'T HAVE MUCH TIME!
I'LL BE RIGHT BACK.
DON'T GO ANYWHERE.
YOU'VE HEARD THE ONE ABOUT BEING BLACK AND WHITE AND RED ALL OVER, RIGHT?
RRNFF!
I DON'T WANT TO HURRY YOU, LADY D...BUT THE WORLD IS...Y'KNOW... ENDING ALL AROUND US.
I KNOW... I KNOW...
BUT YOU'LL NEED WEAPONS FOR WHAT YOU'RE GONNA FACE NEXT!

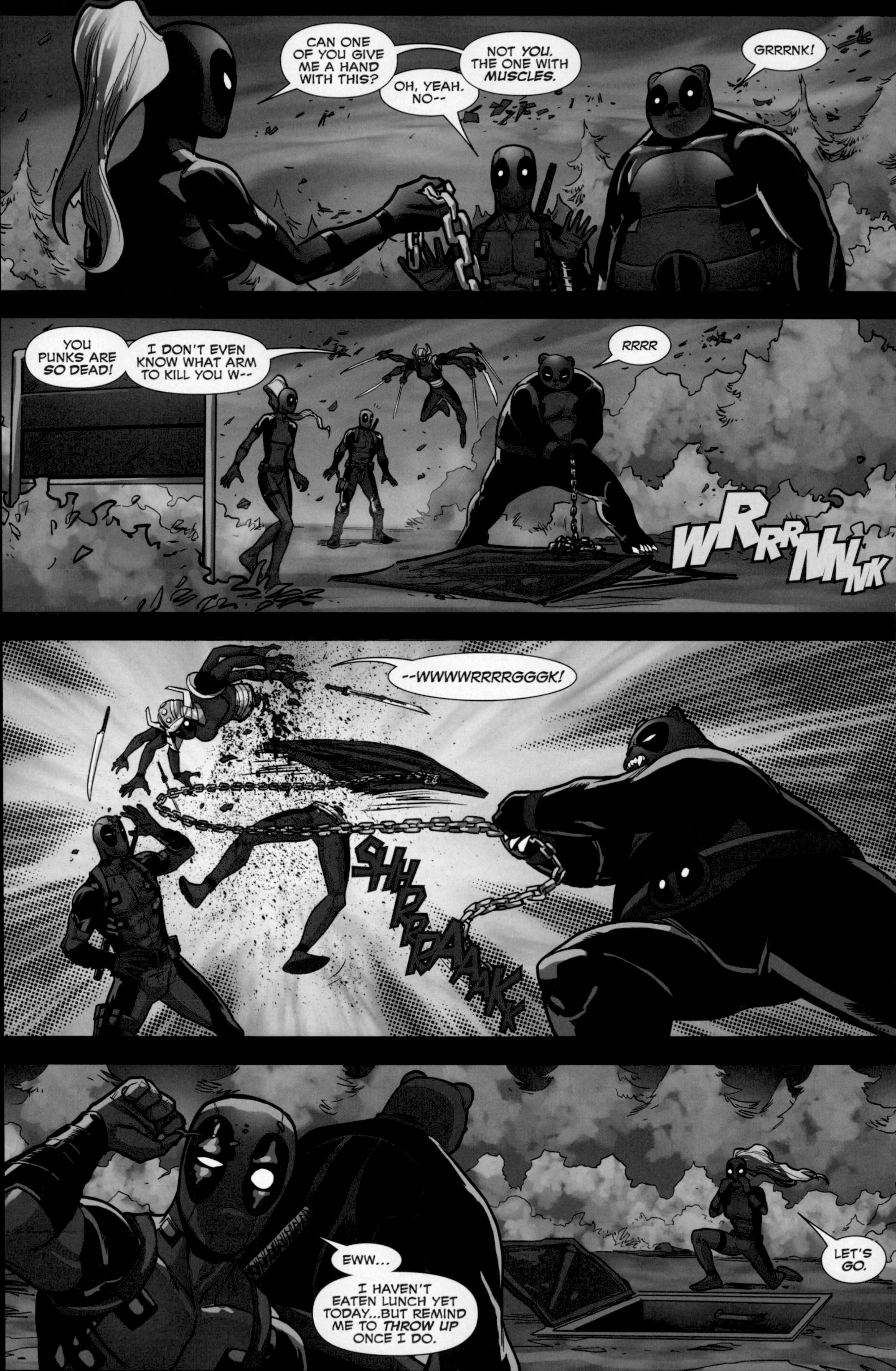

CAN ONE OF YOU GIVE ME A HAND WITH THIS?
NOT YOU. THE ONE WITH MUSCLES.
OH, YEAH. NO--
GRRRNK!
YOU PUNKS ARE SO DEAD!
I DON'T EVEN KNOW WHAT ARM TO KILL YOU W--
RRRR
WRRRNNNK
--WWWWRRRRGGGK!
SHRRRAAAKK
EWW...
I HAVEN'T EATEN LUNCH YET TODAY...BUT REMIND ME TO THROW UP ONCE I DO.
LET'S GO.

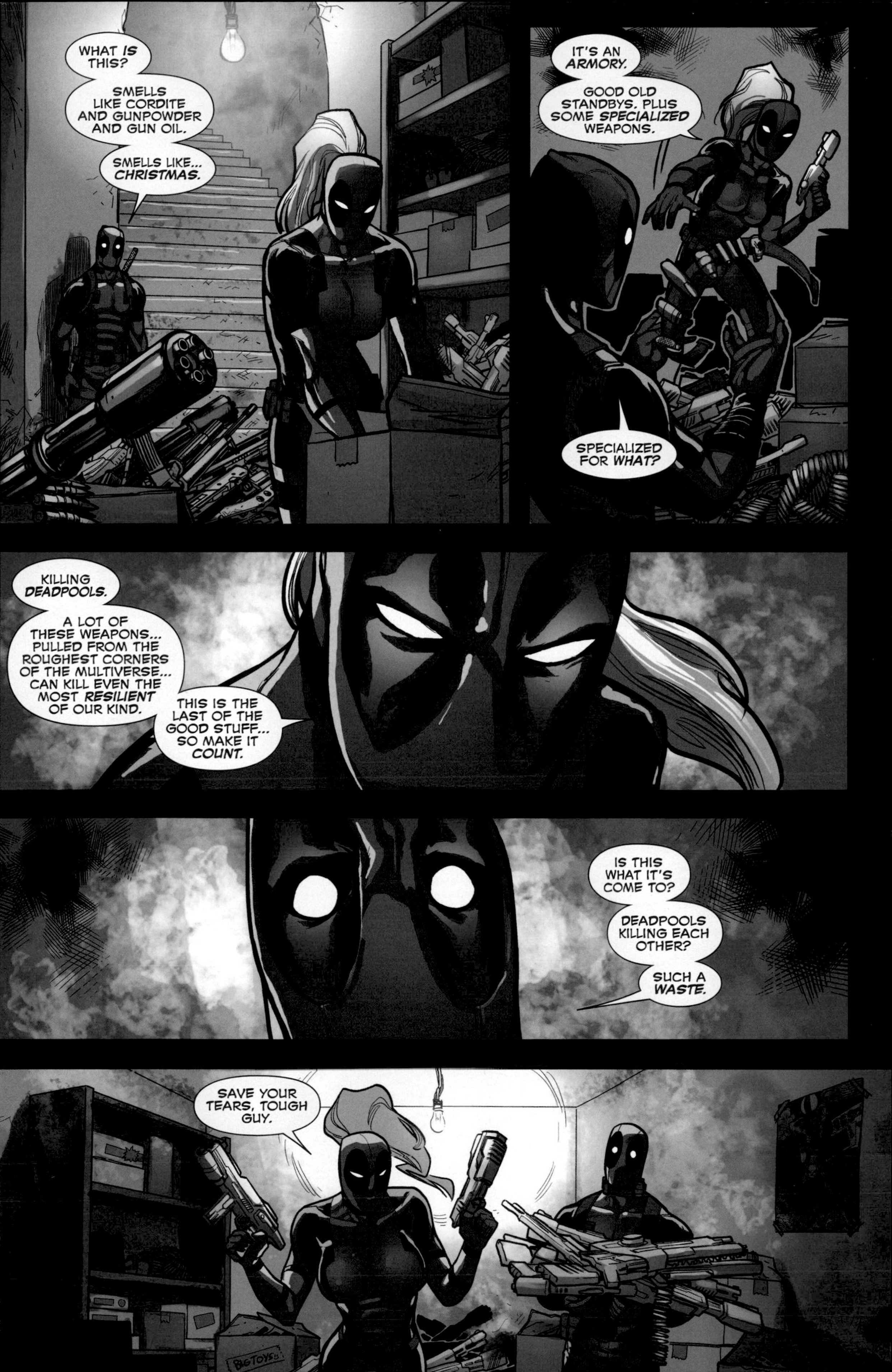
WHAT *IS* THIS?
SMELLS LIKE CORDITE AND GUNPOWDER AND GUN OIL.
SMELLS LIKE... *CHRISTMAS.*
IT'S AN *ARMORY.*
GOOD OLD STANDBYS. PLUS SOME *SPECIALIZED* WEAPONS.
SPECIALIZED FOR *WHAT?*
KILLING *DEADPOOLS.*
A LOT OF THESE WEAPONS... PULLED FROM THE ROUGHEST CORNERS OF THE MULTIVERSE... CAN KILL EVEN THE MOST *RESILIENT* OF OUR KIND.
THIS IS THE LAST OF THE GOOD STUFF... SO MAKE IT *COUNT.*
IS THIS WHAT IT'S COME TO?
DEADPOOLS KILLING EACH OTHER?
SUCH A *WASTE.*
SAVE YOUR TEARS, TOUGH GUY.
BIG TOYS

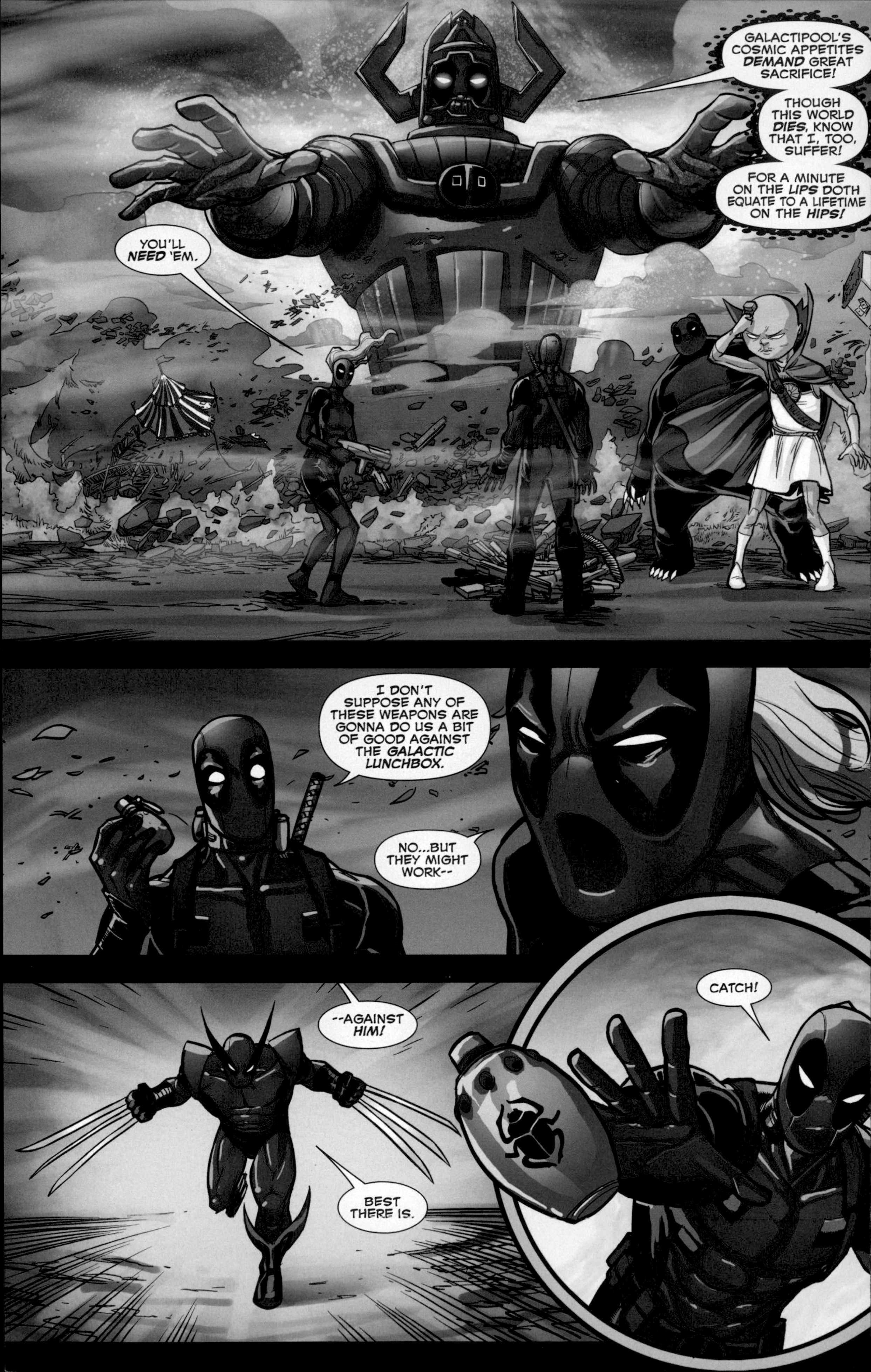
GALACTIPOOL'S COSMIC APPETITES DEMAND GREAT SACRIFICE!
THOUGH THIS WORLD DIES, KNOW THAT I, TOO, SUFFER!
FOR A MINUTE ON THE LIPS DOTH EQUATE TO A LIFETIME ON THE HIPS!
YOU'LL NEED 'EM.
I DON'T SUPPOSE ANY OF THESE WEAPONS ARE GONNA DO US A BIT OF GOOD AGAINST THE GALACTIC LUNCHBOX.
NO...BUT THEY MIGHT WORK--
--AGAINST HIM!
BEST THERE IS.
CATCH!

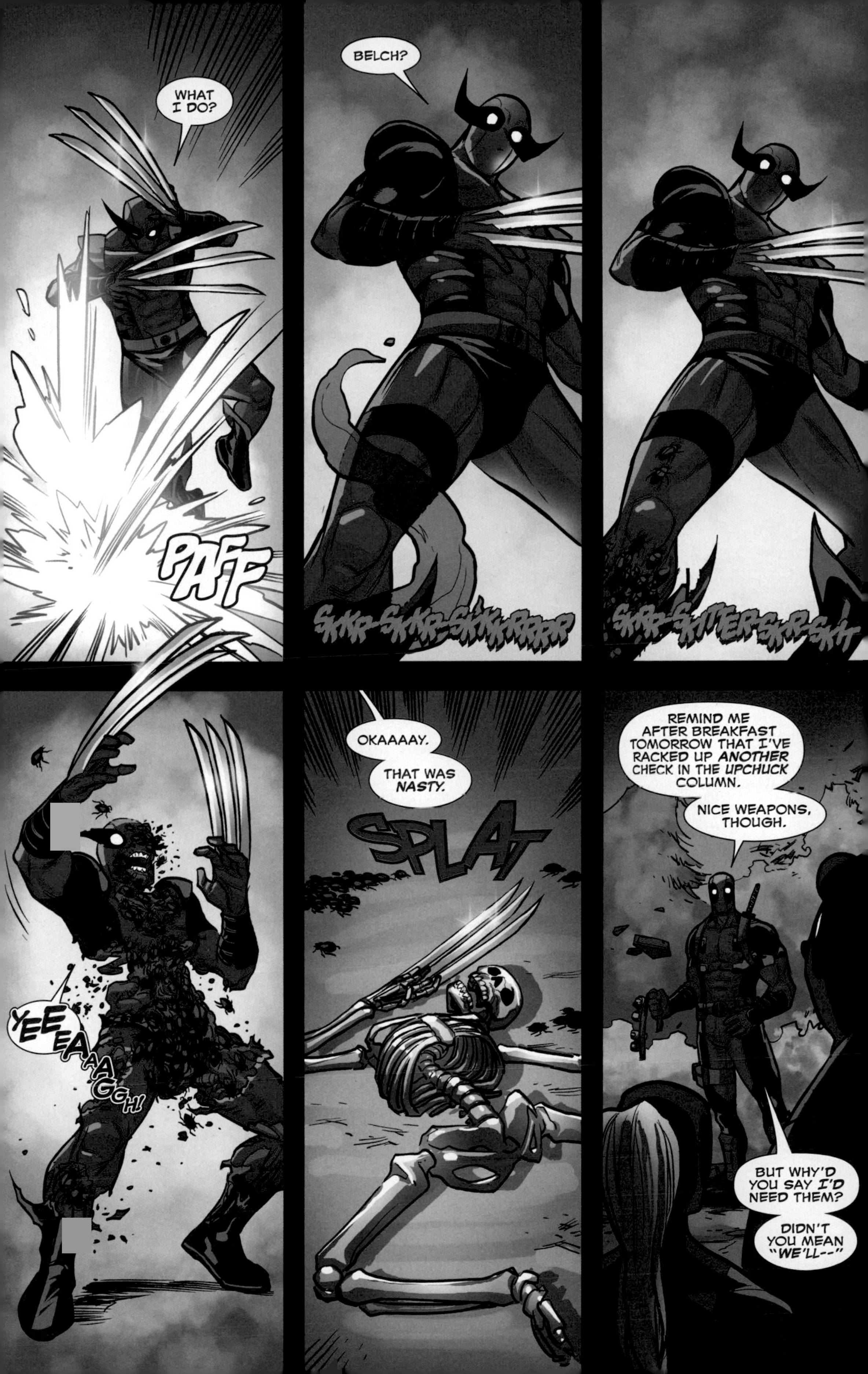
WHAT I DO?
PAFF
BELCH?
SKKR-SKKR-SKKKRRRR
SKRR-SKITTER-SKR-SKIT
YEEEAAAGGH!
OKAAAAY.
THAT WAS NASTY.
SPLAT
REMIND ME AFTER BREAKFAST TOMORROW THAT I'VE RACKED UP ANOTHER CHECK IN THE UPCHUCK COLUMN.
NICE WEAPONS, THOUGH.
BUT WHY'D YOU SAY I'D NEED THEM?
DIDN'T YOU MEAN "WE'LL--"

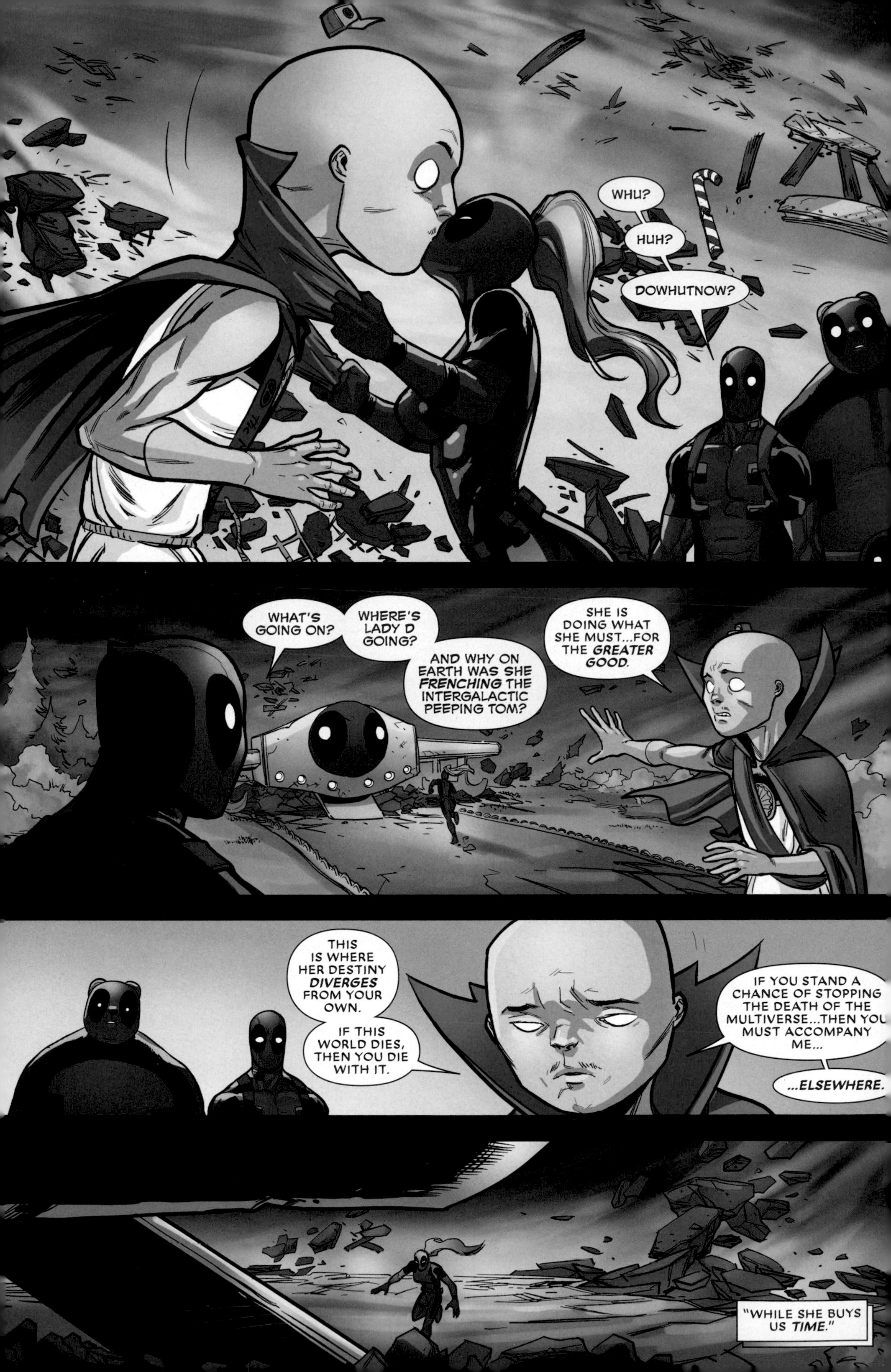
WHU?
HUH?
DOWHUTNOW?
WHAT'S GOING ON?
WHERE'S LADY D GOING?
AND WHY ON EARTH WAS SHE *FRENCHING* THE INTERGALACTIC PEEPING TOM?
SHE IS DOING WHAT SHE MUST...FOR THE *GREATER GOOD*.
THIS IS WHERE HER DESTINY *DIVERGES* FROM YOUR OWN.
IF THIS WORLD DIES, THEN YOU DIE WITH IT.
IF YOU STAND A CHANCE OF STOPPING THE DEATH OF THE MULTIVERSE...THEN YOU MUST ACCOMPANY ME...
...ELSEWHERE.
"WHILE SHE BUYS US *TIME*."

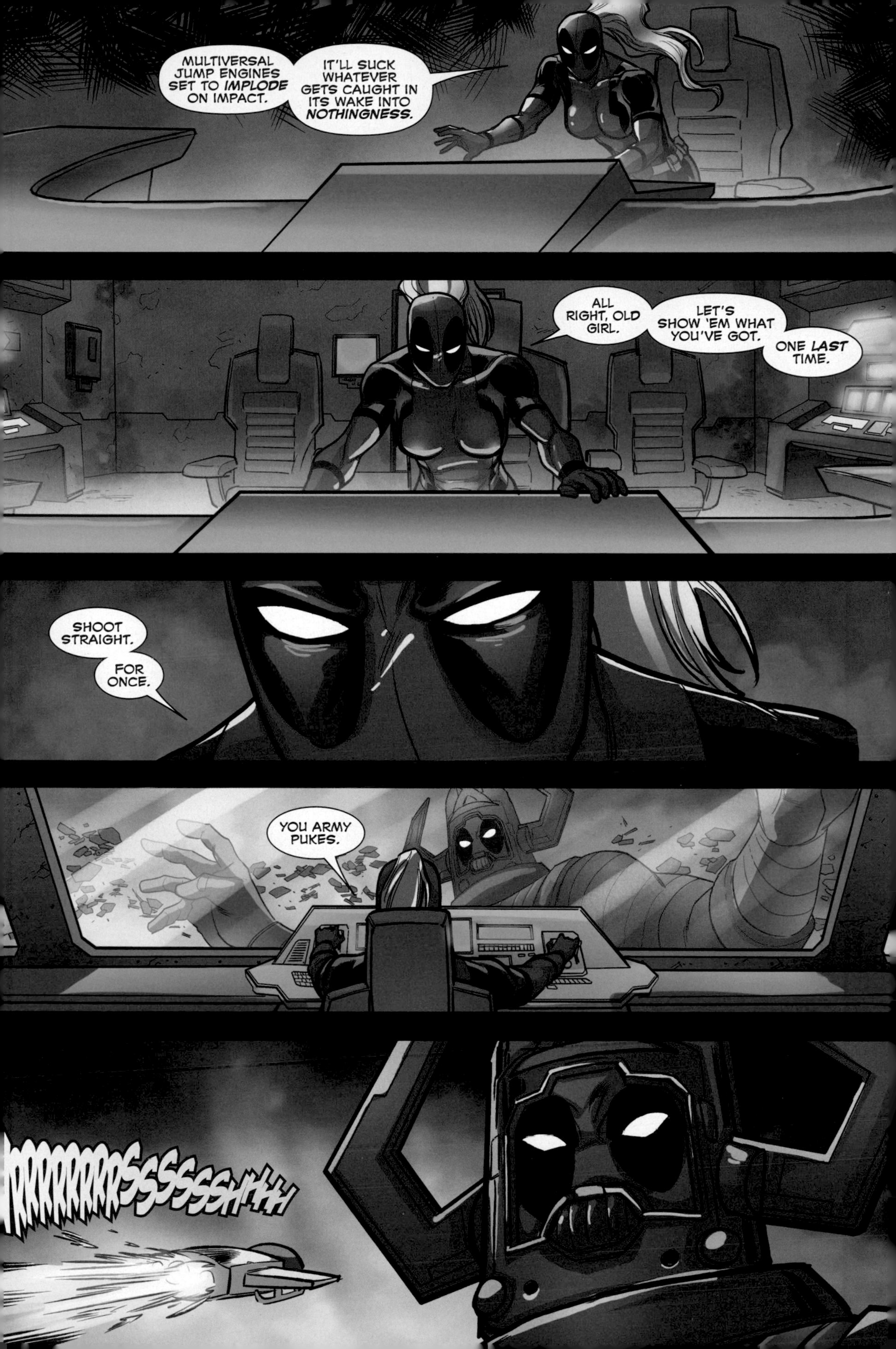
MULTIVERSAL JUMP ENGINES SET TO *IMPLODE* ON IMPACT.
IT'LL SUCK WHATEVER GETS CAUGHT IN ITS WAKE INTO ***NOTHINGNESS.***
ALL RIGHT, OLD GIRL.
LET'S SHOW 'EM WHAT YOU'VE GOT.
ONE *LAST* TIME.
SHOOT STRAIGHT.
FOR ONCE.
YOU ARMY PUKES.
RRRRRRRRRSSSSSSHHHH

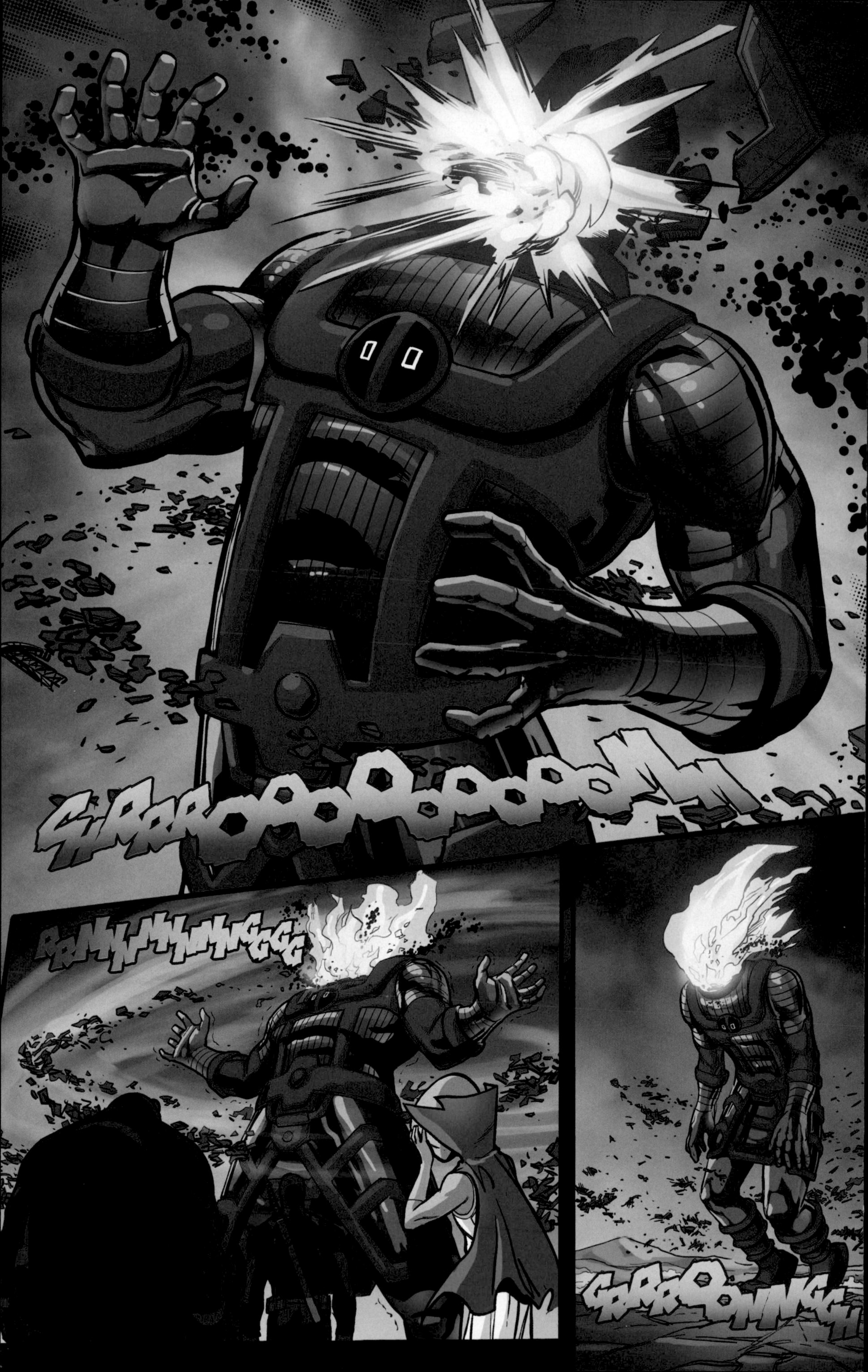
SHRRROOOOOOOOOOM
RRMMMMMMMNGGG
GRRROONNGGH

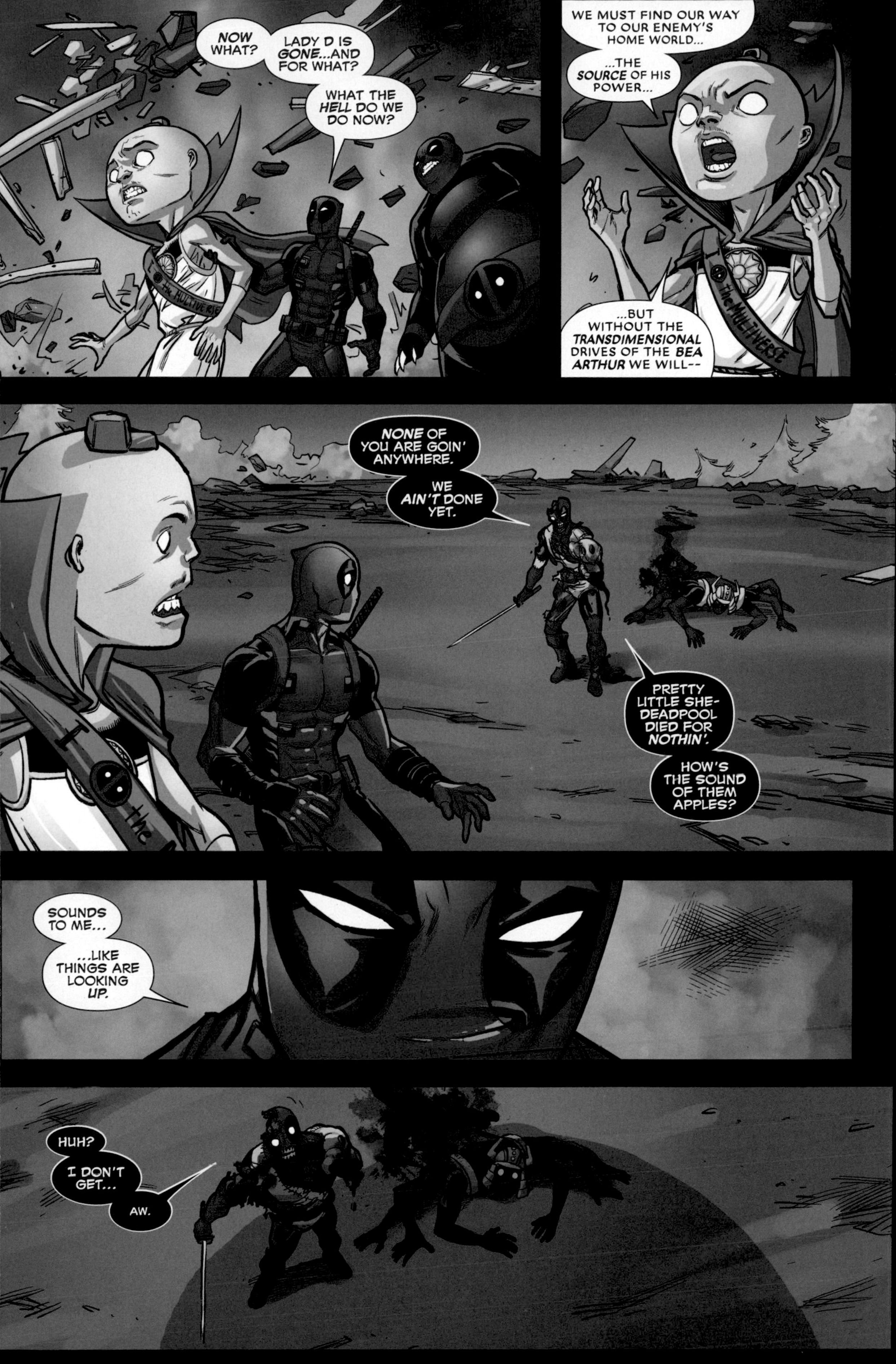
NOW WHAT?
LADY D IS GONE...AND FOR WHAT?
WHAT THE HELL DO WE DO NOW?
WE MUST FIND OUR WAY TO OUR ENEMY'S HOME WORLD...
...THE SOURCE OF HIS POWER...
...BUT WITHOUT THE TRANSDIMENSIONAL DRIVES OF THE BEA ARTHUR WE WILL--
NONE OF YOU ARE GOIN' ANYWHERE.
WE AIN'T DONE YET.
PRETTY LITTLE SHE-DEADPOOL DIED FOR NOTHIN'.
HOW'S THE SOUND OF THEM APPLES?
SOUNDS TO ME...
...LIKE THINGS ARE LOOKING UP.
HUH?
I DON'T GET...
AW.

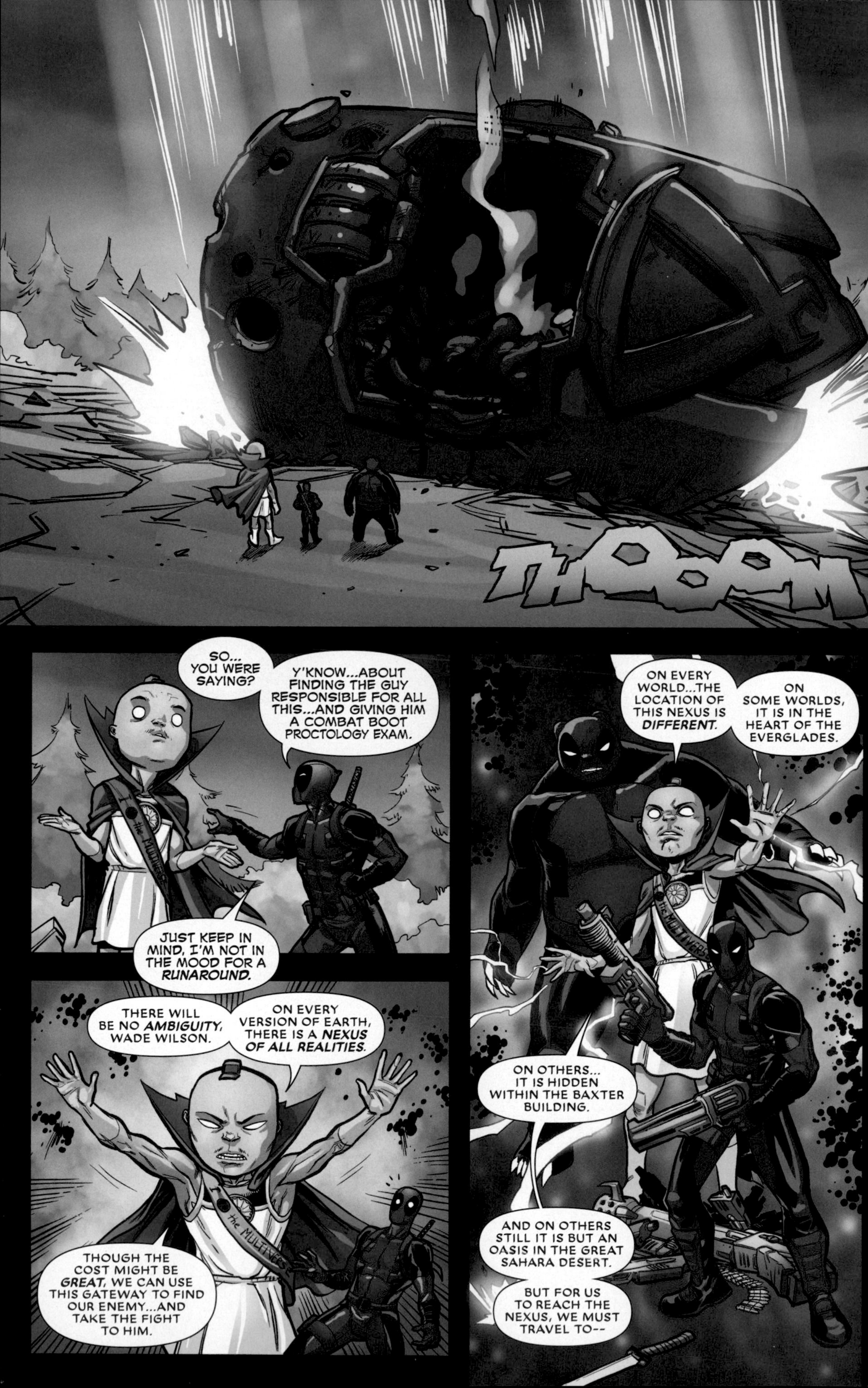
THOOOM
SO... YOU WERE SAYING?
Y'KNOW...ABOUT FINDING THE GUY RESPONSIBLE FOR ALL THIS...AND GIVING HIM A COMBAT BOOT PROCTOLOGY EXAM.
JUST KEEP IN MIND, I'M NOT IN THE MOOD FOR A RUNAROUND.
THERE WILL BE NO AMBIGUITY, WADE WILSON.
ON EVERY VERSION OF EARTH, THERE IS A NEXUS OF ALL REALITIES.
THOUGH THE COST MIGHT BE GREAT, WE CAN USE THIS GATEWAY TO FIND OUR ENEMY...AND TAKE THE FIGHT TO HIM.
ON EVERY WORLD...THE LOCATION OF THIS NEXUS IS DIFFERENT.
ON SOME WORLDS, IT IS IN THE HEART OF THE EVERGLADES.
ON OTHERS... IT IS HIDDEN WITHIN THE BAXTER BUILDING.
AND ON OTHERS STILL IT IS BUT AN OASIS IN THE GREAT SAHARA DESERT.
BUT FOR US TO REACH THE NEXUS, WE MUST TRAVEL TO--

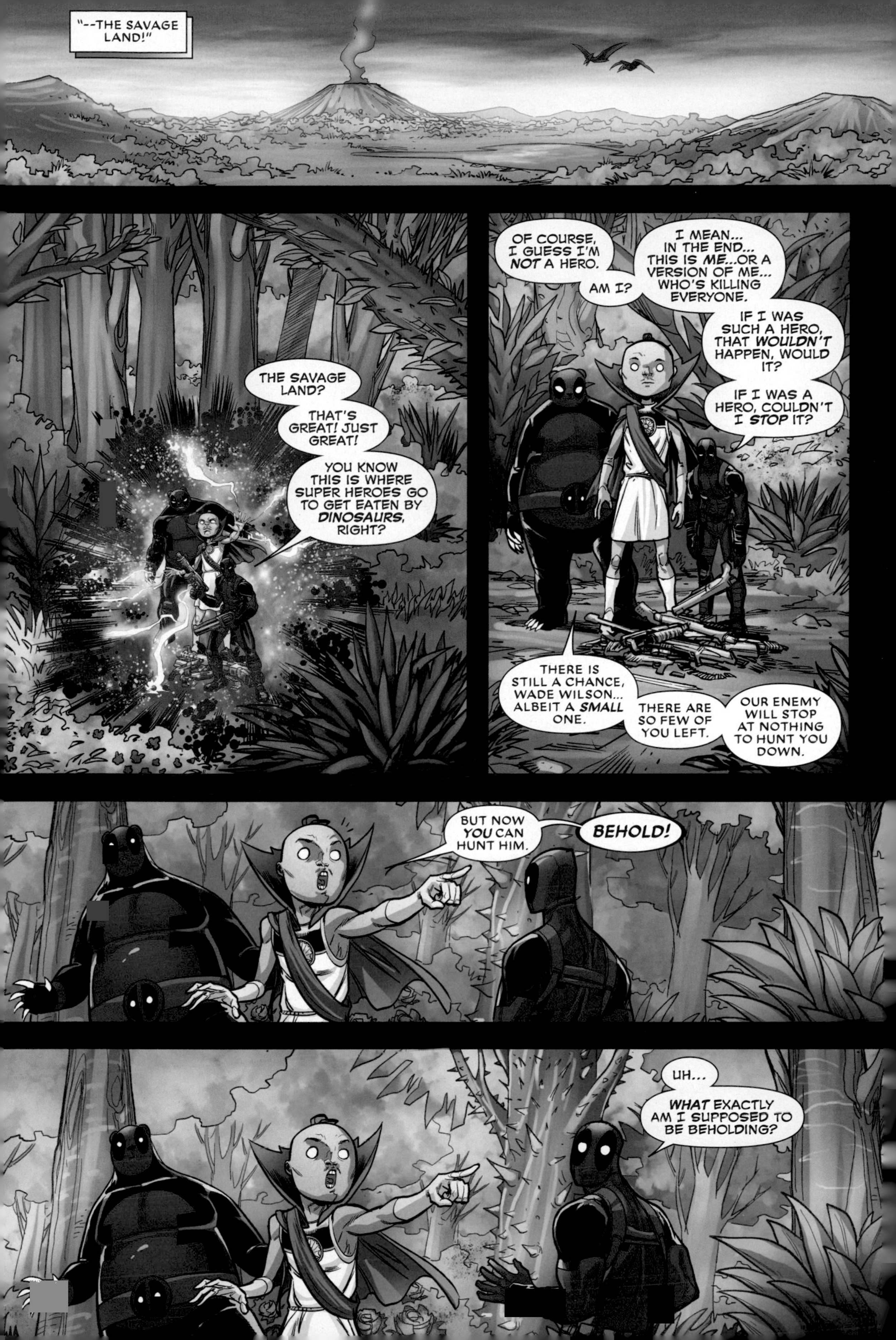
"--THE SAVAGE LAND!"
THE SAVAGE LAND?
THAT'S GREAT! JUST GREAT!
YOU KNOW THIS IS WHERE SUPER HEROES GO TO GET EATEN BY *DINOSAURS*, RIGHT?
OF COURSE, I GUESS I'M *NOT* A HERO.
AM I?
I MEAN... IN THE END... THIS IS *ME*...OR A VERSION OF ME... WHO'S KILLING EVERYONE.
IF I WAS SUCH A HERO, THAT *WOULDN'T* HAPPEN, WOULD IT?
IF I WAS A HERO, COULDN'T I *STOP* IT?
THERE IS STILL A CHANCE, WADE WILSON... ALBEIT A *SMALL* ONE.
THERE ARE SO FEW OF YOU LEFT.
OUR ENEMY WILL STOP AT NOTHING TO HUNT YOU DOWN.
BUT NOW *YOU* CAN HUNT HIM.
BEHOLD!
UH...
WHAT EXACTLY AM I SUPPOSED TO BE BEHOLDING?

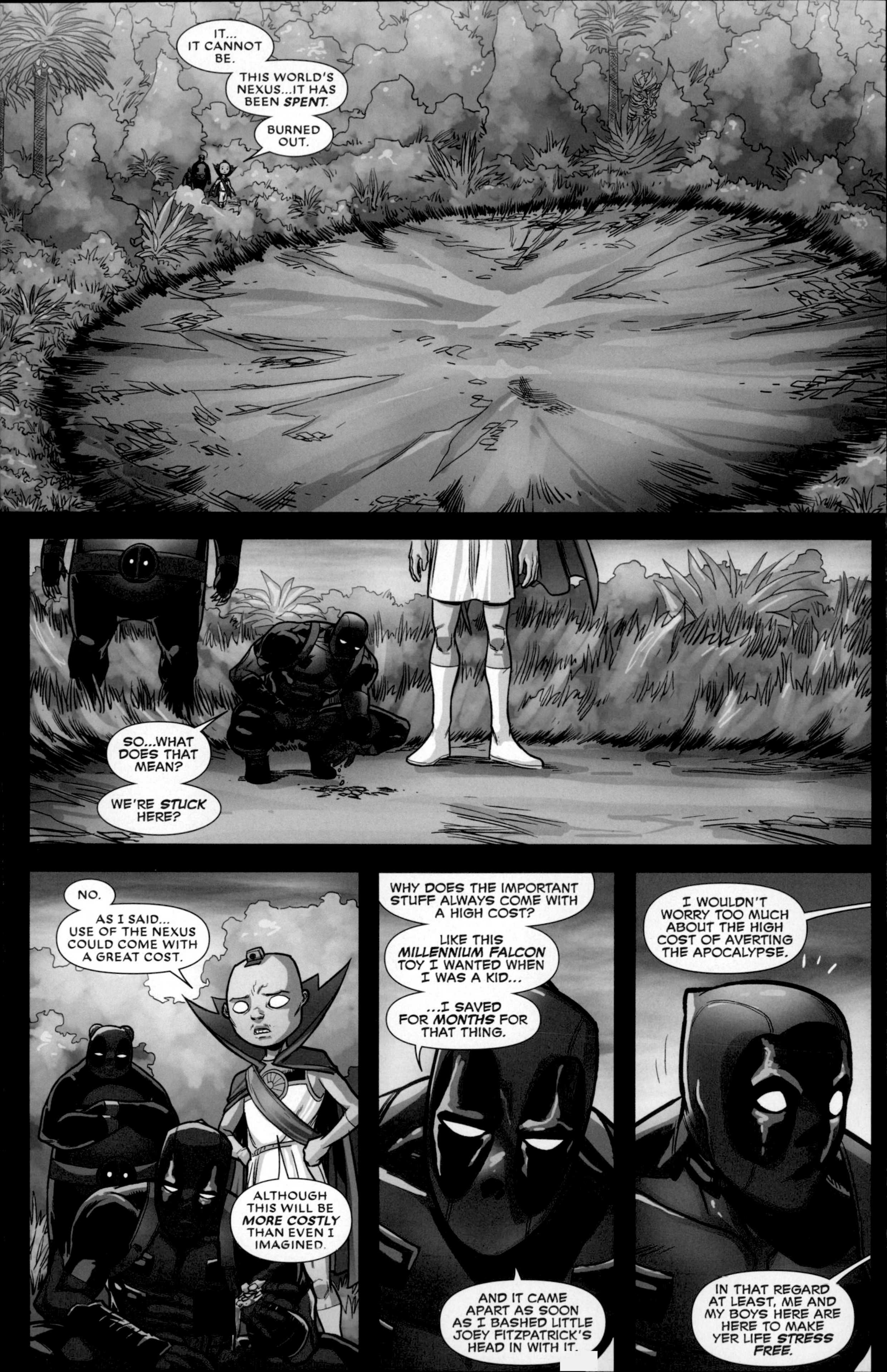
IT... IT CANNOT BE.
THIS WORLD'S NEXUS...IT HAS BEEN *SPENT*.
BURNED OUT.
SO...WHAT DOES THAT MEAN?
WE'RE *STUCK* HERE?
NO.
AS I SAID... USE OF THE NEXUS COULD COME WITH A GREAT COST.
ALTHOUGH THIS WILL BE *MORE COSTLY* THAN EVEN I IMAGINED.
WHY DOES THE IMPORTANT STUFF ALWAYS COME WITH A HIGH COST?
LIKE THIS *MILLENNIUM FALCON* TOY I WANTED WHEN I WAS A KID...
...I SAVED FOR *MONTHS* FOR THAT THING.
AND IT CAME APART AS SOON AS I BASHED LITTLE JOEY FITZPATRICK'S HEAD IN WITH IT.
I WOULDN'T WORRY TOO MUCH ABOUT THE HIGH COST OF AVERTING THE APOCALYPSE.
IN THAT REGARD AT LEAST, ME AND MY BOYS HERE ARE HERE TO MAKE YER LIFE *STRESS FREE*.

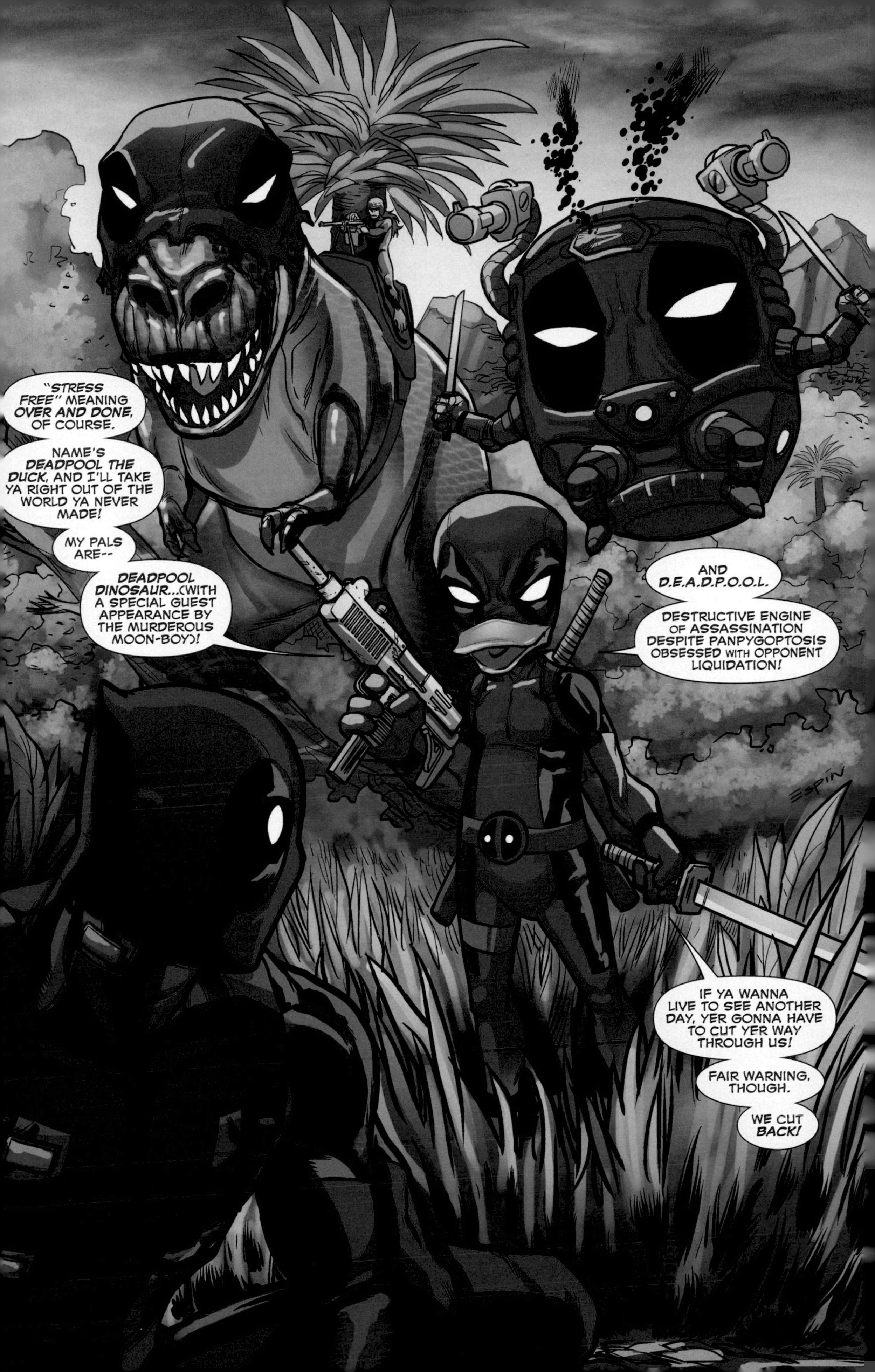
"STRESS FREE" MEANING OVER AND DONE, OF COURSE.
NAME'S DEADPOOL THE DUCK, AND I'LL TAKE YA RIGHT OUT OF THE WORLD YA NEVER MADE!
MY PALS ARE--
DEADPOOL DINOSAUR...(WITH A SPECIAL GUEST APPEARANCE BY THE MURDEROUS MOON-BOY)!
AND D.E.A.D.P.O.O.L.
DESTRUCTIVE ENGINE OF ASSASSINATION DESPITE PANPYGOPTOSIS OBSESSED WITH OPPONENT LIQUIDATION!
IF YA WANNA LIVE TO SEE ANOTHER DAY, YER GONNA HAVE TO CUT YER WAY THROUGH US!
FAIR WARNING, THOUGH.
WE CUT BACK!
ESPIN

FOUR

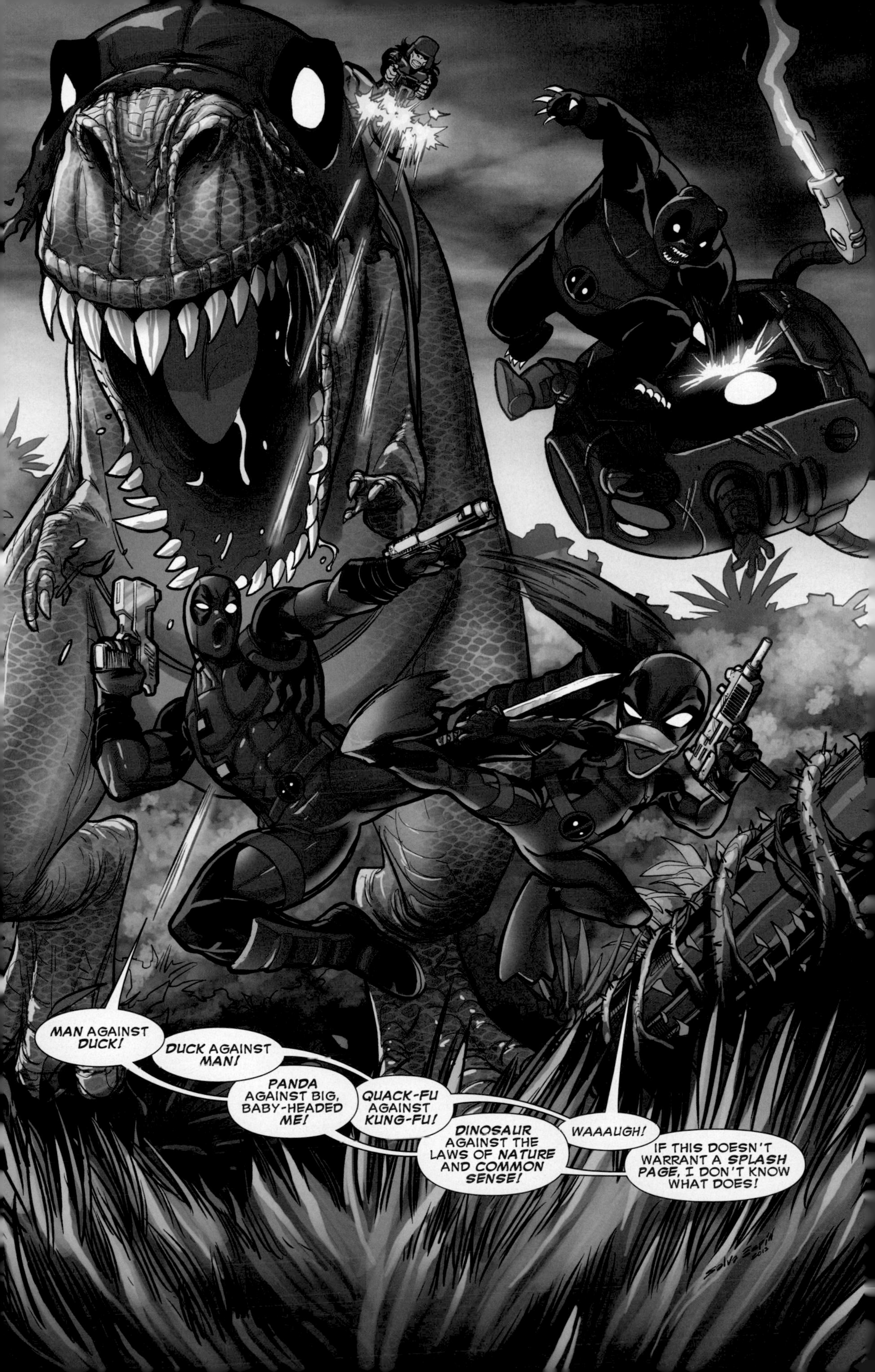
MAN AGAINST DUCK!
DUCK AGAINST MAN!
PANDA AGAINST BIG, BABY-HEADED ME!
QUACK-FU AGAINST KUNG-FU!
DINOSAUR AGAINST THE LAWS OF NATURE AND COMMON SENSE!
WAAAUGH!
IF THIS DOESN'T WARRANT A SPLASH PAGE, I DON'T KNOW WHAT DOES!

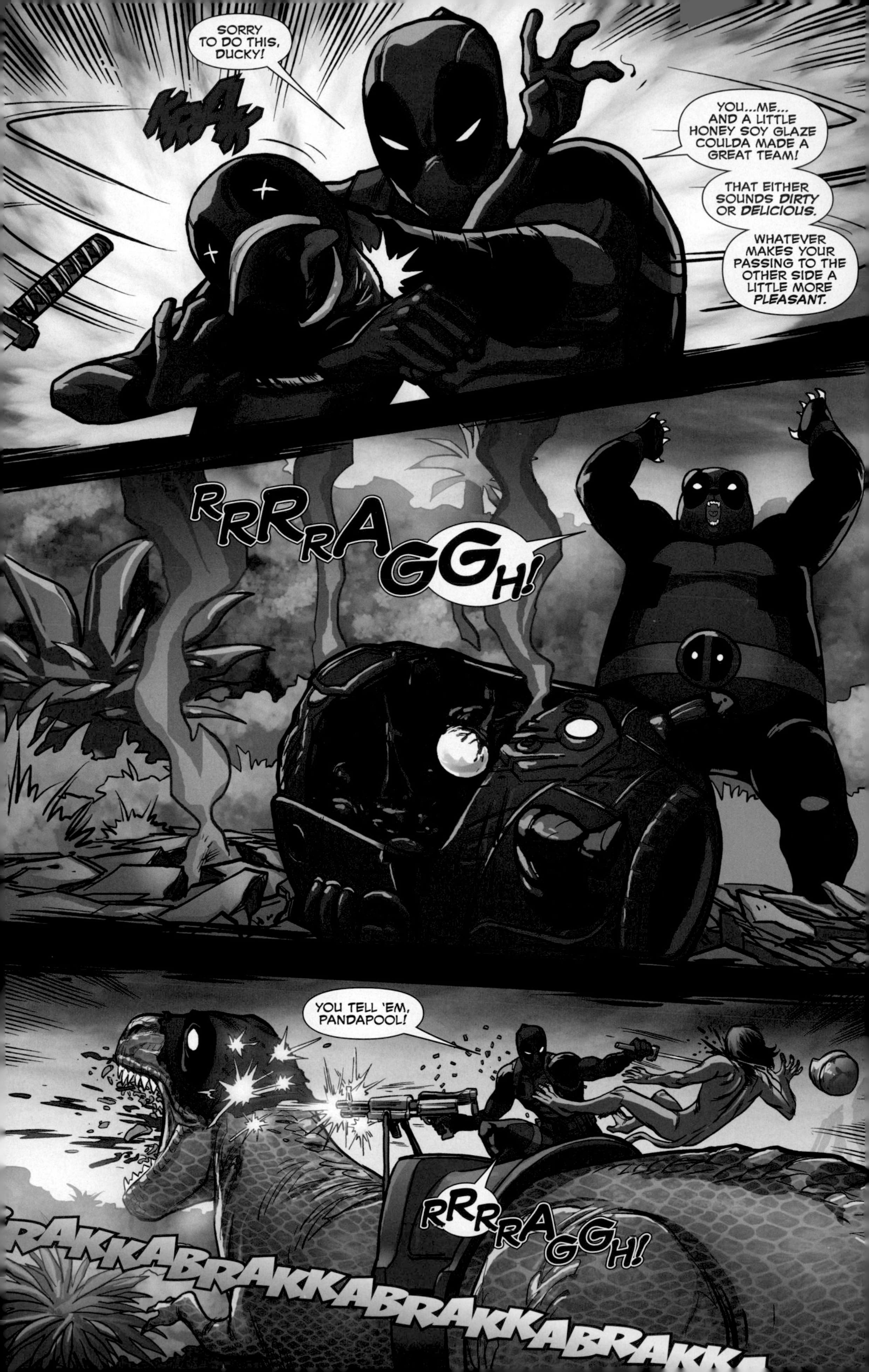
SORRY TO DO THIS, DUCKY!
KRAK
YOU...ME... AND A LITTLE HONEY SOY GLAZE COULDA MADE A GREAT TEAM!
THAT EITHER SOUNDS DIRTY OR DELICIOUS.
WHATEVER MAKES YOUR PASSING TO THE OTHER SIDE A LITTLE MORE PLEASANT.
RRRRRAGGGH!
YOU TELL 'EM, PANDAPOOL!
RRRRRAGGGH!
RAKKABRAKKABRAKKABRAKKA

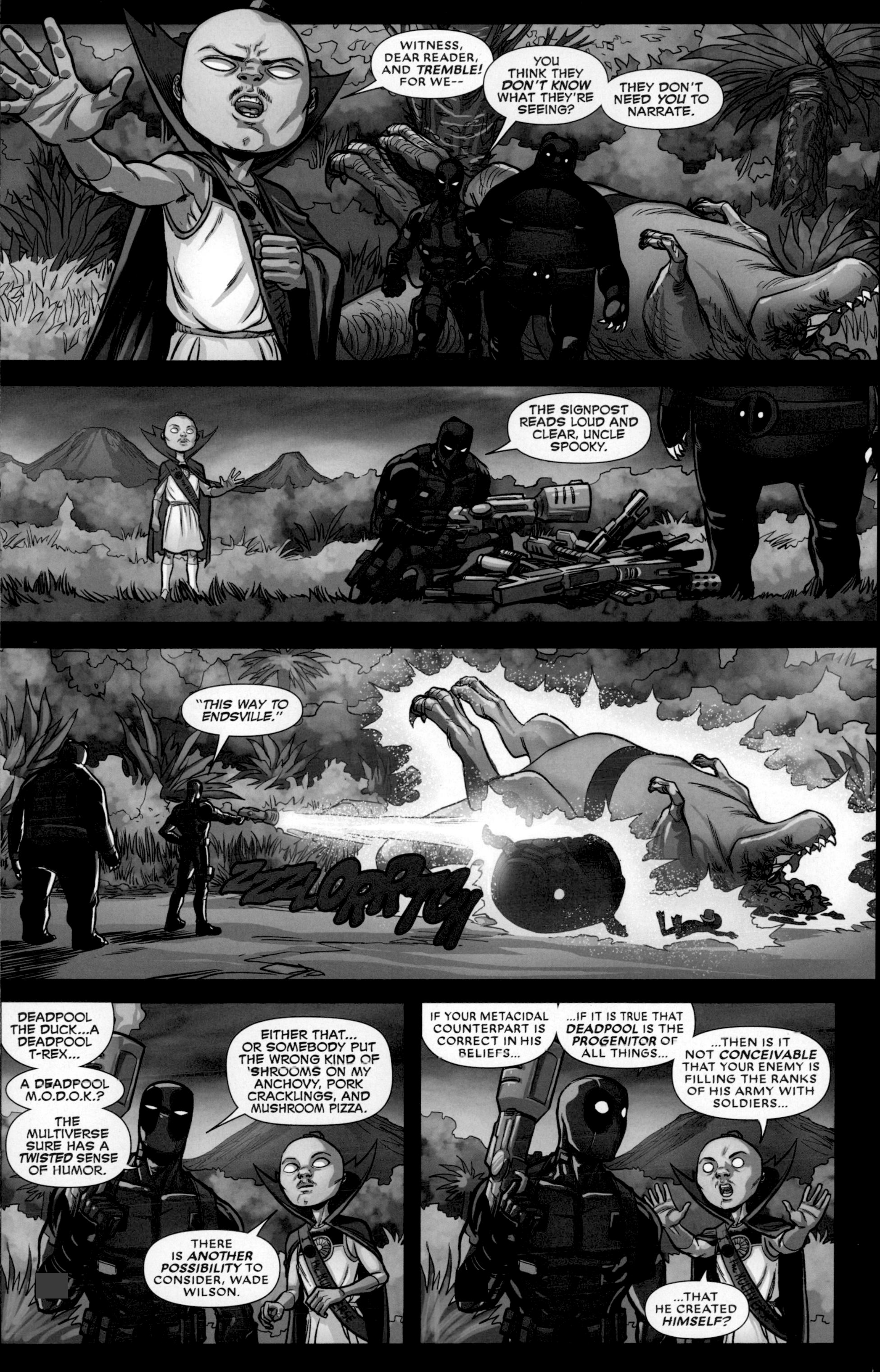
WITNESS, DEAR READER, AND TREMBLE! FOR WE--
YOU THINK THEY DON'T KNOW WHAT THEY'RE SEEING?
THEY DON'T NEED YOU TO NARRATE.
THE SIGNPOST READS LOUD AND CLEAR, UNCLE SPOOKY.
"THIS WAY TO ENDSVILLE."
ZZZZLORRRZZ
DEADPOOL THE DUCK...A DEADPOOL T-REX...
A DEADPOOL M.O.D.O.K.?
THE MULTIVERSE SURE HAS A TWISTED SENSE OF HUMOR.
EITHER THAT... OR SOMEBODY PUT THE WRONG KIND OF 'SHROOMS ON MY ANCHOVY, PORK CRACKLINGS, AND MUSHROOM PIZZA.
THERE IS ANOTHER POSSIBILITY TO CONSIDER, WADE WILSON.
IF YOUR METACIDAL COUNTERPART IS CORRECT IN HIS BELIEFS...
...IF IT IS TRUE THAT DEADPOOL IS THE PROGENITOR OF ALL THINGS...
...THEN IS IT NOT CONCEIVABLE THAT YOUR ENEMY IS FILLING THE RANKS OF HIS ARMY WITH SOLDIERS...
...THAT HE CREATED HIMSELF?

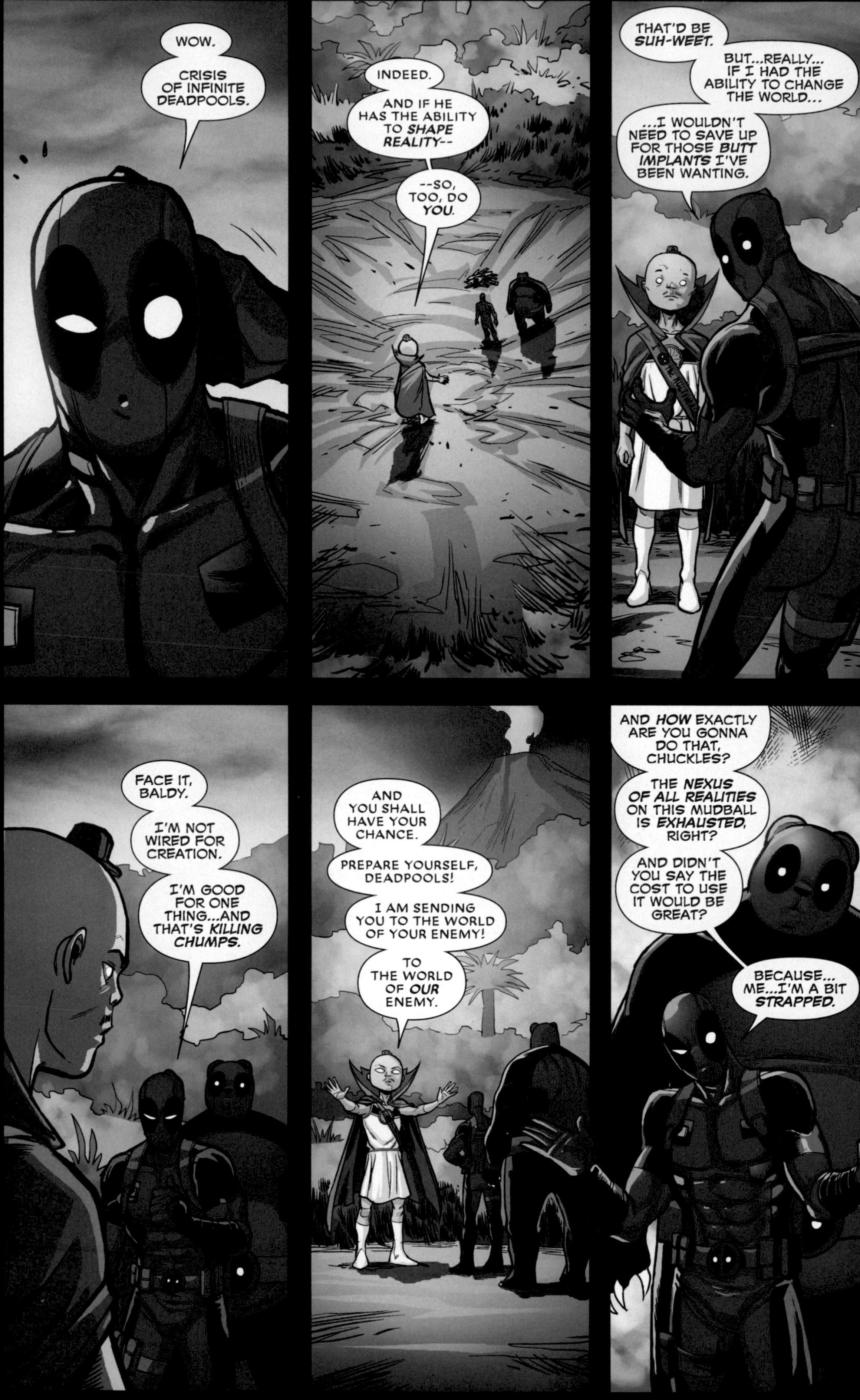
WOW.
CRISIS OF INFINITE DEADPOOLS.
INDEED.
AND IF HE HAS THE ABILITY TO SHAPE REALITY--
--SO, TOO, DO YOU.
THAT'D BE SUH-WEET.
BUT...REALLY... IF I HAD THE ABILITY TO CHANGE THE WORLD...
...I WOULDN'T NEED TO SAVE UP FOR THOSE BUTT IMPLANTS I'VE BEEN WANTING.
FACE IT, BALDY.
I'M NOT WIRED FOR CREATION.
I'M GOOD FOR ONE THING...AND THAT'S KILLING CHUMPS.
AND YOU SHALL HAVE YOUR CHANCE.
PREPARE YOURSELF, DEADPOOLS!
I AM SENDING YOU TO THE WORLD OF YOUR ENEMY!
TO THE WORLD OF OUR ENEMY.
AND HOW EXACTLY ARE YOU GONNA DO THAT, CHUCKLES?
THE NEXUS OF ALL REALITIES ON THIS MUDBALL IS EXHAUSTED, RIGHT?
AND DIDN'T YOU SAY THE COST TO USE IT WOULD BE GREAT?
BECAUSE... ME...I'M A BIT STRAPPED.

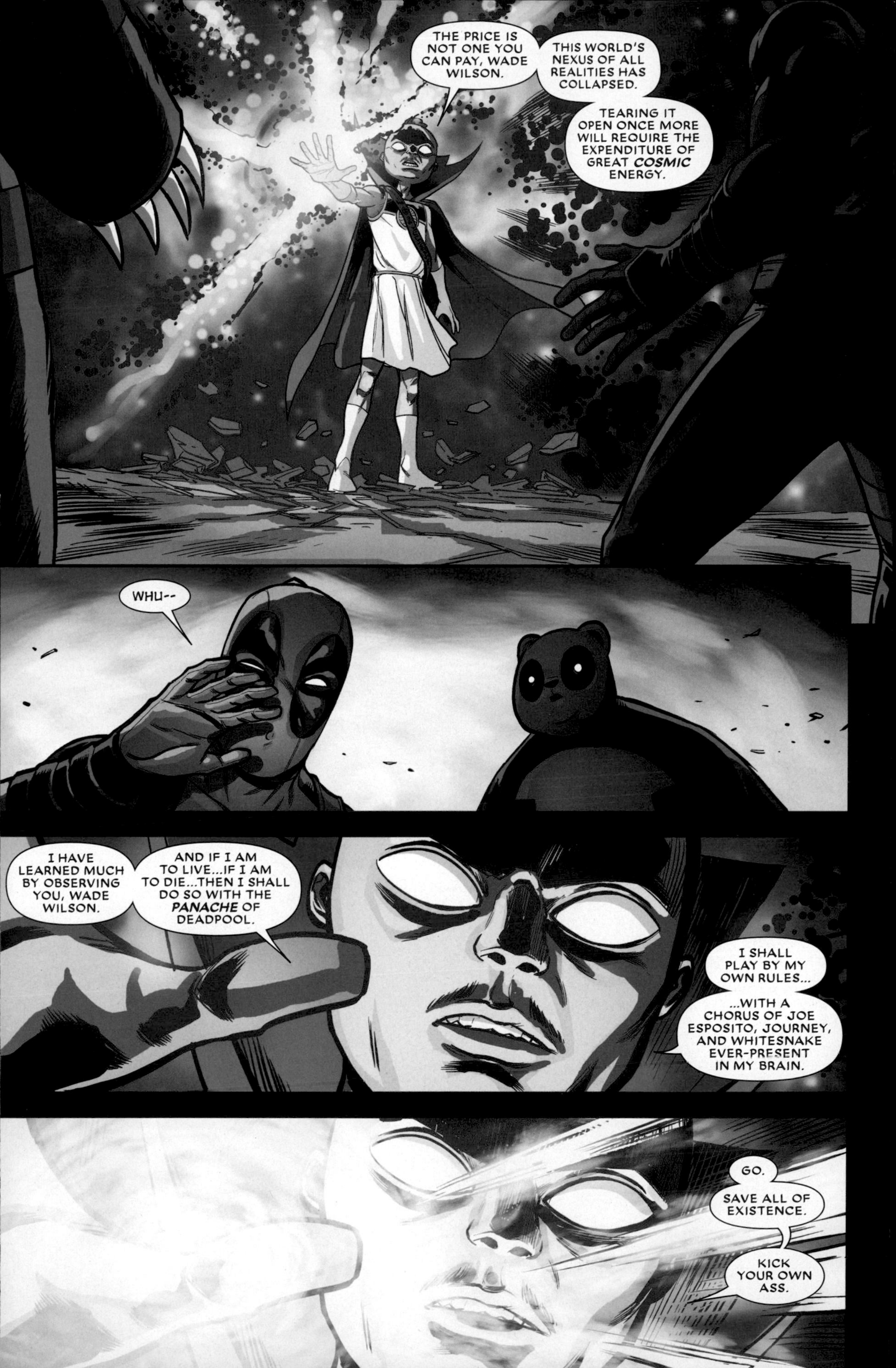
THE PRICE IS NOT ONE YOU CAN PAY, WADE WILSON.
THIS WORLD'S NEXUS OF ALL REALITIES HAS COLLAPSED.
TEARING IT OPEN ONCE MORE WILL REQUIRE THE EXPENDITURE OF GREAT *COSMIC* ENERGY.
WHU--
I HAVE LEARNED MUCH BY OBSERVING YOU, WADE WILSON.
AND IF I AM TO LIVE...IF I AM TO DIE...THEN I SHALL DO SO WITH THE *PANACHE* OF DEADPOOL.
I SHALL PLAY BY MY OWN RULES...
...WITH A CHORUS OF JOE ESPOSITO, JOURNEY, AND WHITESNAKE EVER-PRESENT IN MY BRAIN.
GO.
SAVE ALL OF EXISTENCE.
KICK YOUR OWN ASS.

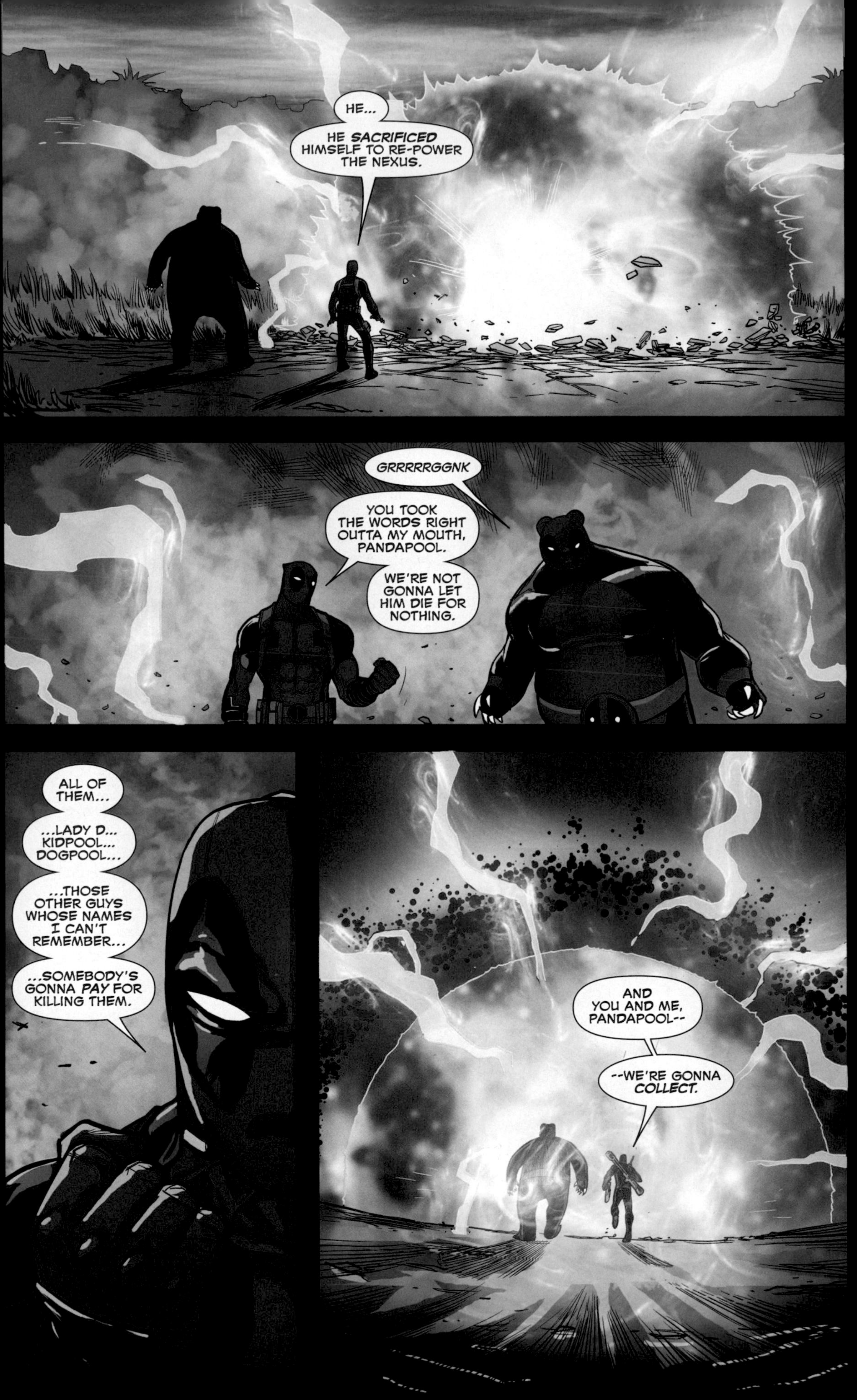
HE...
HE SACRIFICED HIMSELF TO RE-POWER THE NEXUS.
GRRRRRGGNK
YOU TOOK THE WORDS RIGHT OUTTA MY MOUTH, PANDAPOOL.
WE'RE NOT GONNA LET HIM DIE FOR NOTHING.
ALL OF THEM...
...LADY D... KIDPOOL... DOGPOOL...
...THOSE OTHER GUYS WHOSE NAMES I CAN'T REMEMBER...
...SOMEBODY'S GONNA PAY FOR KILLING THEM.
AND YOU AND ME, PANDAPOOL--
--WE'RE GONNA COLLECT.

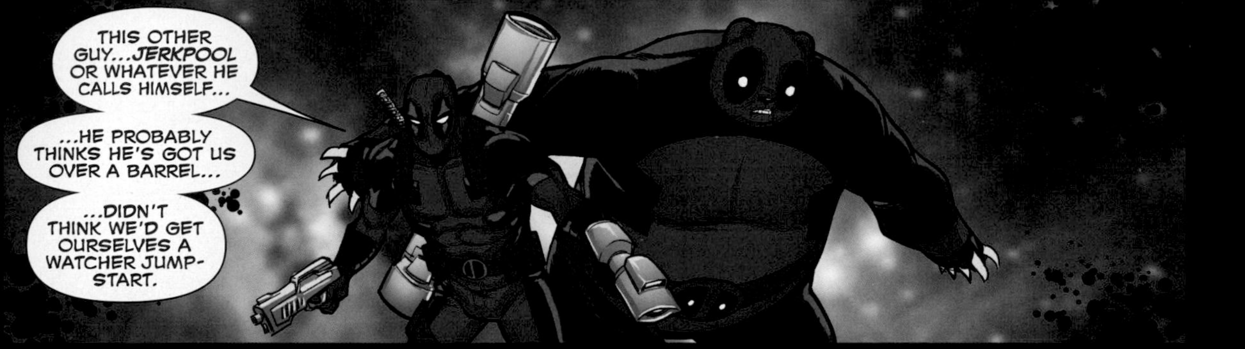
THIS OTHER GUY...JERKPOOL OR WHATEVER HE CALLS HIMSELF...
...HE PROBABLY THINKS HE'S GOT US OVER A BARREL...
...DIDN'T THINK WE'D GET OURSELVES A WATCHER JUMP-START.

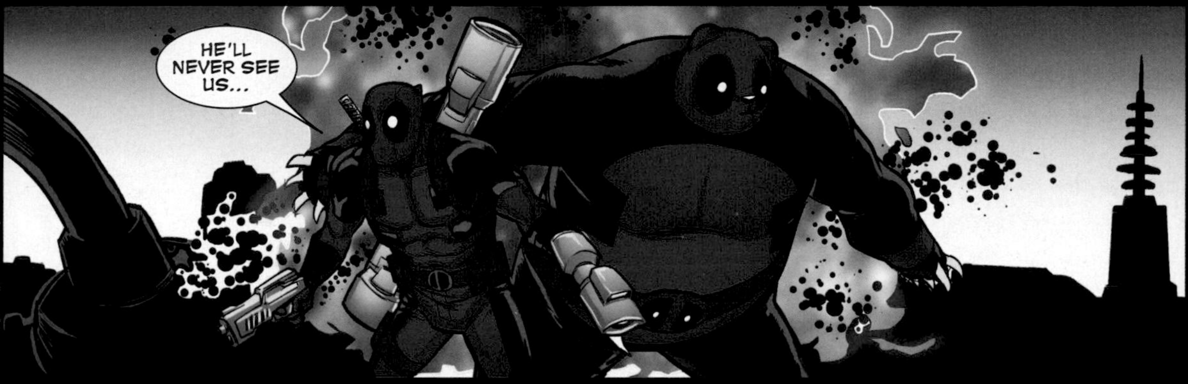
HE'LL NEVER SEE US...

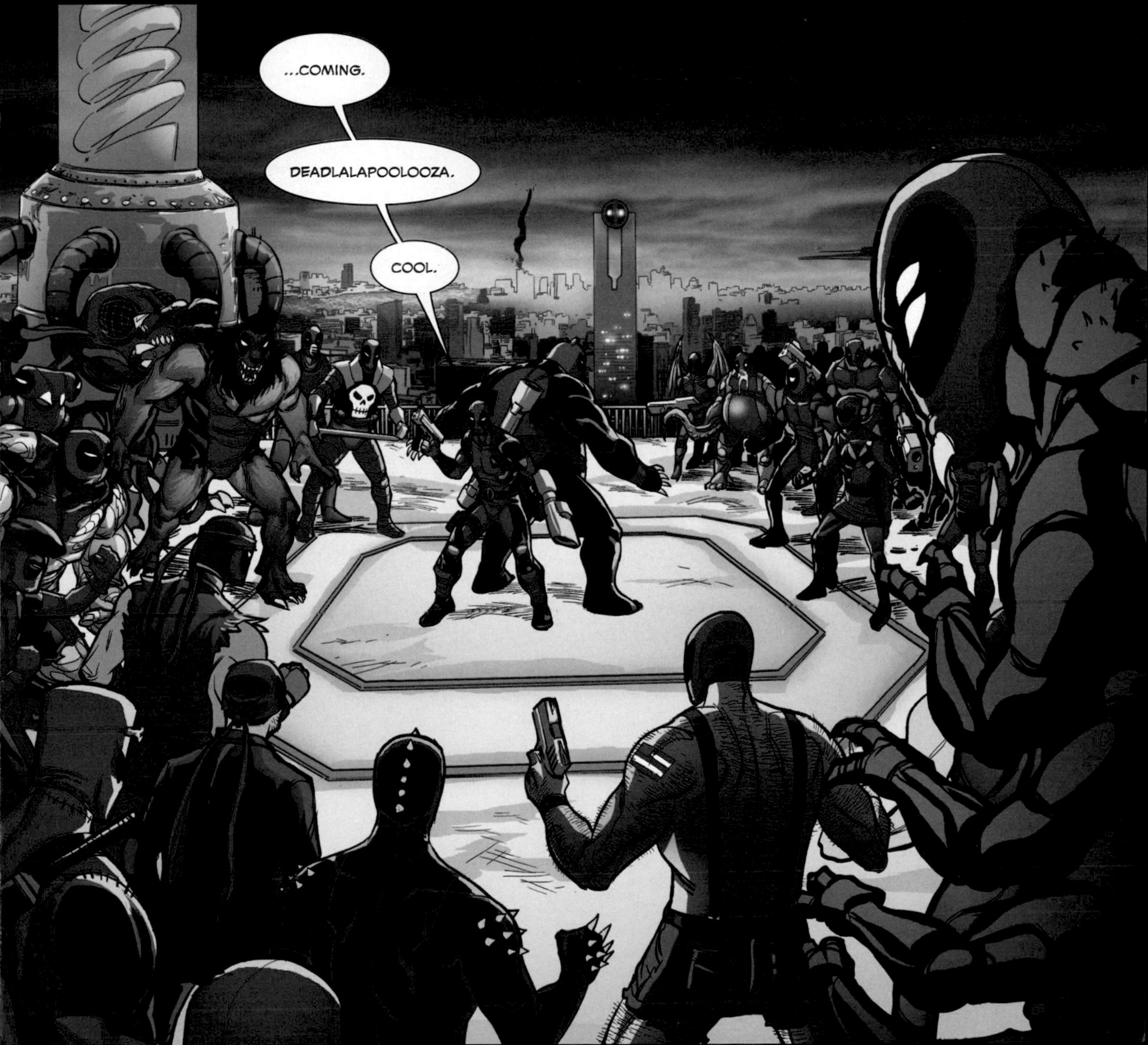
...COMING.
DEADLALAPOOLOOZA.
COOL.

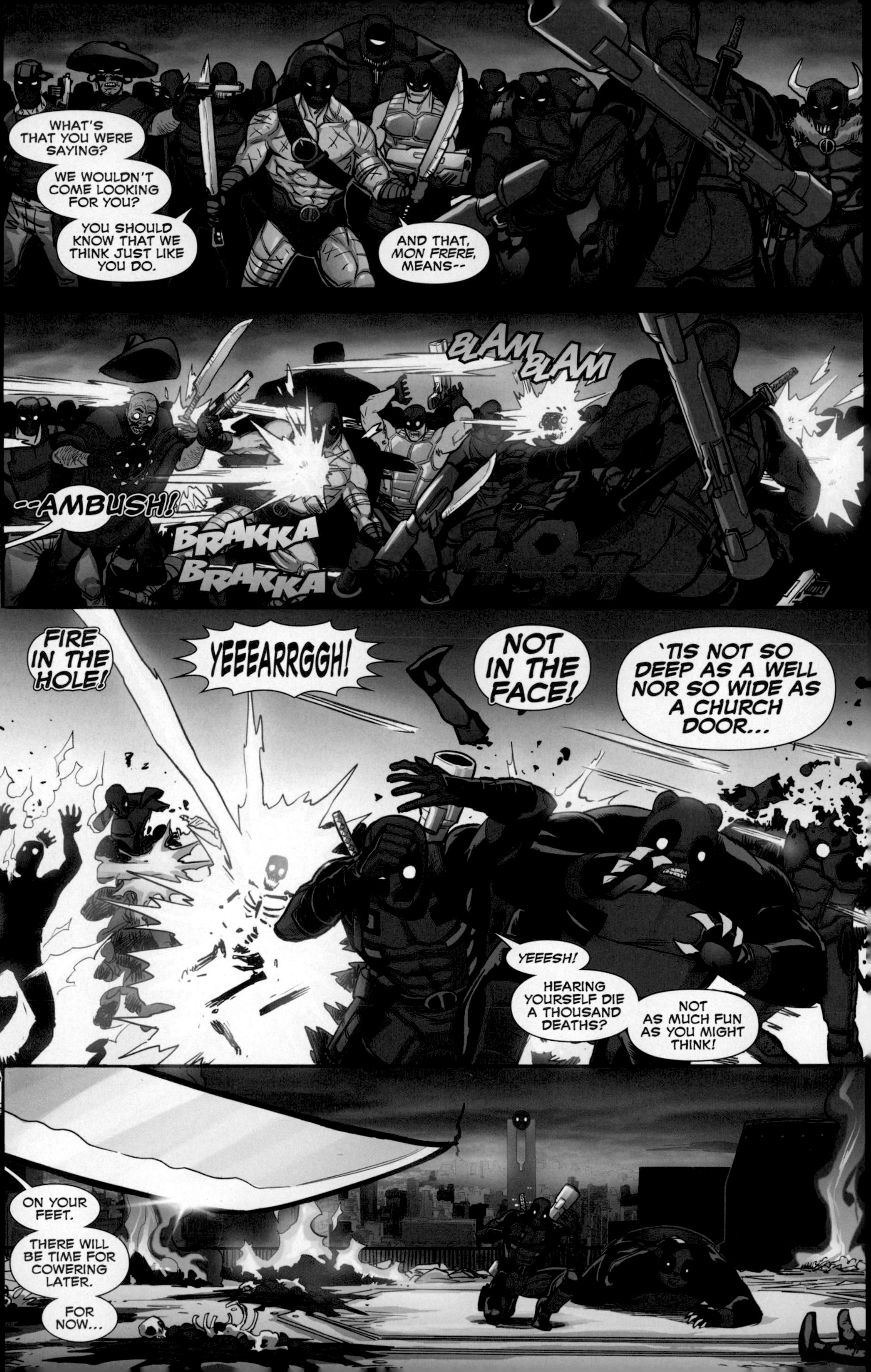
WHAT'S THAT YOU WERE SAYING?
WE WOULDN'T COME LOOKING FOR YOU?
YOU SHOULD KNOW THAT WE THINK JUST LIKE YOU DO.
AND THAT, MON FRERE, MEANS--
BLAM BLAM
--AMBUSH!
BRAKKA BRAKKA
FIRE IN THE HOLE!
YEEEARRGGH!
NOT IN THE FACE!
'TIS NOT SO DEEP AS A WELL NOR SO WIDE AS A CHURCH DOOR...
YEEESH!
HEARING YOURSELF DIE A THOUSAND DEATHS?
NOT AS MUCH FUN AS YOU MIGHT THINK!
ON YOUR FEET.
THERE WILL BE TIME FOR COWERING LATER.
FOR NOW...

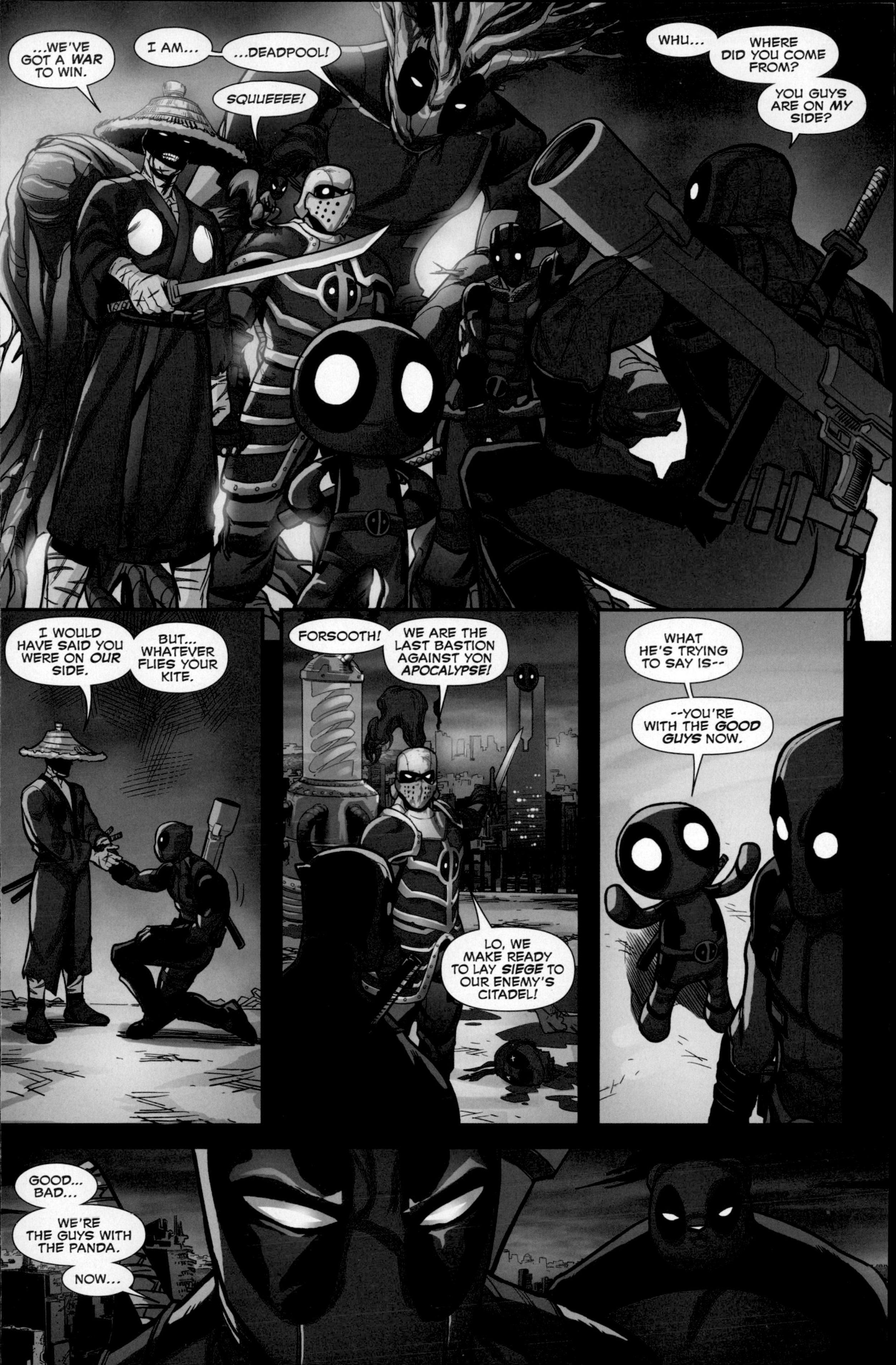
...WE'VE GOT A WAR TO WIN.
I AM...
...DEADPOOL!
SQUUEEEE!
WHU...
WHERE DID YOU COME FROM?
YOU GUYS ARE ON MY SIDE?
I WOULD HAVE SAID YOU WERE ON OUR SIDE.
BUT... WHATEVER FLIES YOUR KITE.
FORSOOTH!
WE ARE THE LAST BASTION AGAINST YON APOCALYPSE!
LO, WE MAKE READY TO LAY SIEGE TO OUR ENEMY'S CITADEL!
WHAT HE'S TRYING TO SAY IS--
--YOU'RE WITH THE GOOD GUYS NOW.
GOOD... BAD...
WE'RE THE GUYS WITH THE PANDA.
NOW...

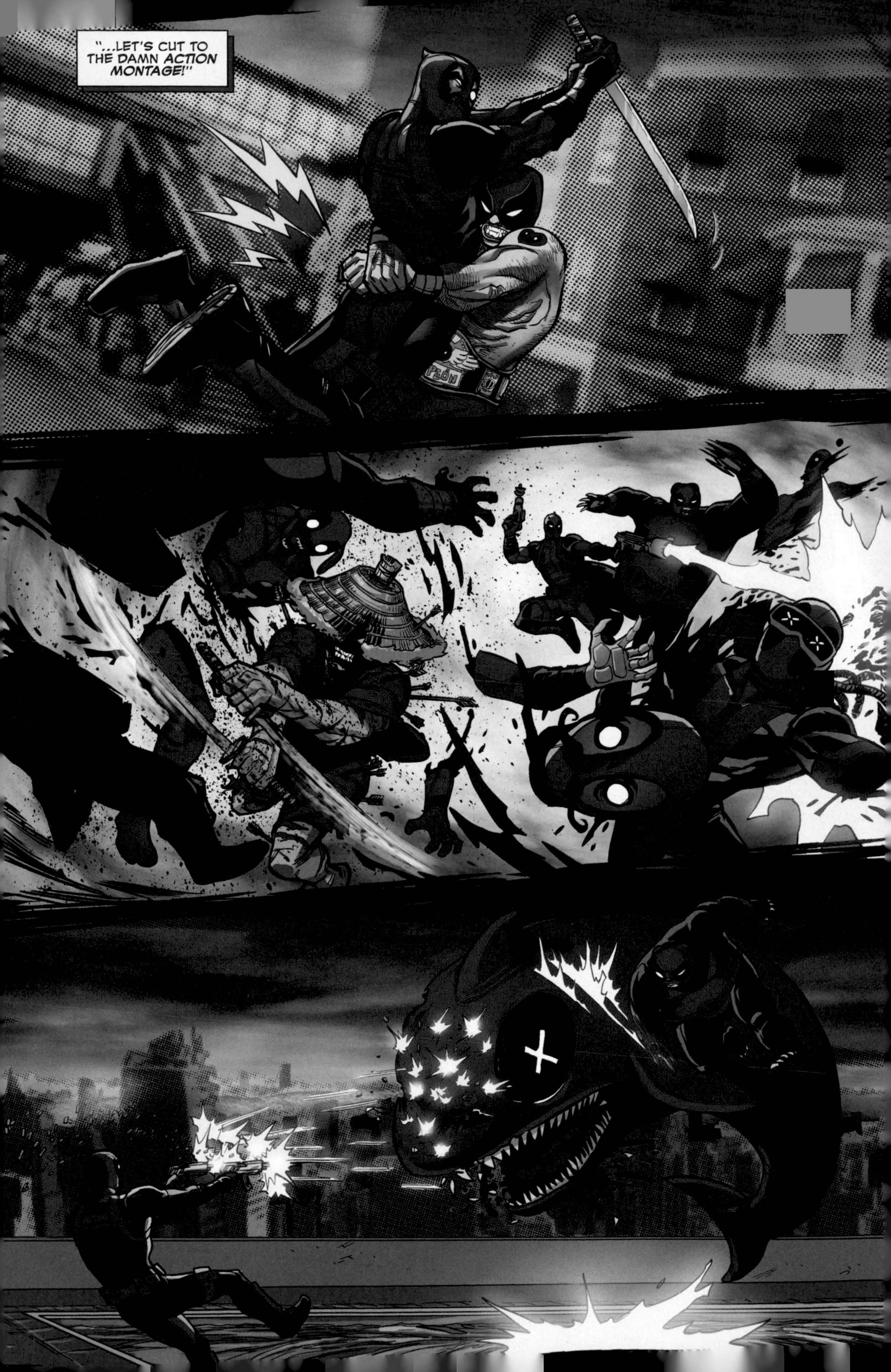
"...LET'S CUT TO THE DAMN ACTION MONTAGE!"

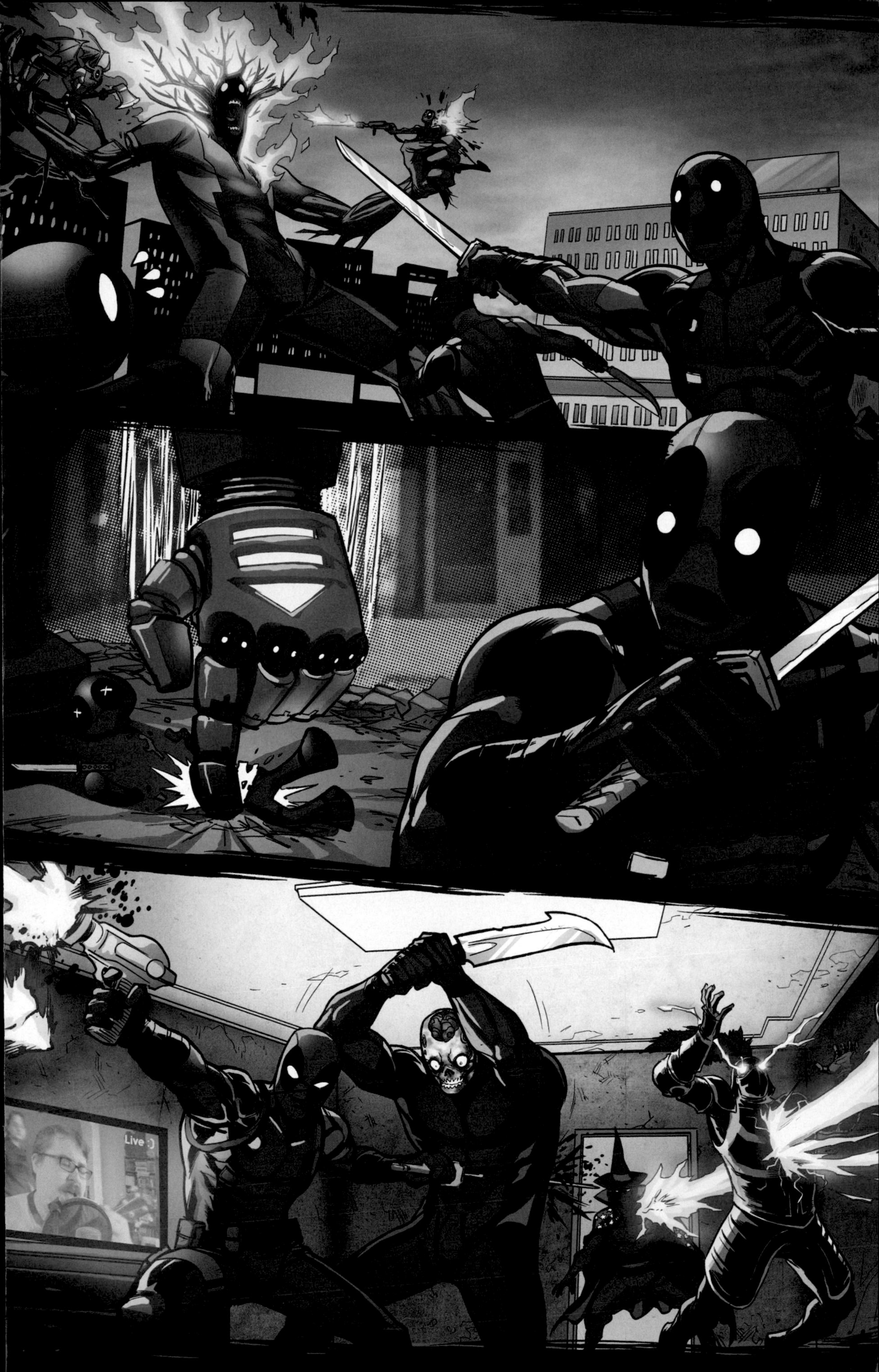
Live :)

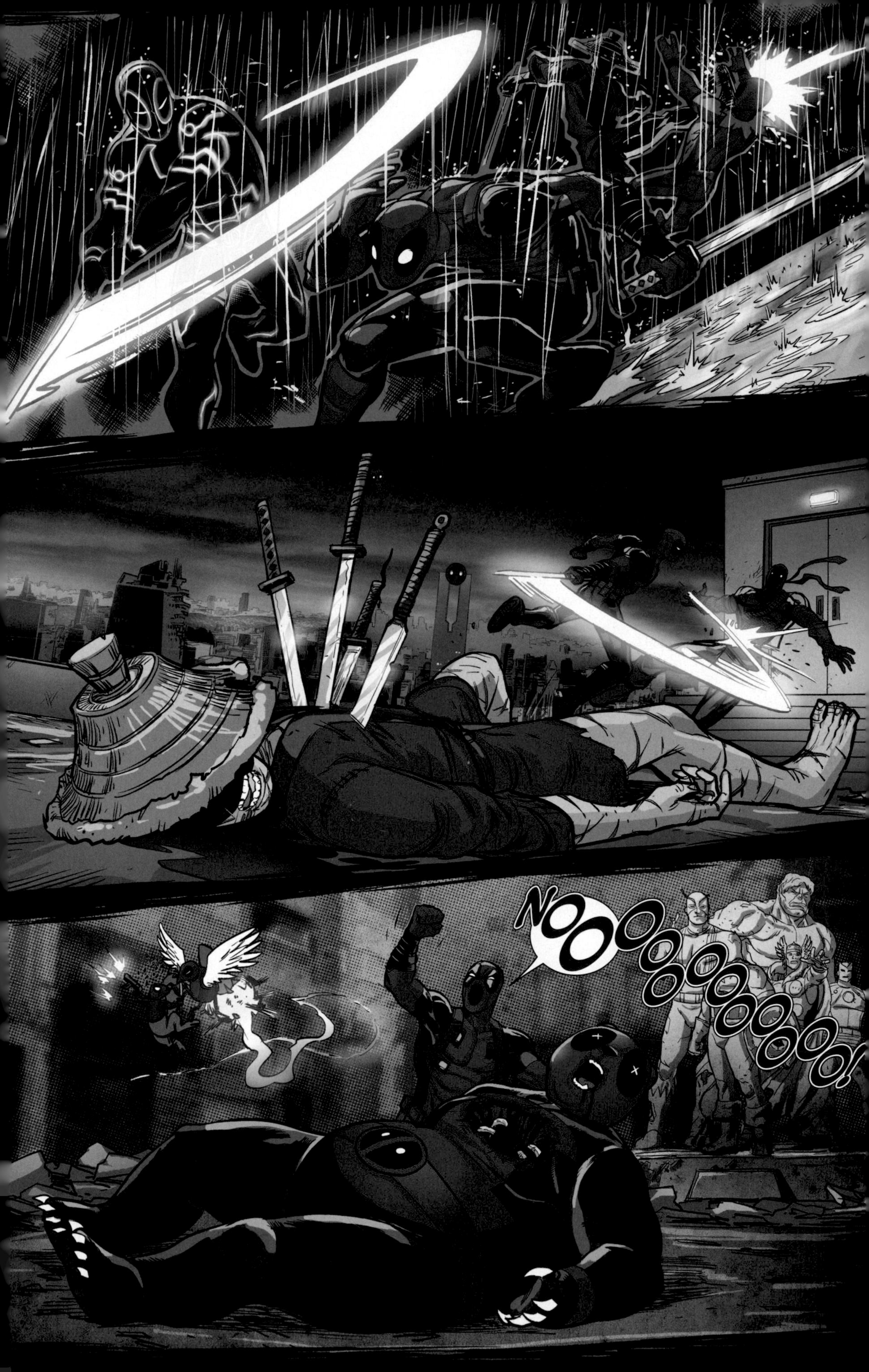
NOOOOOOOOOOOOOOO!

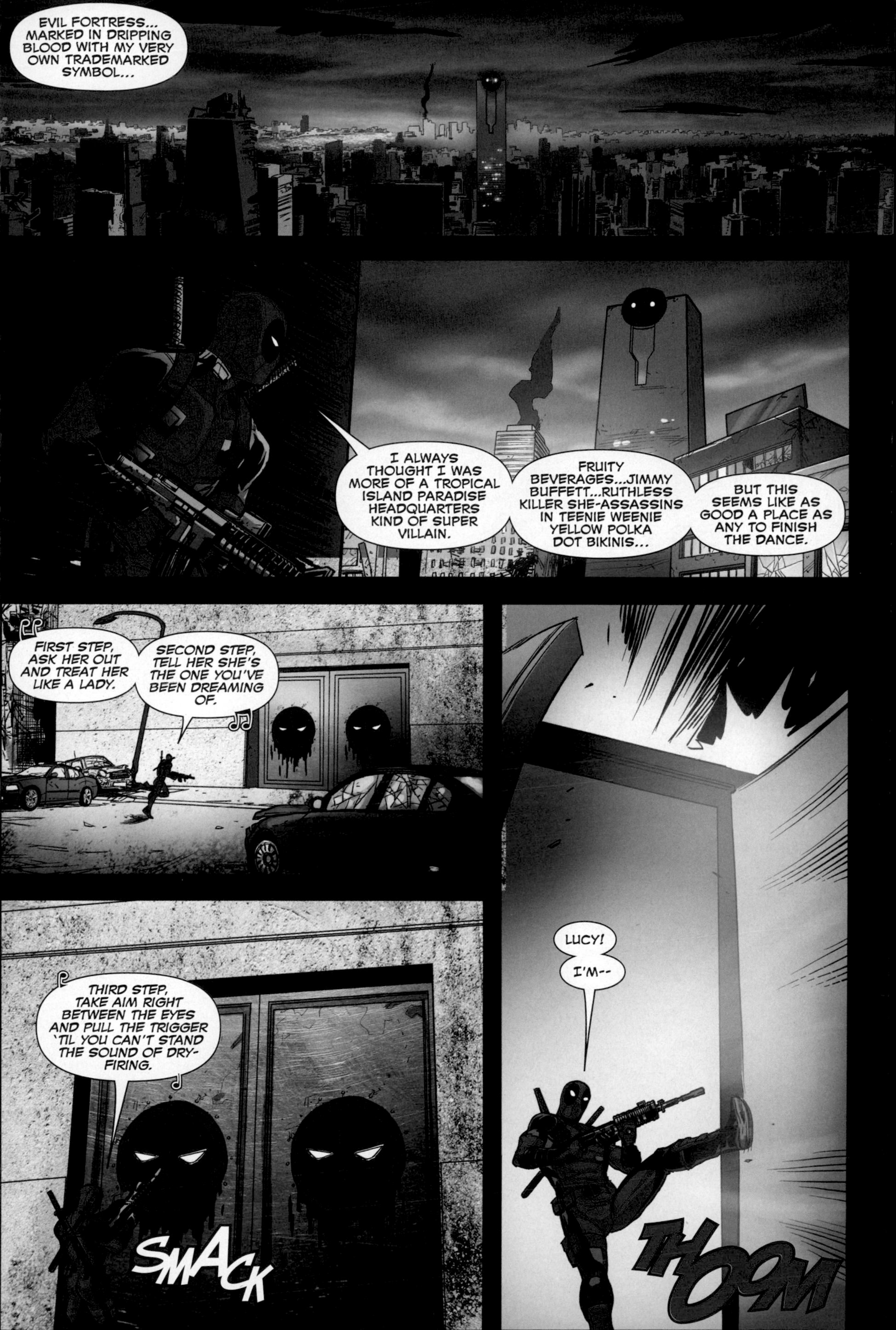
EVIL FORTRESS... MARKED IN DRIPPING BLOOD WITH MY VERY OWN TRADEMARKED SYMBOL...
I ALWAYS THOUGHT I WAS MORE OF A TROPICAL ISLAND PARADISE HEADQUARTERS KIND OF SUPER VILLAIN.
FRUITY BEVERAGES...JIMMY BUFFETT...RUTHLESS KILLER SHE-ASSASSINS IN TEENIE WEENIE YELLOW POLKA DOT BIKINIS...
BUT THIS SEEMS LIKE AS GOOD A PLACE AS ANY TO FINISH THE DANCE.
FIRST STEP, ASK HER OUT AND TREAT HER LIKE A LADY.
SECOND STEP, TELL HER SHE'S THE ONE YOU'VE BEEN DREAMING OF.
THIRD STEP, TAKE AIM RIGHT BETWEEN THE EYES AND PULL THE TRIGGER 'TIL YOU CAN'T STAND THE SOUND OF DRY-FIRING.
SMACK
LUCY!
I'M--
THOOM

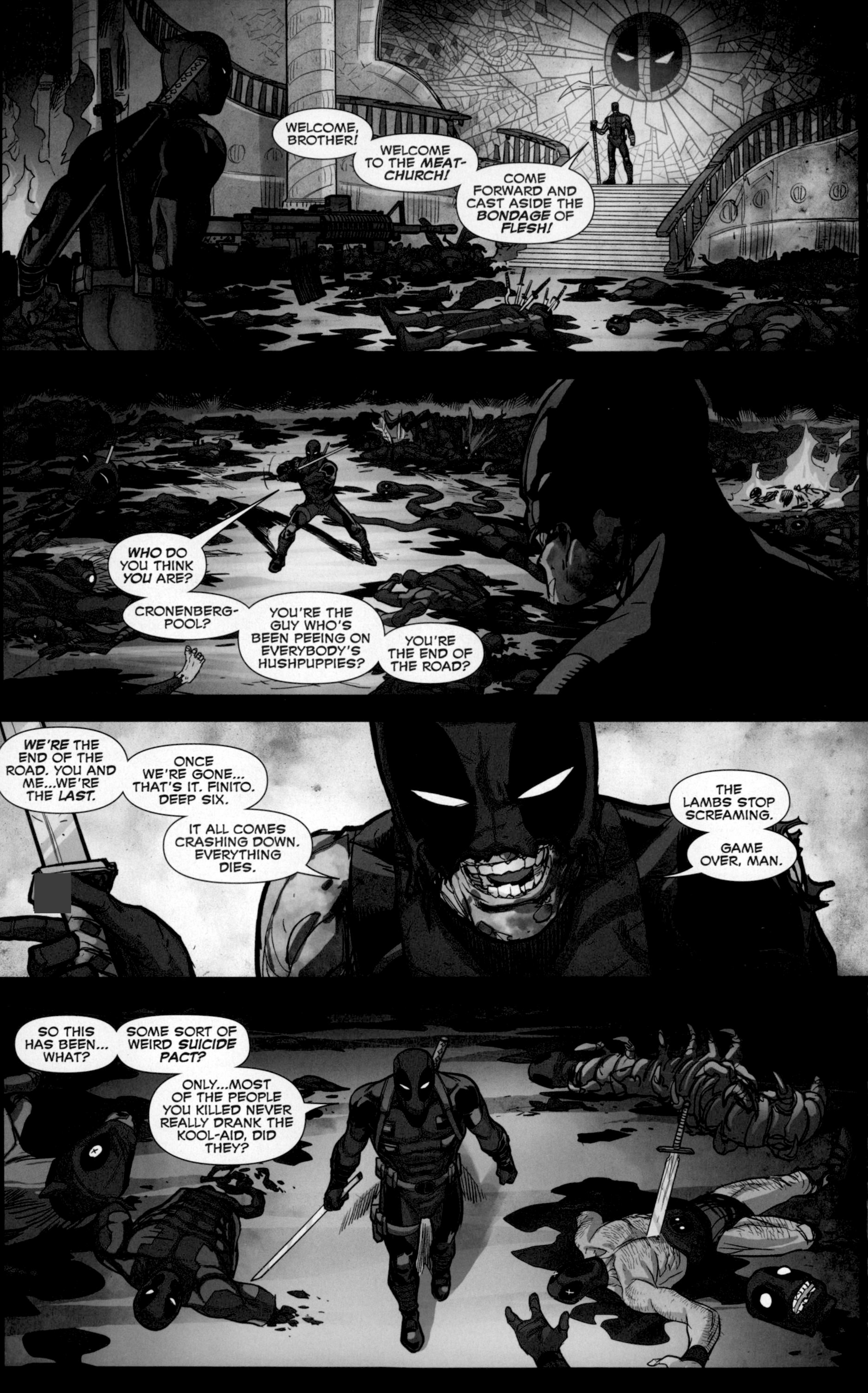
WELCOME, BROTHER!
WELCOME TO THE MEAT-CHURCH!
COME FORWARD AND CAST ASIDE THE BONDAGE OF FLESH!
WHO DO YOU THINK YOU ARE?
CRONENBERG-POOL?
YOU'RE THE GUY WHO'S BEEN PEEING ON EVERYBODY'S HUSHPUPPIES?
YOU'RE THE END OF THE ROAD?
WE'RE THE END OF THE ROAD. YOU AND ME...WE'RE THE LAST.
ONCE WE'RE GONE... THAT'S IT. FINITO. DEEP SIX.
IT ALL COMES CRASHING DOWN. EVERYTHING DIES.
THE LAMBS STOP SCREAMING.
GAME OVER, MAN.
SO THIS HAS BEEN... WHAT?
SOME SORT OF WEIRD SUICIDE PACT?
ONLY...MOST OF THE PEOPLE YOU KILLED NEVER REALLY DRANK THE KOOL-AID, DID THEY?

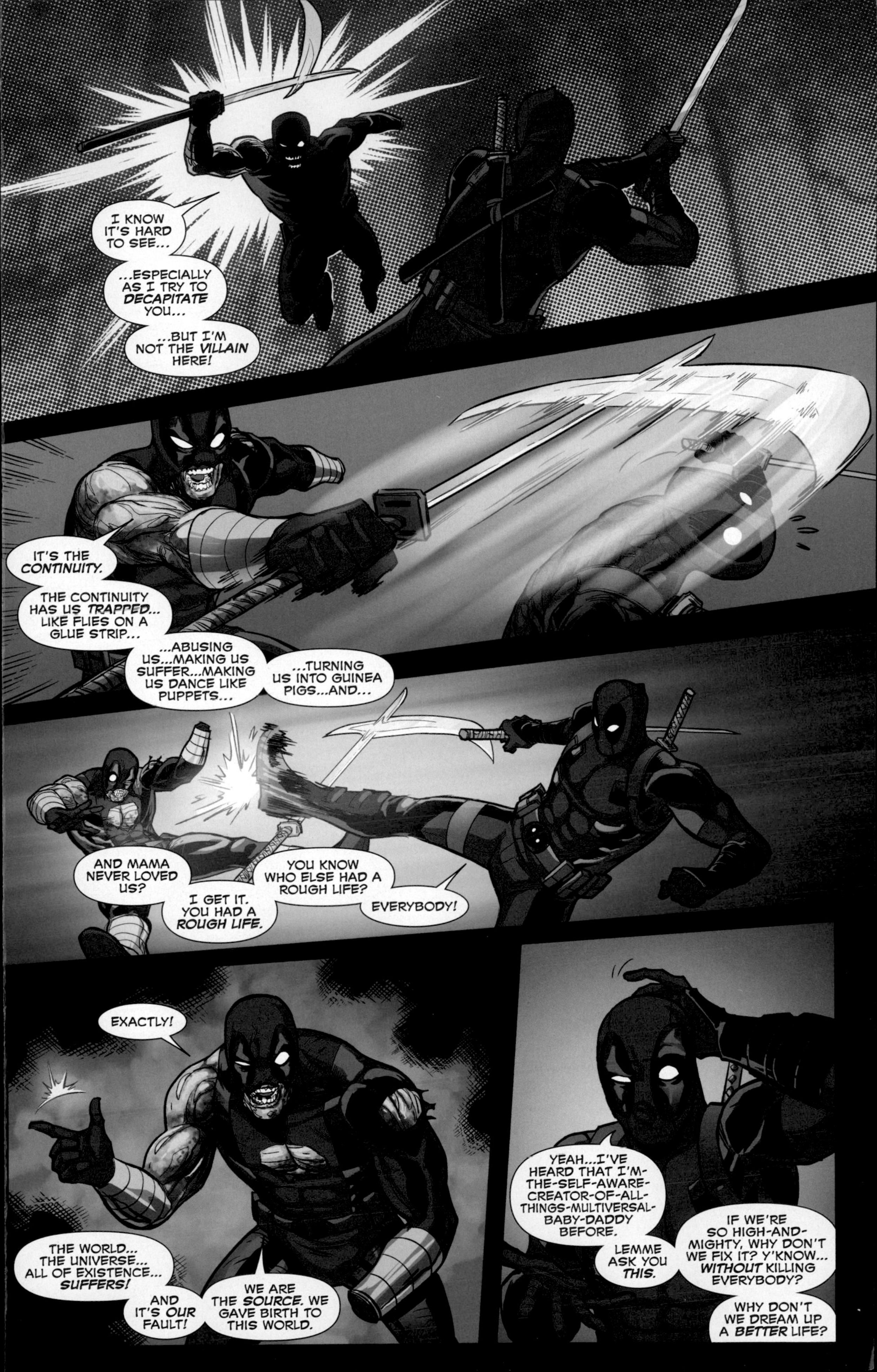

I KNOW IT'S HARD TO SEE...
...ESPECIALLY AS I TRY TO DECAPITATE YOU...
...BUT I'M NOT THE VILLAIN HERE!
IT'S THE CONTINUITY.
THE CONTINUITY HAS US TRAPPED... LIKE FLIES ON A GLUE STRIP...
...ABUSING US...MAKING US SUFFER...MAKING US DANCE LIKE PUPPETS...
...TURNING US INTO GUINEA PIGS...AND...
AND MAMA NEVER LOVED US?
I GET IT. YOU HAD A ROUGH LIFE.
YOU KNOW WHO ELSE HAD A ROUGH LIFE?
EVERYBODY!
EXACTLY!
THE WORLD... THE UNIVERSE... ALL OF EXISTENCE... SUFFERS!
AND IT'S OUR FAULT!
WE ARE THE SOURCE. WE GAVE BIRTH TO THIS WORLD.
YEAH...I'VE HEARD THAT I'M-THE-SELF-AWARE-CREATOR-OF-ALL-THINGS-MULTIVERSAL-BABY-DADDY BEFORE.
LEMME ASK YOU THIS.
IF WE'RE SO HIGH-AND-MIGHTY, WHY DON'T WE FIX IT? Y'KNOW... WITHOUT KILLING EVERYBODY?
WHY DON'T WE DREAM UP A BETTER LIFE?

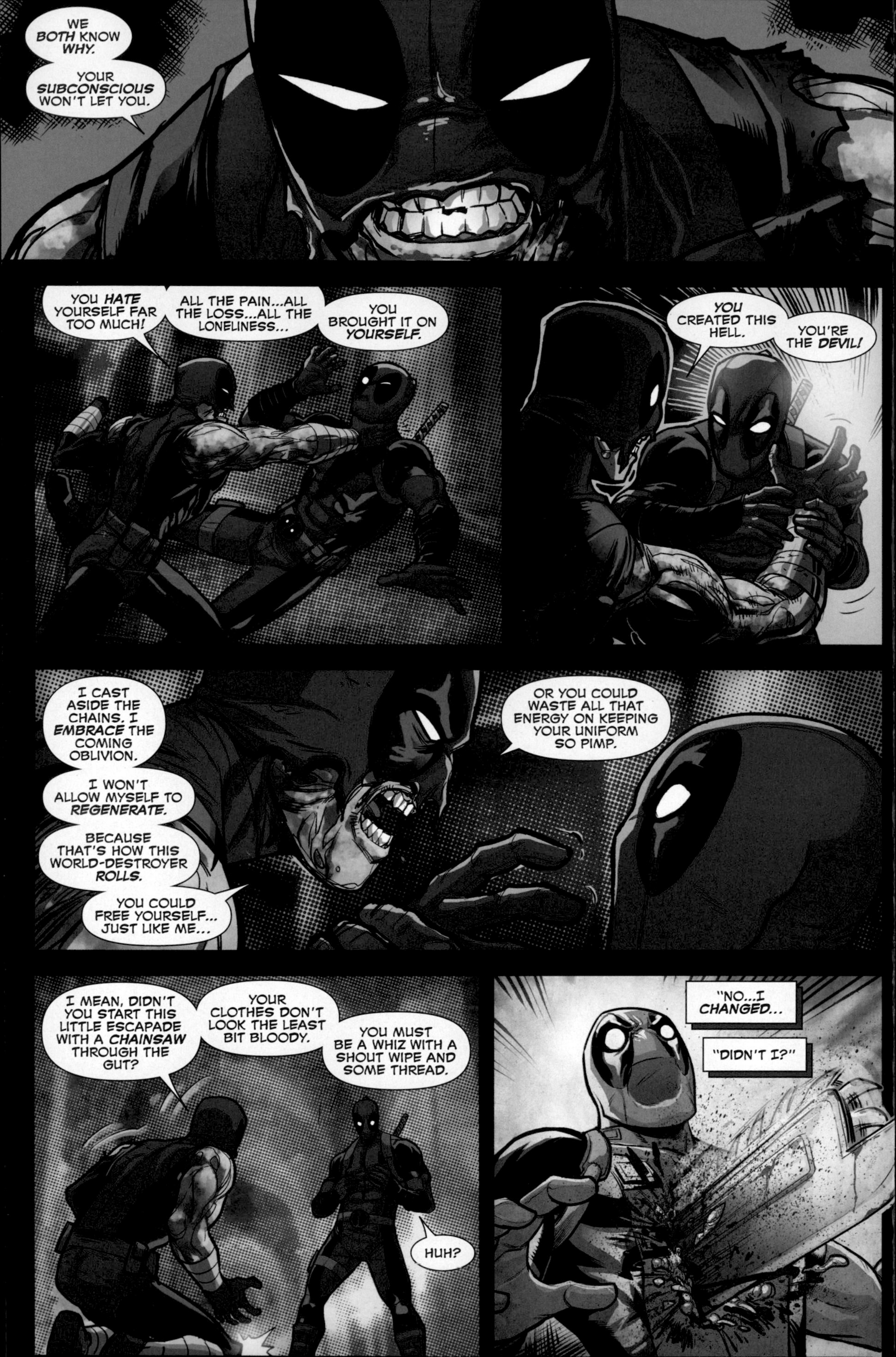
WE BOTH KNOW WHY.
YOUR SUBCONSCIOUS WON'T LET YOU.
YOU HATE YOURSELF FAR TOO MUCH!
ALL THE PAIN...ALL THE LOSS...ALL THE LONELINESS...
YOU BROUGHT IT ON YOURSELF.
YOU CREATED THIS HELL.
YOU'RE THE DEVIL!
I CAST ASIDE THE CHAINS. I EMBRACE THE COMING OBLIVION.
I WON'T ALLOW MYSELF TO REGENERATE.
BECAUSE THAT'S HOW THIS WORLD-DESTROYER ROLLS.
YOU COULD FREE YOURSELF... JUST LIKE ME...
OR YOU COULD WASTE ALL THAT ENERGY ON KEEPING YOUR UNIFORM SO PIMP.
I MEAN, DIDN'T YOU START THIS LITTLE ESCAPADE WITH A CHAINSAW THROUGH THE GUT?
YOUR CLOTHES DON'T LOOK THE LEAST BIT BLOODY.
YOU MUST BE A WHIZ WITH A SHOUT WIPE AND SOME THREAD.
HUH?
"NO...I CHANGED...
"DIDN'T I?"

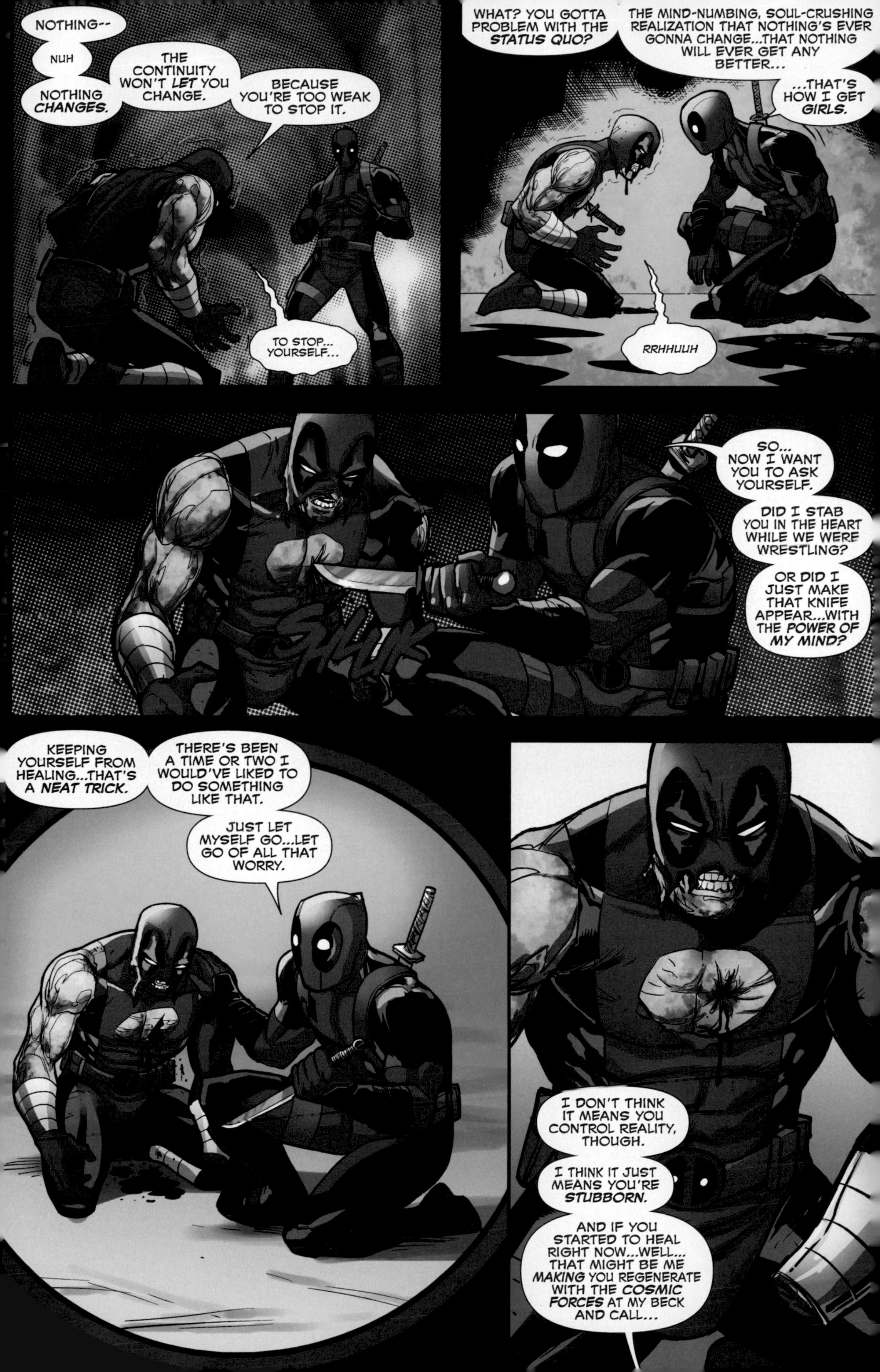
NOTHING--
NUH
NOTHING *CHANGES.*
THE CONTINUITY WON'T *LET* YOU CHANGE.
BECAUSE YOU'RE TOO WEAK TO STOP IT.
TO STOP... YOURSELF...
WHAT? YOU GOTTA PROBLEM WITH THE *STATUS QUO?*
THE MIND-NUMBING, SOUL-CRUSHING REALIZATION THAT NOTHING'S EVER GONNA CHANGE...THAT NOTHING WILL EVER GET ANY BETTER...
...THAT'S HOW I GET *GIRLS.*
RRHHUUH
SO... NOW I WANT YOU TO ASK YOURSELF.
DID I STAB YOU IN THE HEART WHILE WE WERE WRESTLING?
OR DID I JUST MAKE THAT KNIFE APPEAR...WITH THE *POWER OF MY MIND?*
SHLUK
KEEPING YOURSELF FROM HEALING...THAT'S A *NEAT TRICK.*
THERE'S BEEN A TIME OR TWO I WOULD'VE LIKED TO DO SOMETHING LIKE THAT.
JUST LET MYSELF GO...LET GO OF ALL THAT WORRY.
I DON'T THINK IT MEANS YOU CONTROL REALITY, THOUGH.
I THINK IT JUST MEANS YOU'RE *STUBBORN.*
AND IF YOU STARTED TO HEAL RIGHT NOW...WELL... THAT MIGHT BE ME *MAKING* YOU REGENERATE WITH THE *COSMIC FORCES* AT MY BECK AND CALL...

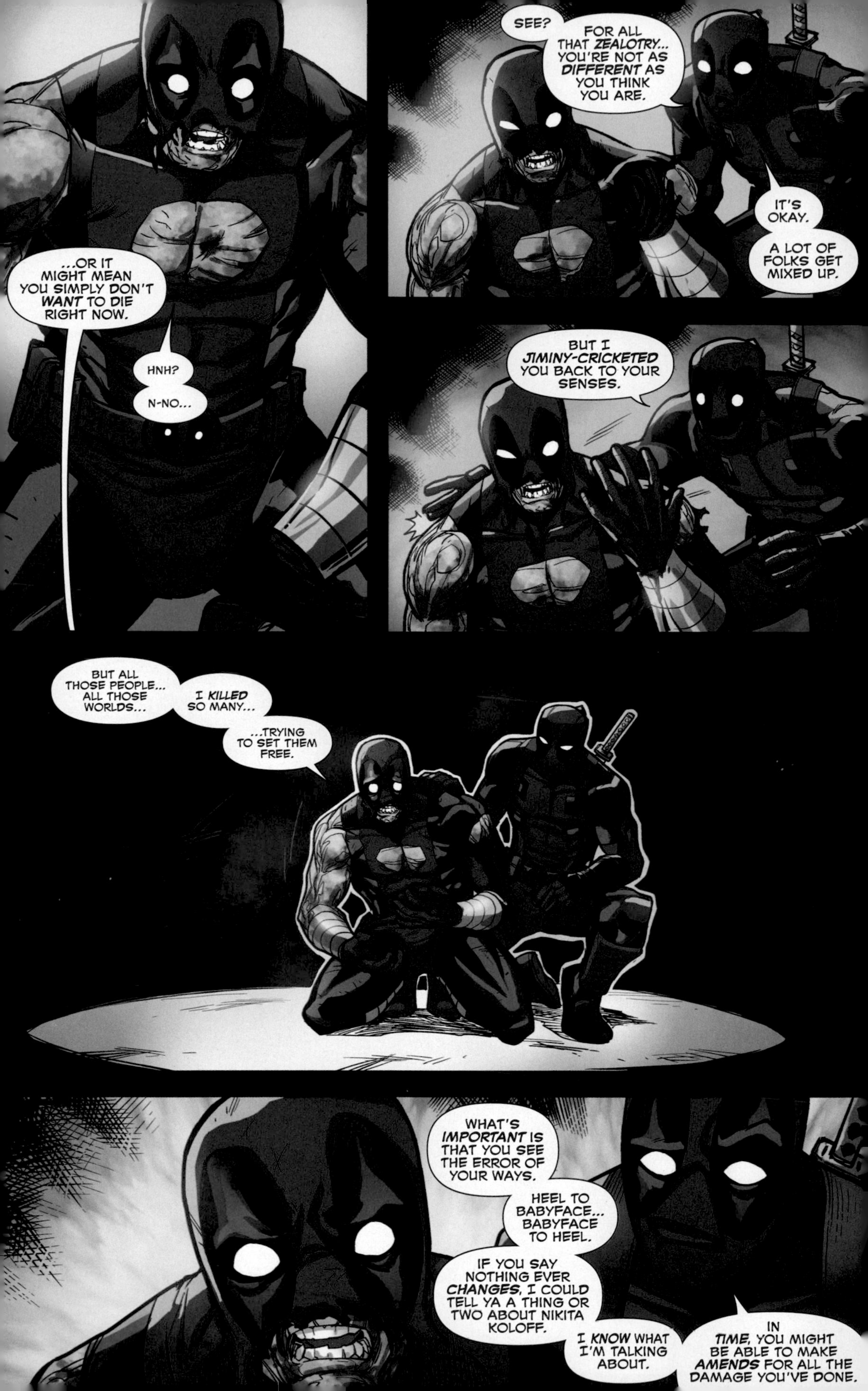
...OR IT MIGHT MEAN YOU SIMPLY DON'T WANT TO DIE RIGHT NOW.
HNH?
N-NO...
SEE?
FOR ALL THAT ZEALOTRY... YOU'RE NOT AS DIFFERENT AS YOU THINK YOU ARE.
IT'S OKAY.
A LOT OF FOLKS GET MIXED UP.
BUT I JIMINY-CRICKETED YOU BACK TO YOUR SENSES.
BUT ALL THOSE PEOPLE... ALL THOSE WORLDS...
I KILLED SO MANY...
...TRYING TO SET THEM FREE.
WHAT'S IMPORTANT IS THAT YOU SEE THE ERROR OF YOUR WAYS.
HEEL TO BABYFACE... BABYFACE TO HEEL.
IF YOU SAY NOTHING EVER CHANGES, I COULD TELL YA A THING OR TWO ABOUT NIKITA KOLOFF.
I KNOW WHAT I'M TALKING ABOUT.
IN TIME, YOU MIGHT BE ABLE TO MAKE AMENDS FOR ALL THE DAMAGE YOU'VE DONE.

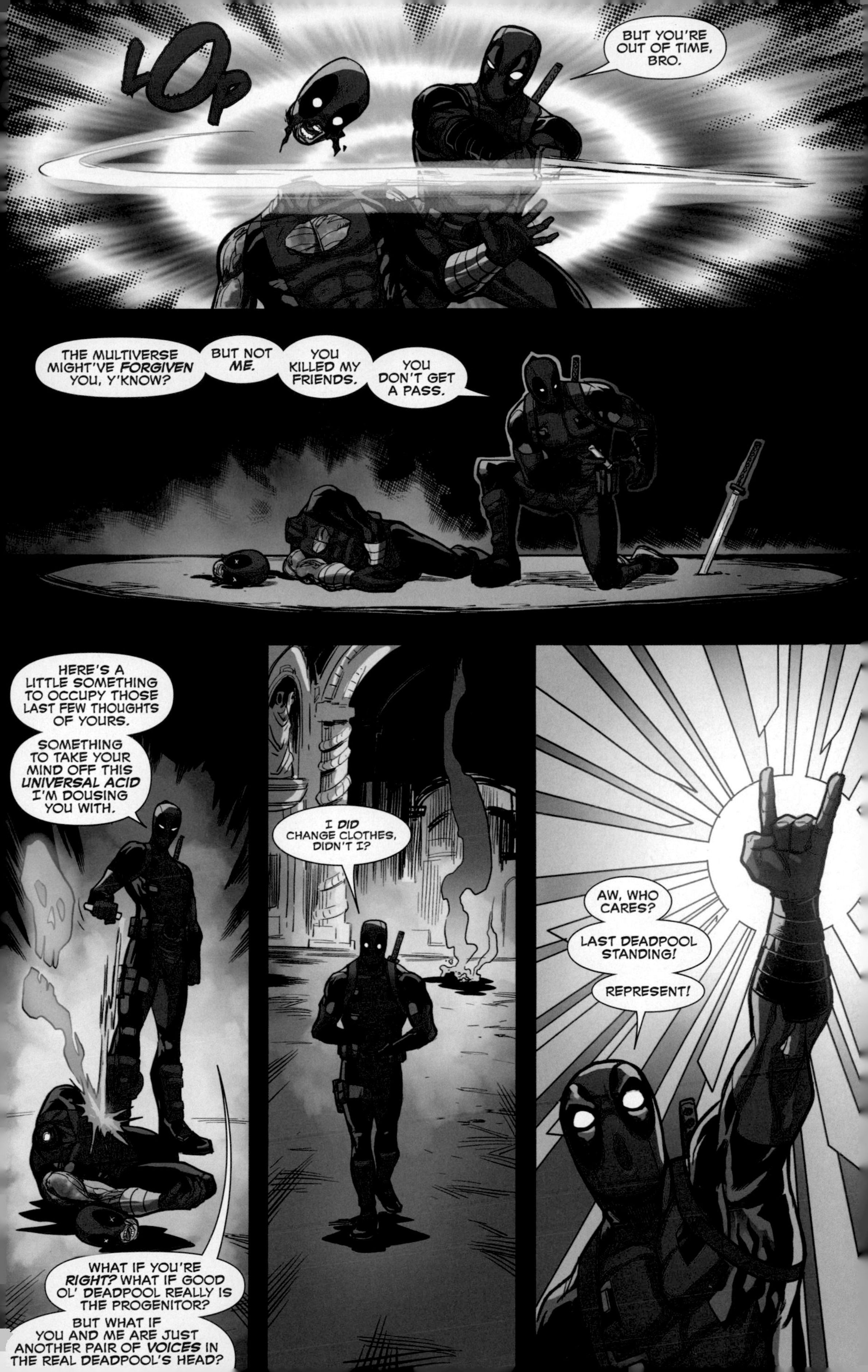

TOP
BUT YOU'RE OUT OF TIME, BRO.
THE MULTIVERSE MIGHT'VE FORGIVEN YOU, Y'KNOW?
BUT NOT ME.
YOU KILLED MY FRIENDS.
YOU DON'T GET A PASS.
HERE'S A LITTLE SOMETHING TO OCCUPY THOSE LAST FEW THOUGHTS OF YOURS.
SOMETHING TO TAKE YOUR MIND OFF THIS UNIVERSAL ACID I'M DOUSING YOU WITH.
WHAT IF YOU'RE RIGHT? WHAT IF GOOD OL' DEADPOOL REALLY IS THE PROGENITOR?
BUT WHAT IF YOU AND ME ARE JUST ANOTHER PAIR OF VOICES IN THE REAL DEADPOOL'S HEAD?
I DID CHANGE CLOTHES, DIDN'T I?
AW, WHO CARES?
LAST DEADPOOL STANDING!
REPRESENT!

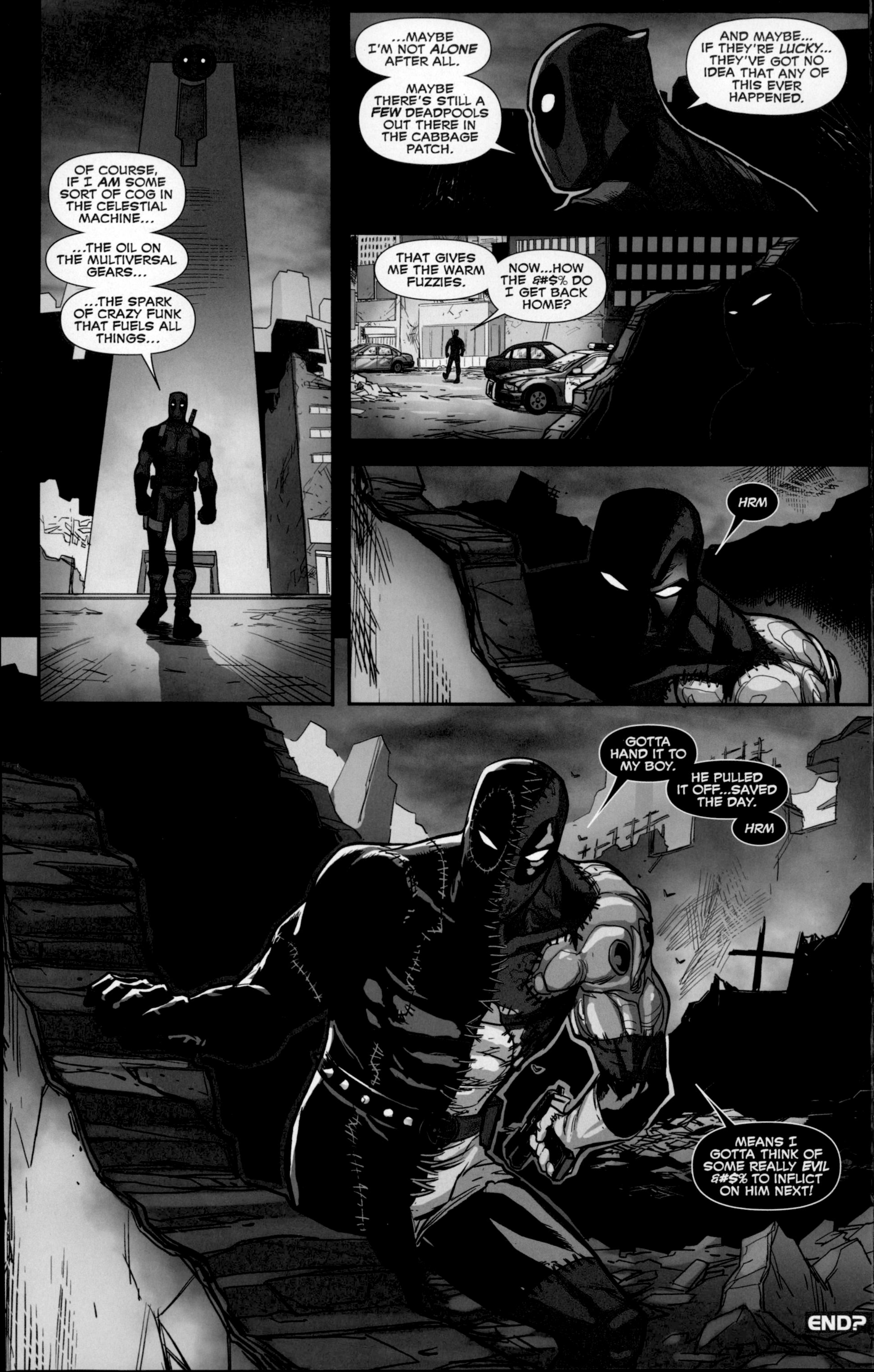
OF COURSE, IF I AM SOME SORT OF COG IN THE CELESTIAL MACHINE...
...THE OIL ON THE MULTIVERSAL GEARS...
...THE SPARK OF CRAZY FUNK THAT FUELS ALL THINGS...
...MAYBE I'M NOT ALONE AFTER ALL.
MAYBE THERE'S STILL A FEW DEADPOOLS OUT THERE IN THE CABBAGE PATCH.
AND MAYBE... IF THEY'RE LUCKY... THEY'VE GOT NO IDEA THAT ANY OF THIS EVER HAPPENED.
THAT GIVES ME THE WARM FUZZIES.
NOW...HOW THE &#$% DO I GET BACK HOME?
HRM
GOTTA HAND IT TO MY BOY.
HE PULLED IT OFF...SAVED THE DAY.
HRM
MEANS I GOTTA THINK OF SOME REALLY EVIL &#$% TO INFLICT ON HIM NEXT!
END?

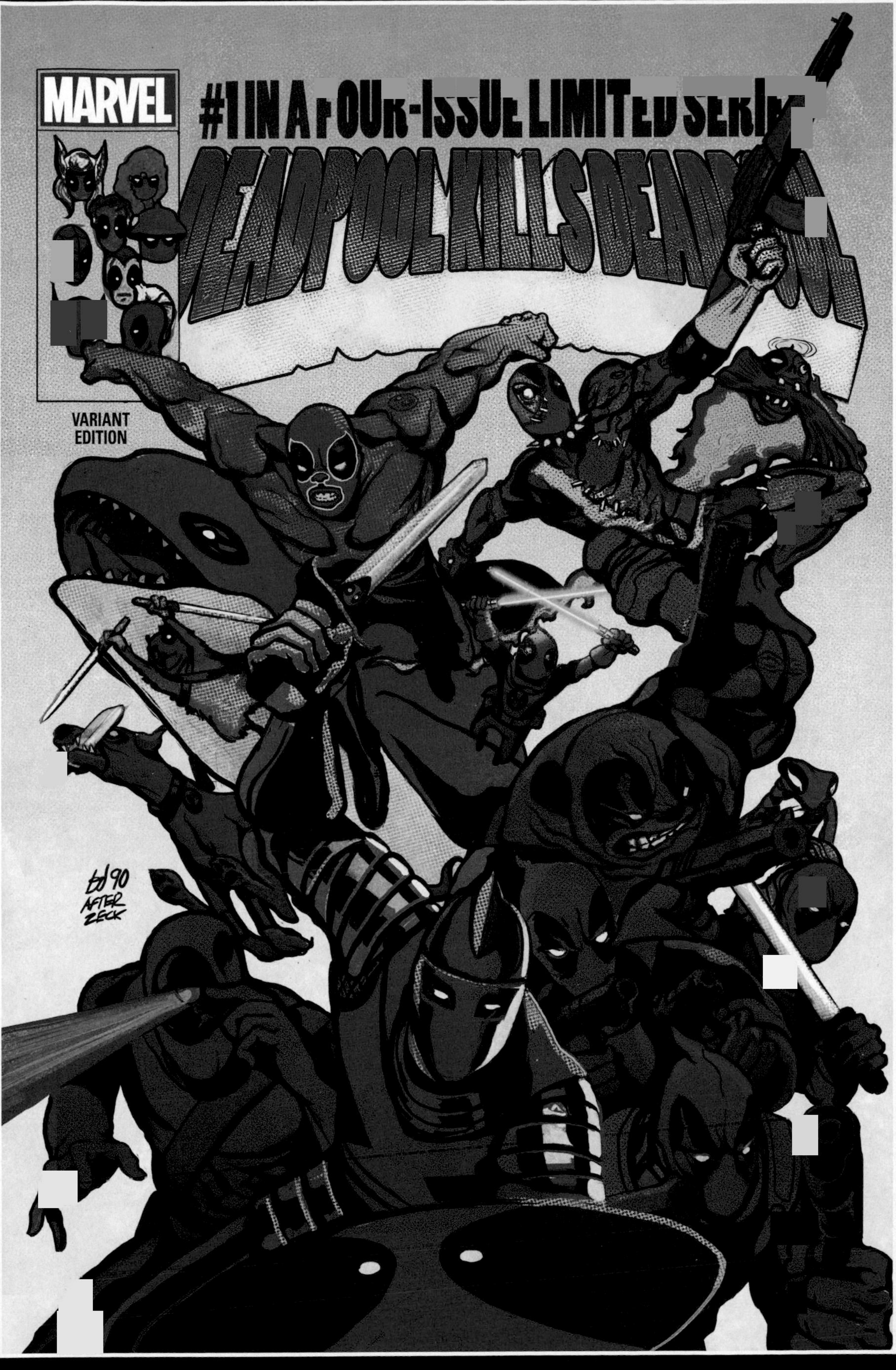
MARVEL
#1 IN A FOUR-ISSUE LIMITED
DEADPOOL KILLS
VARIANT EDITION
bd 90 AFTER ZECK

#1 VARIANT BY **MIKE DEL MUNDO**

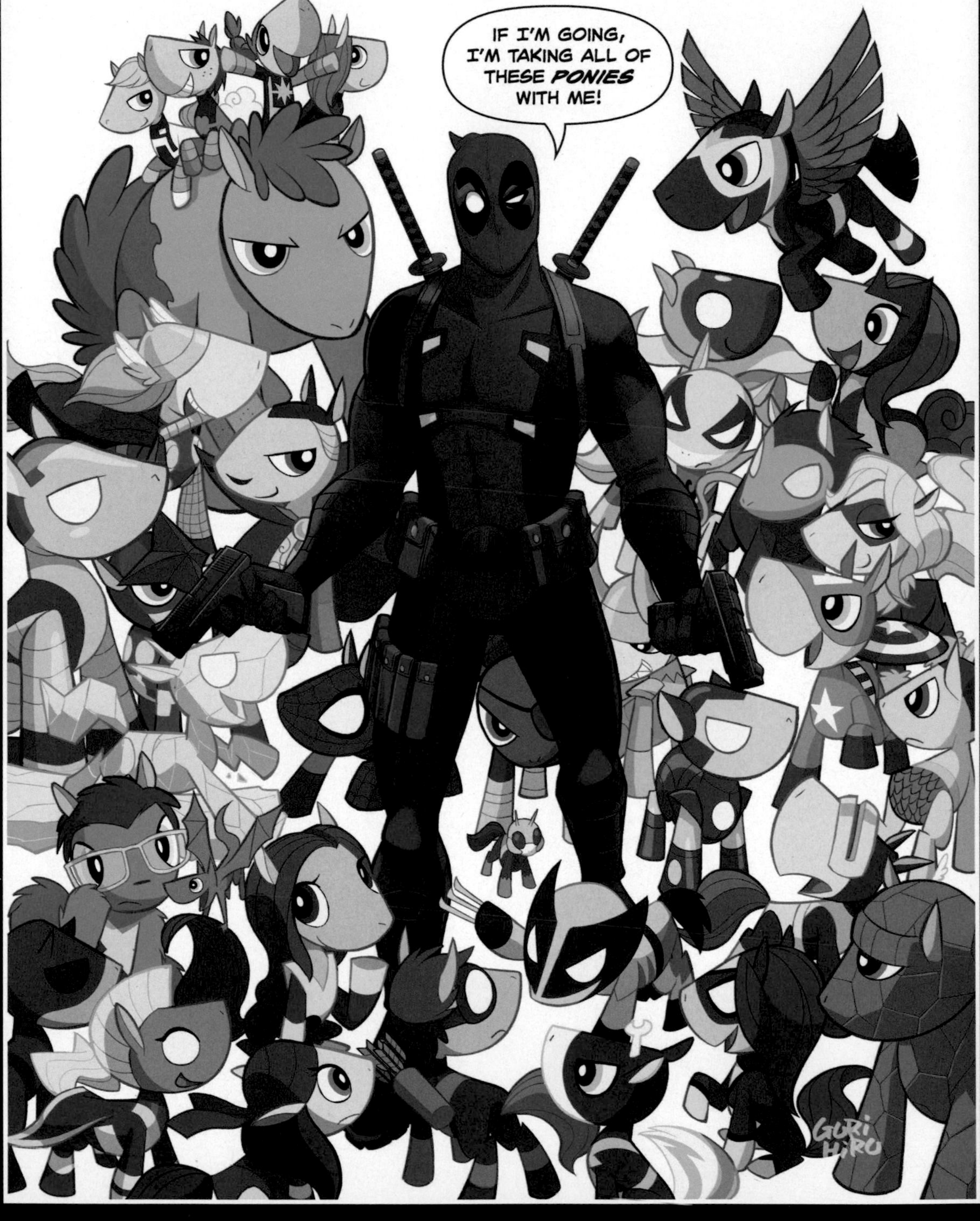
IF I'M GOING, I'M TAKING ALL OF THESE PONIES WITH ME!
GURIHIRU

#1 SAN DIEGO COMIC-CON VARIANT BY **GURIHIRU**

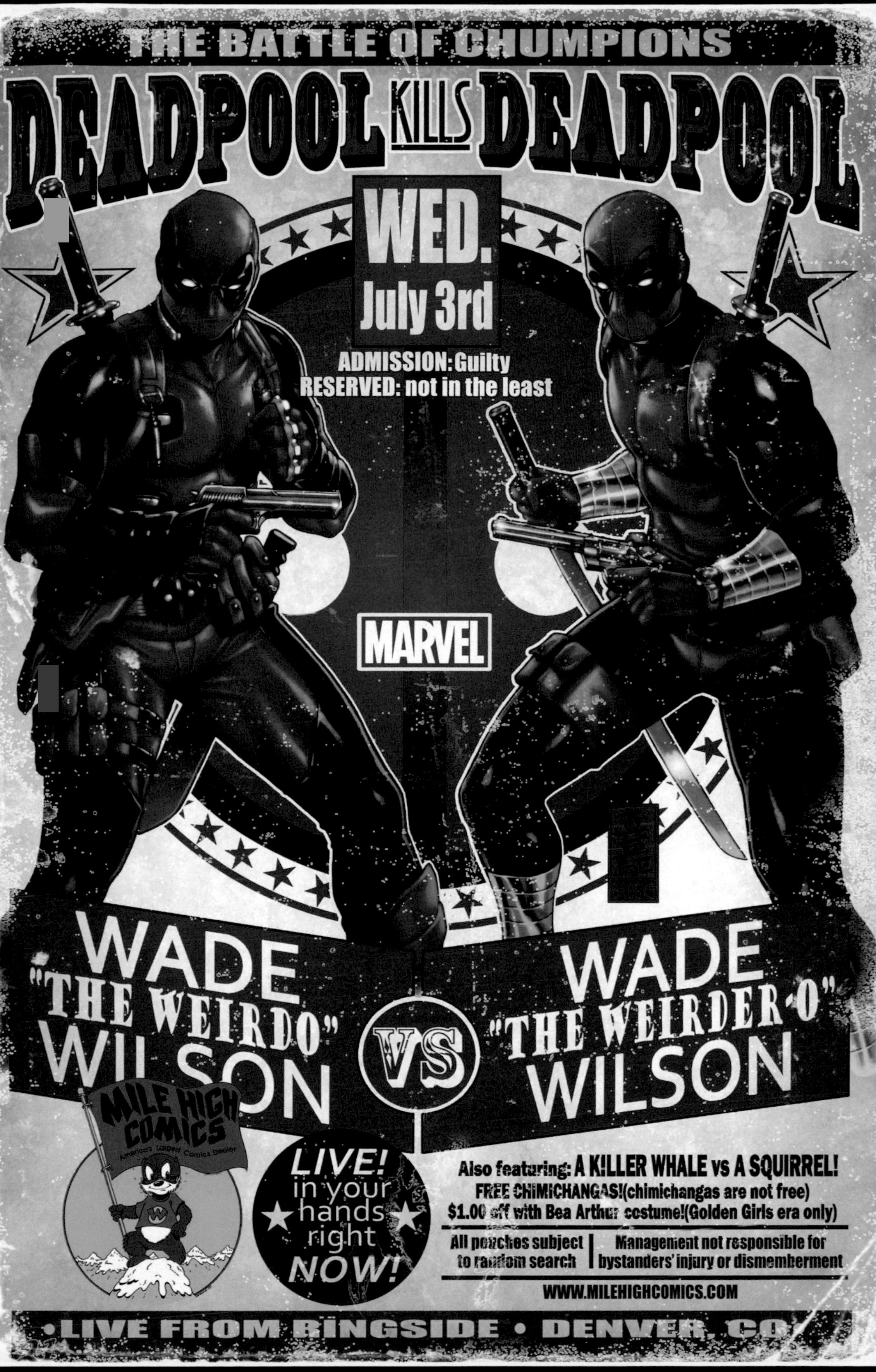
THE BATTLE OF CHUMPIONS
DEADPOOL KILLS DEADPOOL
WED.
July 3rd
ADMISSION: Guilty
RESERVED: not in the least
MARVEL
WADE "THE WEIRDO" WILSON
VS
WADE "THE WEIRDER-O" WILSON
MILE HIGH COMICS
LIVE! in your hands right NOW!
Also featuring: A KILLER WHALE vs A SQUIRREL!
FREE CHIMICHANGAS!(chimichangas are not free)
$1.00 off with Bea Arthur costume!(Golden Girls era only)
All pouches subject to random search
Management not responsible for bystanders' injury or dismemberment
WWW.MILEHIGHCOMICS.COM
•LIVE FROM RINGSIDE • DENVER, CO•

#1 MILE HIGH VARIANT BY **MARK BROOKS**

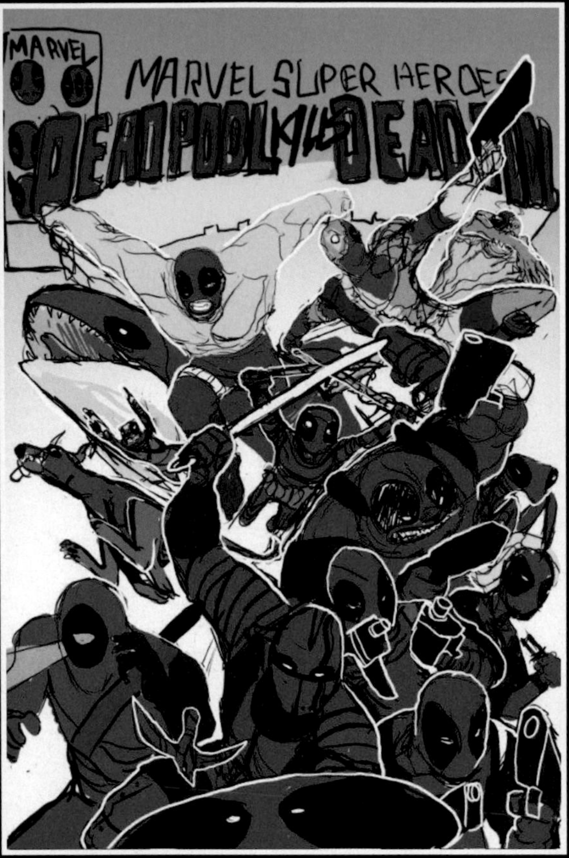
MARVEL
MARVEL SUPER HEROES
DEADPOOL
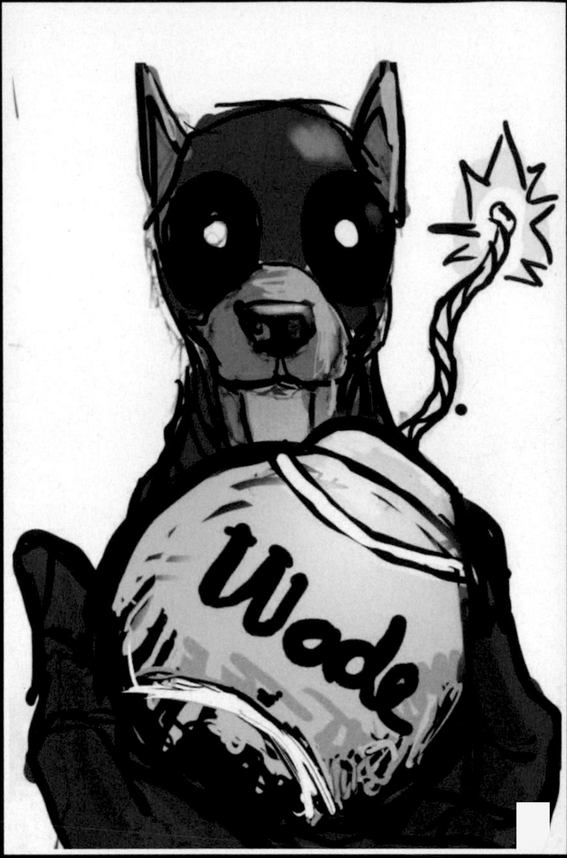
Wade
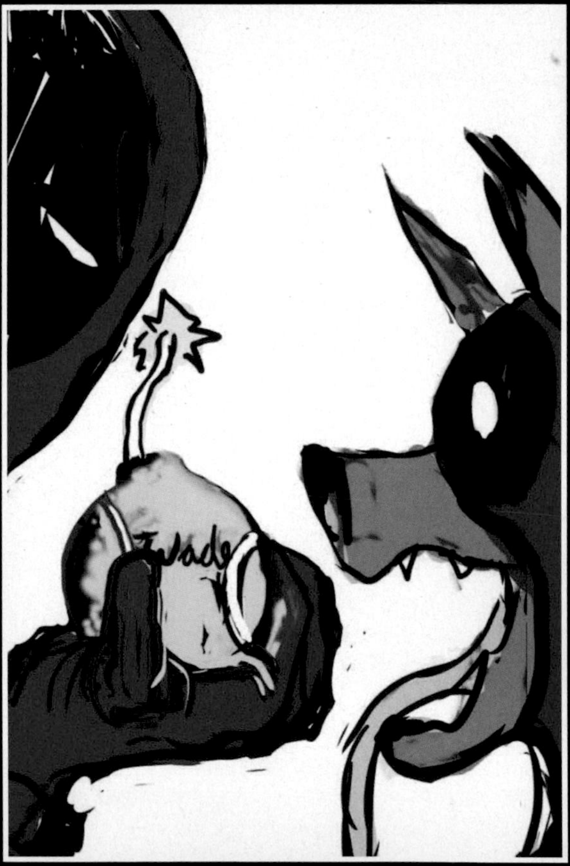
Wade
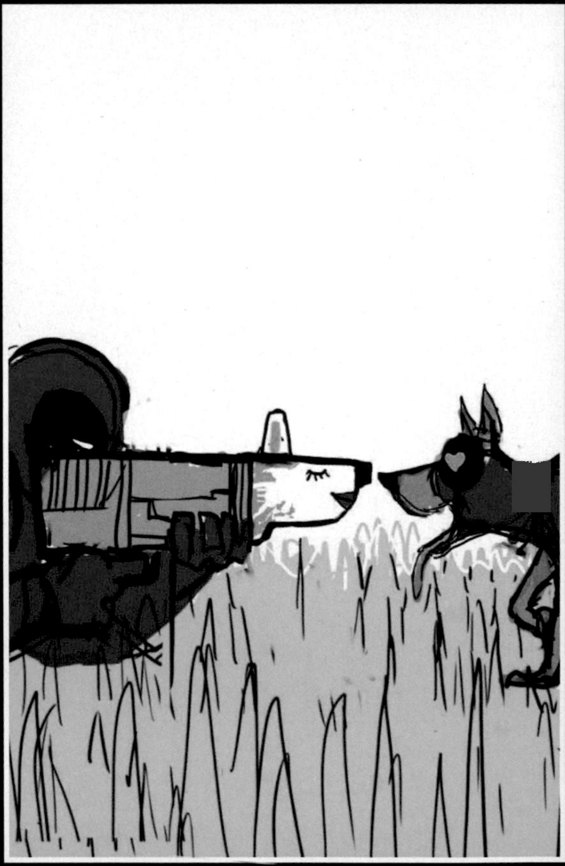

COVER CONCEPTS BY **MIKE DEL MUNDO**

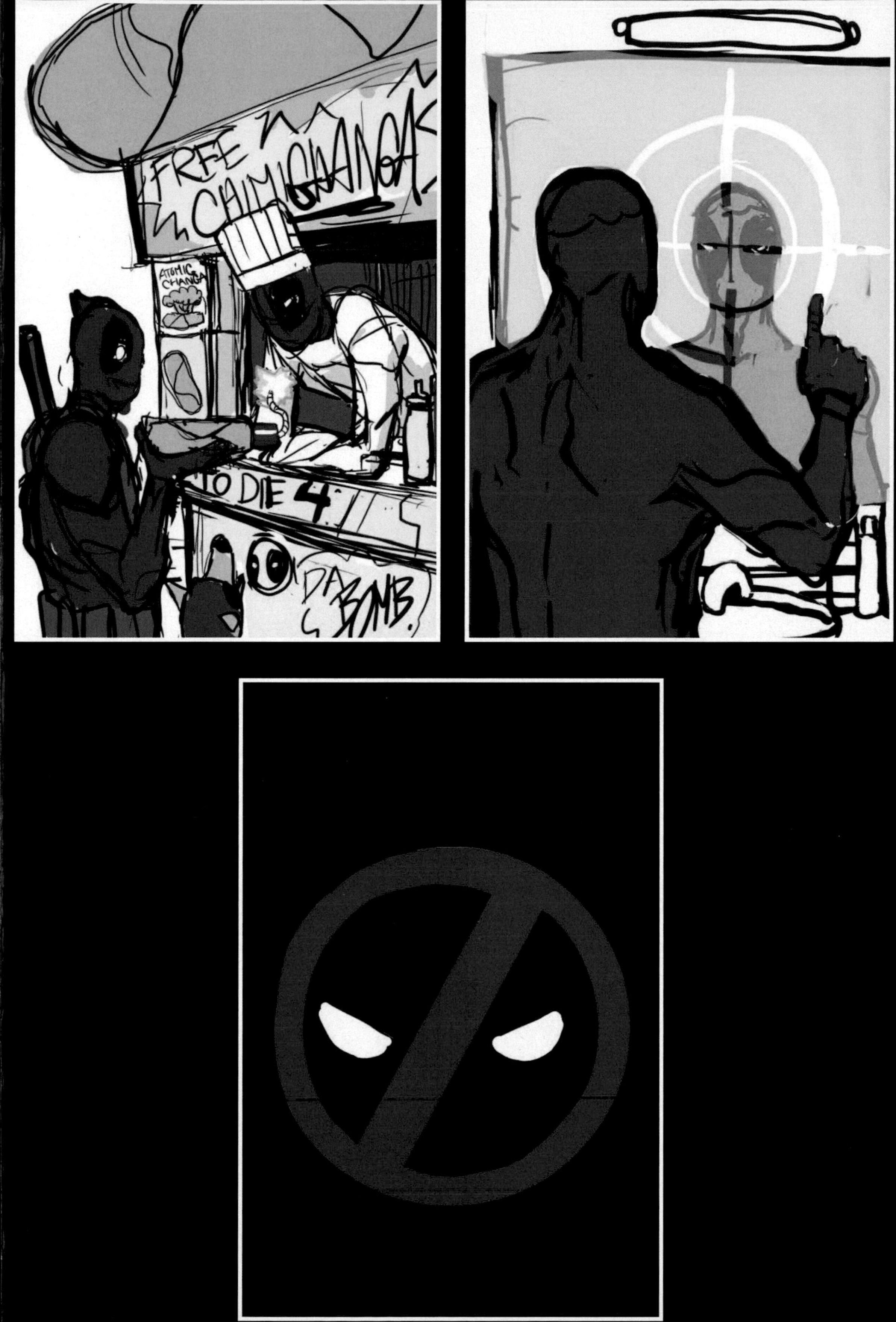
FREE CHIMICHANGAS
ATOMIC CHANGA
TO DIE 4
DA BOMB.

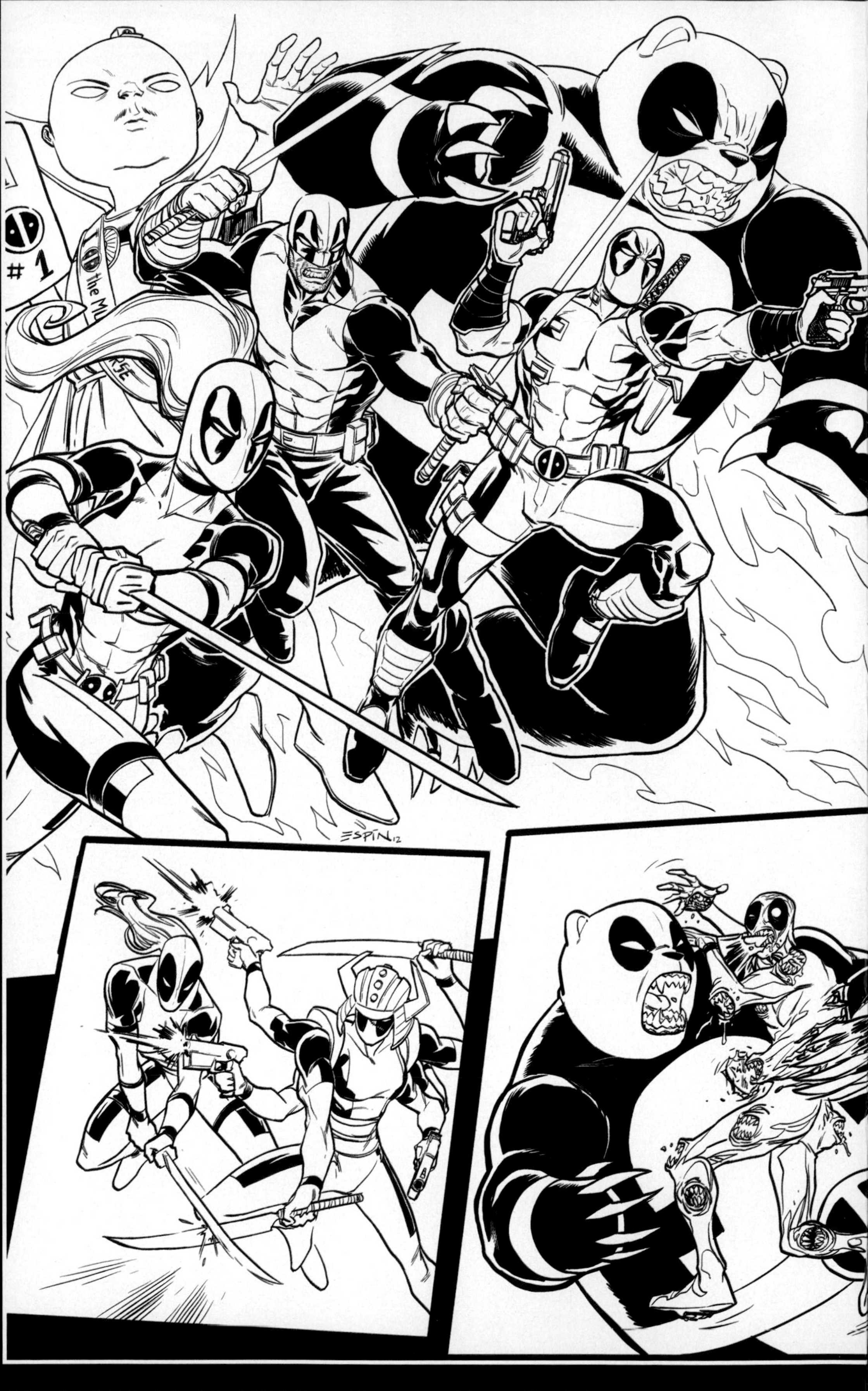

1
ESPIN

#2, PAGES 14-15 ARTWORK BY **SALVA ESPIN**

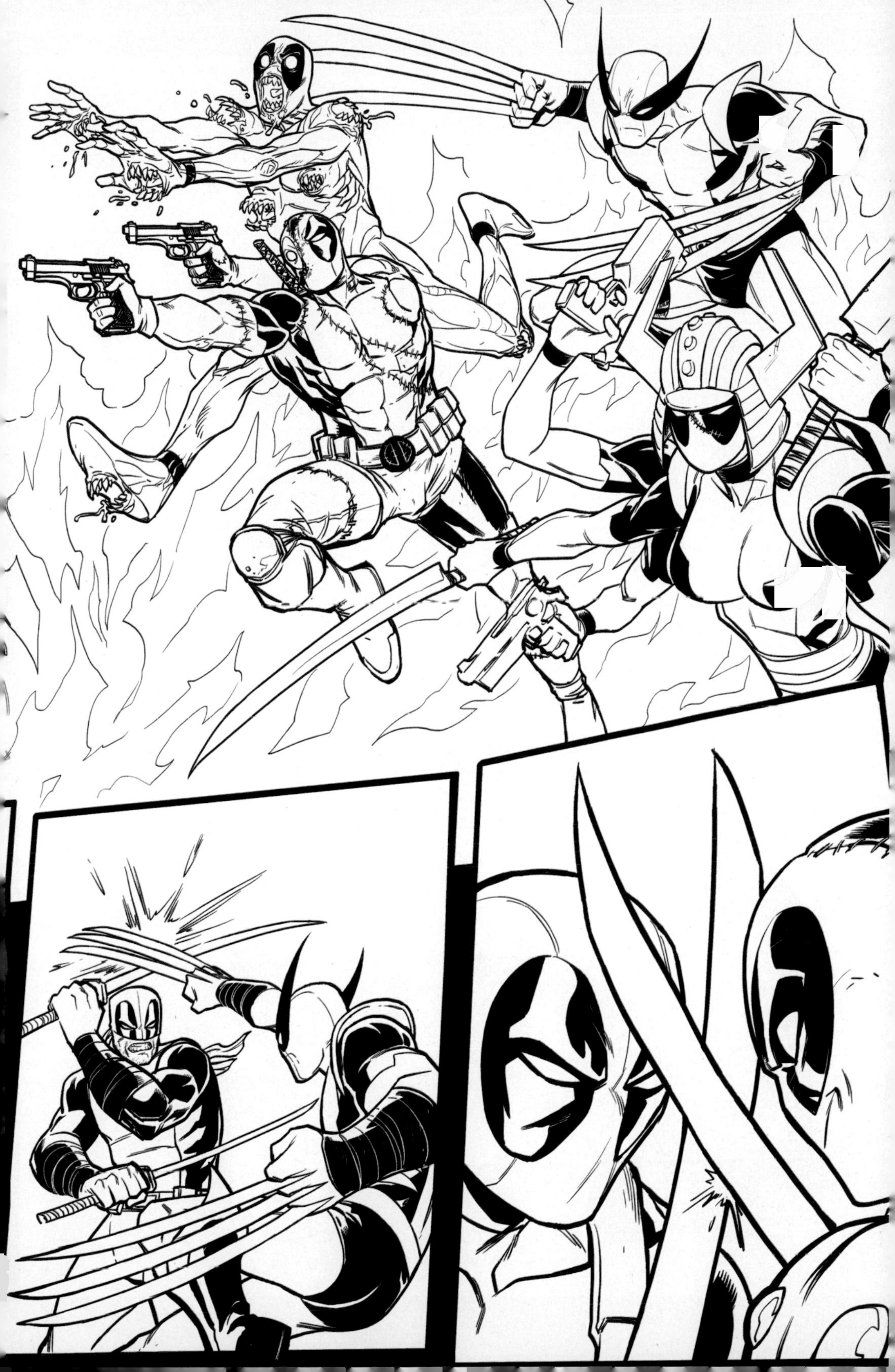

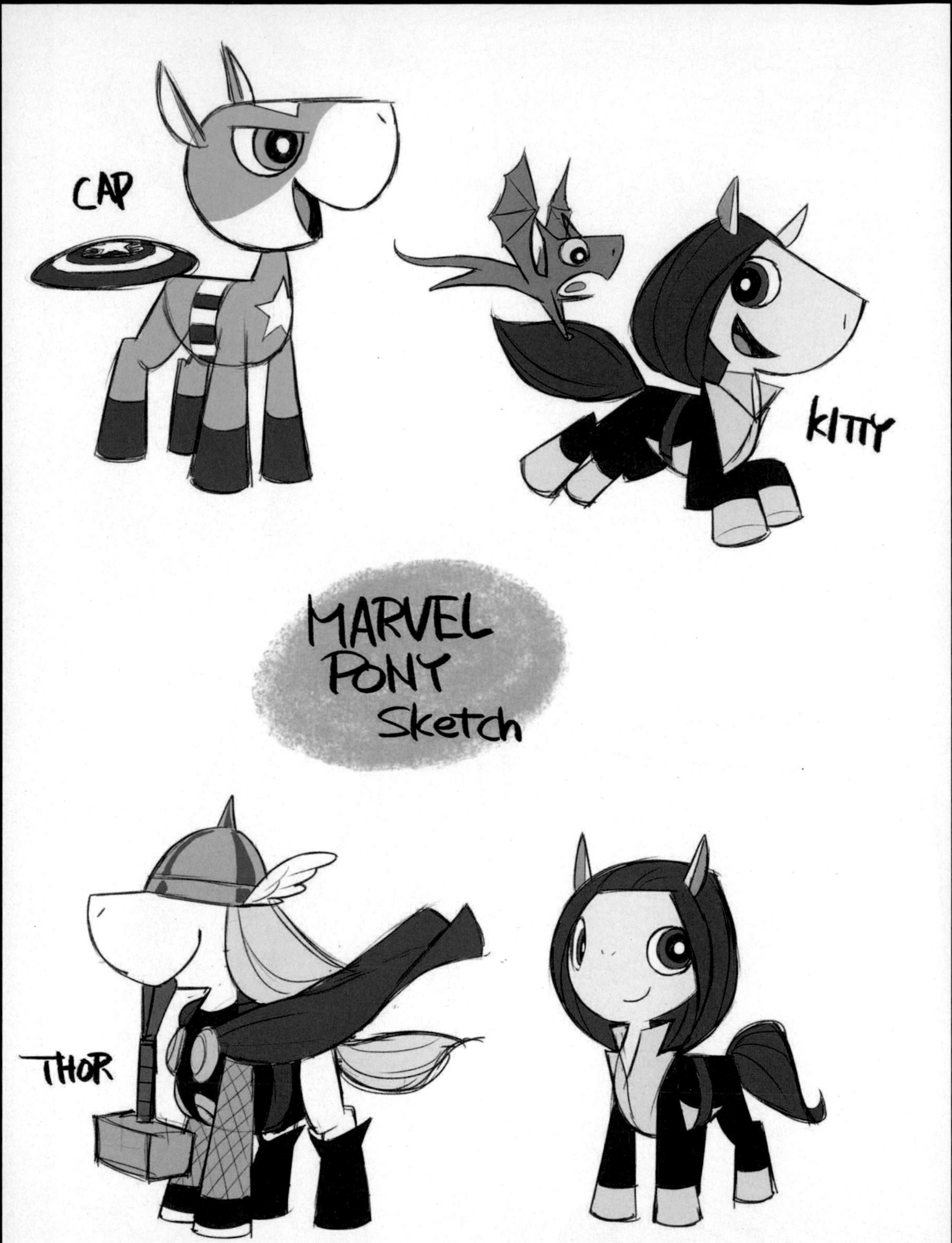
CAP
KITTY
MARVEL PONY Sketch
THOR

MARVEL PONIES SKETCH BY **GURIHIRU**